CW00732063

Letlapa Mphahlele

Child of this Soil
My life as a freedom fighter

KWELA BOOKS

The photograph on the front cover was taken of the author at age 17,
a few months before he went into exile.
It is used with the permission of his brother Seputule.

Cover design by Nazli Jacobs
Designed and set in 10 on 12 pt Plantin
by Teresa Williams
Printed and bound by Mills Litho,
Maitland, Cape Town, South Africa

First edition, first printing 2002
Second printing 2002

ISBN 0-7957-0149-7

http://www.kwela.com

—To Molongoane —

YOUR MAGIC IS INDELIBLE in my mind, you contemplative mountain breathing eternity with the rest of the Kgoahlampa.

To cast your spell, you wove the ugly with the beautiful.

I remember your chilly winter shade maliciously covering my shivering flesh; yet you hoarded it in baking summer when I needed it most.

At night your hooting owls made me tighten the blankets around my naked body, vainly trying to erase the pictures of evil that my mind conjured from the tales I had heard the old people tell.

I remember happily sliding on your broad-backed boulders, my buttocks on the sleigh of tender, leafy branches.

My mouth still waters when I remember the feast of mafaya, manokane and mapshepshane that you decked on your trees.

— Foreword —

INWARDLY I GROANED, "ANOTHER ONE."

A friend had phoned me to ask me to look at Letlapa Mphahlele's manuscript and "give him some advice". There are hundreds of these manuscripts lying in drawers and boxes in our black townships. In the end I have to gently tell the author that he or she still needs to put more work into it. These exercises cost me time but I seldom refuse, because there are profound stories out there that need to be told.

Letlapa brought the manuscript and I turned the pages with growing excitement. At last, I was hearing a new African voice. His prose is poetic in the tradition of our maboko, saying much more than the literal meaning on the surface. He was giving me insights into the dark world of the guerrilla.

I read it again and wrote questions on a pad when I bumped into a confusing or unclear section. When he came back, he had the answers to my questions, and I said they needed to be in the manuscript. I asked for the computer disc with the manuscript on it. That is when I discovered that the discs he was carrying were not computer discs – they were for an ancient electric typewriter, possibly a grandparent of today's word processors – and that his friend in Umtata had typed the manuscript for him.

I helped him put it onto computer, and along the way answer the questions I asked. It was work I loved doing and working with him was humbling. He is a simple and honest man who loves his country and his people.

A new voice? Perhaps I should say a new literary voice. What he says can be heard daily in our black townships. Letlapa merely gives it form and is sending it out to the wide world.

He says what thousands of men and women are mumbling under their breath. In 1976, armed with stones and petrol bombs, they defended themselves against policemen and soldiers who brandished the most sophisticated of weapons. They went into exile and military training. They returned to live precarious lives in the underground armies of the PAC, the ANC and the Black Consciousness Movement of Azania.

7

We have heard the leaders of these organisations. They have written books and other publications and have made speeches in rallies and parliaments since the demise of apartheid. We haven't heard their foot soldiers, the people who did not live in hotels but rather in holes in the ground.

What drove them to go into territory many of us were scared even to imagine? What kept a Letlapa focused even in the darkest hours of life underground? What do they feel about what has happened in our great land since 1989?

I've had long debates with Letlapa on these issues. You and I might think some of his arguments are romantic. But if we are to catapult this country to a higher level, we'll have to start by listening to people like Letlapa.

JOE THLOLOE, Editor-in-chief, e-tv
Johannesburg, July 2002

— A point in history —

SOUTH AFRICA WAS PREPARING for the first democratic elections. The lion and the lamb had been transformed and were jostling in friendly combat, and the world was marvelling at the miracle of the 'peaceful' demise of apartheid.

In the late morning, I lay fully clothed on a bed in a house in Umtata, watching Nozi tearfully preparing my things for my departure. She was tough, and this was the first time I had seen her cry.

"Are you really leaving me, dear?" she asked, sobbing.

Nozi's slant eyes had earned her the nickname of 'Chinaeyes' among her friends. Her firm body was a result of a strict dietary regime and regular exercise. Falling in love with her introduced me to what I had always dismissed as capitalist indulgences: on Valentine's Day she would spoil me with gifts, flowers and cards, and I had to reciprocate. I regretted the day I didn't send her a card on Secretary's Day. She scolded me because she had told me the date a few days earlier; I hadn't known about it.

The wall of her bedroom just above the headboard was covered with cards from her former boyfriend and from me. They resembled one-winged, colourful butterflies.

The pillow on which I rested my head had wisps of my hair on it – I had developed the habit of pulling out my hair while I was in exile. Days before, Nozi had lamented that she would miss those strands of hair.

The bedroom was on the first floor of a double-storey house in Fort Gale in Umtata. Over the last few days I had helped Nozi tend the yard and plant flowers. She had asked me to plant a red rose so she could remember me through it.

She had always demanded my complete attention, which I found difficult to give because of my shadowy existence. She loved me and was my anchor and comfort in a turbulent world.

"You mean you are really leaving me, dear?"

"Yes," I replied, keeping my face hidden behind the newspaper I was pretending to read.

She grabbed it and threw it on the dressing table. "Yes what? You don't even say 'yes dear'. You have no feelings."

"Yes, dear," I obeyed her orders, and it struck me that these could be the last I'd take from her.

"But why are you leaving? Your leaders are sorting things out with the government."

"I know, but that is a farce. I'll settle for nothing less than the return of my land. My leaders are discussing indemnity and integration: I did not dedicate my life to winning such trifles."

I had watched events in Azania – a name for South Africa adopted by a section of the liberation movement, including the PAC – from 1990, when FW de Klerk had unbanned the liberation movements. I had followed the talks at the Convention for a Democratic South Africa, Codesa, in Kempton Park. I had also felt the excitement around me as the country prepared for the first post-apartheid elections, now only a few days away.

In Umtata, I heard people speaking animatedly about the coming elections and liberation in a way that implied that the two were synonymous. The faithful of all parties swarmed the town putting up posters with their colours, slogans and the faces of their leaders.

If elections are a game of numbers, the African National Congress was going to win convincingly. Multitudes attended its rallies; thousands wore its T-shirts and sang its songs.

My own party, the Pan Africanist Congress, was split in the middle, with some members saying no to the elections and vowing to continue the armed struggle, while others supported participation in the elections.

A handful of us supported both the elections and the continuation of the armed struggle. Generations of serious revolutionaries have known that the two are not mutually exclusive: you use parliament for barking and the army for biting. I was one of the very few in the PAC who believed in this bark and bite strategy.

These elections were not a guarantee of democracy. A true democracy fulfils the material needs of the people it serves. In this case, the landless and those without property would not enjoy the fruits of democracy however many times they voted.

While political democracy was a welcome breeze in the suffocating neo-Nazi atmosphere of South Africa, economic tyranny was not shaken by the Codesa agreements. The Codesa process was cleverly designed to protect whites and help them retain what they had taken away from Africans by force.

The tree of democracy should be planted in soil that nurtures it –

that is, land and property fairly distributed among the workers. Only radical action would bring about true democracy. I believed the liberation movements needed to retain their arms to ensure a swift movement to that goal.

For me personally, there was no freedom in sight. I'd just read in the newspapers that the Attorneys General of the Orange Free State and the North-Eastern Cape had issued warrants for my arrest for "terrorism, murder, attempted murder and arson". My photograph had been published in newspapers and shown on TV, and a reward of one hundred thousand rand was promised for information leading to my arrest and conviction. All this just a few days before the elections.

"You don't love me," Nozi cried.

I couldn't hold back my tears. I cried too and we locked our arms in firm embrace.

Her house had been my home on and off over the years. I was leaving it with dim prospects of ever returning, just as I had left scores of other houses scattered through Azania, Botswana, Lesotho, Zimbabwe and Swaziland.

That evening Nozi finished packing my bags. In the early hours of the morning she cooked two chickens and lots of porridge for the road. Before dawn, we again embraced and exchanged good wishes; then I drove off in the Corolla that Transkeian leader General Bantu Holomisa had lent the PAC. The journey back into exile had started.

I was leaving to avoid arrest, since there was no general amnesty for freedom fighters – not to regroup and continue war against South Africa. War is a corollary of politics: if politically you are outnumbered a hundred to one, you have no justification for waging a war. I was convinced that the war was over, and what was left for me to do was to persuade other combatants and militant members of the organisation that this was so.

The PAC had suspended its armed struggle in February 1994 (although some of its leaders continued telling supporters at rallies that they would be intensifying the armed struggle in the new year). The last orders I had given were that the units should keep their arms, but not attack.

I drove to the University of the Transkei three km away and picked up Freakout Ntlanganiso, who was to drive me to Lesotho. Freakout was studying commerce at the university. Besides his nerves of steel, he was multilingual. His light complexion, medium height and moderate built concealed a deadly warrior.

We left the Corolla in Umtata and transferred to a Nissan four-wheel-drive vehicle, with its back neatly covered with black canvas. It was owned by the Azanian People's Liberation Army (Apla), the PAC's armed wing. It was air-conditioned and among other things was equipped with an altimeter, enabling us to read how high above sea-level we were driving. Its windows were tinted and its exhaust pipe elongated for extra power. I called it the Blue Monster.

The Monster had already done service, concealing anything from secret documents to light machine guns in her body.

The ride from Umtata to Mount Frere was smooth because the road was tarred. From Mount Frere, as the sun was rising, we turned north and braced ourselves for a long stretch of bumpy road that ultimately led us to the Ongeluksnek border post, one of the friendliest I have ever used.

Jazzman, an immigration officer I knew well, was not on duty that day, but the mere mention of his name evoked warmth from his colleagues. We gave them the food we had brought along for Jazzman, but asked them to pass the liquor on to him.

As we bid them farewell, one immigration officer jubilantly said, "Brothers, this could be the last time we serve you in our capacity as Transkeian civil servants. Come April 27, we'll be a new and united country. There'll no longer be a Transkei. We'll all be Azanians in the Republic of Azania, with Comrade Nelson Mandela as our president. I'm just wondering what the passports of Azania will look like."

"They'll be beautiful," I said and waved them goodbye as Freakout eased the car into Lesotho.

My poor countrymen. They had pitched their expectations far above what was in store for them.

— Chapter One —

I WAS TOLD that I was born on December 8, 1960 in my mother's village of Rosenkrantz in the northern Transvaal. Although she had a son before me, who died in his first year, she still gave birth to me at her parents' village, in the Sesotho tradition of bearing firstborns at their maternal grandparents' homes.

I was given my late brother's status and name – Ngoato; but a relative called me Letlapa, and that was so popular it became my official name. Ngoato remains my salutation name, used when I'm addressed at traditional ceremonies and rituals.

Nine months after my birth my mother and I went to Manaleng. We were soon joined by my aunt Machuene, my mother's younger sister. Machuene was a mofepi, a family member who joined a new mother to help her raise a child.

I had three other brothers and three sisters. Throughout my days underground I believed I had only two brothers, only to discover in 1996 that I had another, Kagisho, born during my absence from my fatherland.

My early memories are only of my village of Manaleng, one of numerous villages in GaMphahlele. By design rather than by accident it is situated at the foot of Molongoane, part of the Kgoahlampa – what white South Africans call the Drakensberg – chain that stretches into Natal, rising in Lesotho and coming to rest in the Western Cape. In winter Molongoane cast a chilly shadow over our poorly thatched rondavel huts. In summer when it was very hot, it hoarded its shade.

The mountain was used as a communal toilet. When pigs saw someone disappearing into the bush, they followed. The swine would grunt around the person as he relieved himself, and before he pulled his pants up, would gobble up the steamy lump and grunt for more.

Childhood memories are a patchy collage. I remember the mophane worms and grasshoppers that made good additions to our porridge dishes. We boys and girls would go to the neighbouring village of Molalaneng to catch grasshoppers – lempo, mammati, letlorontlope and saborokong. Lempo was big and delicious. We plucked their wings and severed their legs before we roasted them.

We considered families that ate white maize meal all the time to be wealthy; nothing was as joyous as seeing a truck stop in front of one's home to deliver a bag of it. The poorer families had to eat sorghum porridge when we had no money for maize meal. Sorghum, dark brown and rough and said to be highly nutritious by its pundits, was never my favourite: it may have been nutritious but it was not palatable. It used to fill pots when pockets were empty.

I remember playing with my friends under the huge morula tree in front of our house. There was a big stone at its base, and the child who got to it first would sit on it. The older boys would come later and push us away.

We would be chattering away happily and our elders would be sitting under the shade too, away from us, drinking their beer.

I remember weddings; and in the weeks before, going to watch people older than me, from teenagers to grown men and women, practising songs and dances in the moonlight. "Dikuku di monate, lenyalo le boima – the cakes are delicious but marriage is difficult," they would sing, and the women would ululate.

Among those early songs, one rang constantly in my head: "Afrika lefase la bo ntat'arona le tserwe ke makgowa" – Africa, our fathers' land, has been taken away by whites.

This song was to shape my life.

I remember going with my father, Radikubu, to visit the village of Lekushoaneng. He drank sorghum beer and whisky with his friends while I went to play with other boys in the bush. When we returned at sunset, I found Father had left me behind.

I insisted on walking back to Manaleng, about seven km away, through bush and other villages.

Home at last. Nkone, my mother, rushed out joyfully and swooped me up in her arms. "Sputnik! Sony! Sony, Kamiti. Kancati. Ka dairy meleke!" She chanted the nicknames and endearments she always used when she talked to me.

There was a crowd around us. My tipsy father had come back without me and announced that he didn't know where I was. There was anxiety and panic and before long the neighbours were gathered in my home, trying to decide where to look for me. Father thought the hullabaloo was a joke, because this was the way boys grew up to be tough men: I had to find my way home.

We knew that Father was home when we heard his shout of "Sony, Sony!" – one of my nicknames – long before we saw him. He didn't call out the names of the other children.

In his way he loved me but because he was a man, he was not as demonstrative as Mother. We saw him at weekends and when he was on leave. For the rest he was away at work.

Mohlolatlala, my brother, and Nthabiseng, my sister, sometimes complained that I was the favourite, but Mother would respond by telling them that I was obedient and did my chores without complaining. They were loved just as much as I was.

I remember a journey by bus to far-off New Look township in Pietersburg, now renamed Polokwane. The crowds, the confusing bustle and noise and finally the room that my father rented in the backyard of a house in the township: at last I got to know where he went to on weekdays. This is where he stayed to be near his workplace; he was a driver in the town.

Ah, the opulence of the town. In the weeks we were in Pietersburg, we didn't have to eat morogo (wild spinach) with our porridge – we had meat. There were fish and chips. A visit to a supermarket in Pietersburg left me with the impression that towns were certainly wealthy. We filled our baskets with all sorts of goodies from the shelves and because I didn't notice Father paying, I thought they were free.

It was during this exciting visit that we stopped calling Father Radikubu. Mother insisted that we call him Tate, Father.

Back to Manaleng, where the only car in the village was owned by the sangoma Matane. The previous owner had used it as a taxi, because it still had the sign saying "Nie-Blankes" on its roof. We would scream and run after this fascinating machine, shouting "Nie-Blankes, Nie-Blankes!" as Matane drove in and out of the village.

I don't know how my paternal grandmother earned the name Ntate, Sesotho for father. I never thought of asking the family elders, but I assumed she got it because of her resourcefulness. When she was out visiting and was given food, she would eat a little and then bring the rest back for Mohlolatlala and me. The Lord's Prayer in Northern Sesotho opens with the phrase, "Ntate wesho wa magodimong," and she was a father who saw to it that her children got their daily meal.

Mother didn't like the habit. She couldn't stop it and she didn't try; she just frowned when Ntate brought the food.

Mother and Tate would use a belt, a stick or even a wooden clothes hanger to hit us when they were angry. Ntate, tall and strong, would get angry when we were beaten, especially if it was by Father.

She would wrap her protective arms around us and scream at Father: "Who beat you when you were that small?"

As I grew up, I discovered Ntate's popularity in the house was limited. Rumour had it that contrary to tribal customs, she used to fight back tigerishly against her late husband. No man her age would take chances fighting her.

The old people in the village would shake their heads and murmur that she would not live long because of the internal and external bleeding she sustained during the fights with her husband. Mother agreed with them.

Ntate was not the only grandparent in the house. There was ancient Great-grandmother Tsokoane, who had outlived every soul in Manaleng and the surrounding villages. In fact, I have yet to see a human being as old as Matladi, Tsokoane's salutation name. I wasn't as close to her as was Mohlolatlala. He had resorted to Tsokoane's flabby, dry breasts when Mother weaned him. Ntate told me that Father too had sucked Tsokoane's breasts after weaning.

Tsokoane was like an ambassador of the spirits in the world of flesh and blood.

She fought courageous but fruitless battles with the government over her old age pension. She had been getting it for many years, but things went awry when one of her daughters-in-law burned her dompas, her identity document, during a quarrel. When Tsokoane tried to get another from the authorities in order to continue drawing her pension, she was told to come back later for it. Every time she went, she was told to come back, again and again and again. When I became aware of the world around me she was already in this come-back-to-morrow business. I remember once accompanying her to the authorities at Moshate, the Chief's Great Place, to try and get her pass.

Dr Machupe Mphahlele (no relation), a gynaecologist of note, also tried to help her. I was certain a doctor would achieve what we lay people couldn't deliver. He failed.

Matladi died in the early 1970s, having lost years of old age pension.

After watching her struggle, I was put off passes and vowed not to have one when I grew up. Perhaps I had started my fight even before I realised it, because I didn't have a birth certificate or any other document attesting to my existence.

I wouldn't be the first in this fight against the pass laws: adult men ran to the mountain at the sight of a police van. Rumour had it that they either had no documents, or if they had, they were not in order. I imagined myself forming an alliance with them – an alliance of retreat to the mountains.

The men were not the only ones who panicked at the sight of khwela-mahala – 'free ride', or the police van. The women who brewed tototo also fled when the van appeared. The village children who first spotted the khwelamahala would whistle and shout "Copper, copper!" The women would hide their drums of liquor in holes and cover them up, or if the van was too close, they would simply pour the liquor out and destroy any evidence the police might hold on to.

Ordinary sorghum beer was brewed in my home and not the illicit stuff, and the men had their passes, but we were not spared from fear. In the house we had a long, rusty spear that would have made a good museum piece, which had to be hidden under the big clay pots whenever rumour of a house-to-house search reached us. The police never searched our house and the spear survived.

The police, the courts, the magistrates and the commissioners were the authorities that were respected and feared in the village, not Mogalatjane, who was the chief of Manaleng. The village bell on a tree in front of his house was the only visible sign that he was the chief. Besides that Mogalatjane was ordinary; no, perhaps a degree less than ordinary, as he had continual conversations with companions none of us could see, rebuking them, egging them on and joking and laughing with them. Children followed him and laughed, but I stopped when Mother told me if I kept laughing at him I would be like him when I grew up. Under his strong bones and tall frame lay weakness: not the weakness of an individual but the weakness of the clan, of the nation and of humanity. Mogale (his salutation name) was not made in the mould of Shaka. He had no army at his command. Nor beasts. He went around begging like any of us.

It wasn't just Mogale. People were disrespectful of the new breed of chief. The present crop was susceptible to corruption: a nip of whisky was enough to sway a decision in a dispute. These chiefs were unlike their forebears who had been tough, disciplined warriors who led their armies into glorious battles. Although some of them were tyrants, they carried the decisive last word. They did not defer to a myriad of unscrupulous courts, magistrates and commissioners as the Mogales had to.

The old chiefs were not merely the owners of the soil – they were the soil. Thus when a chief dies the Northern Basotho say, "Mabu a utswitswe – the soil has been stolen."

Once Mogale was judge in a dispute over land – my family and our neighbours clashed over a small plot. It's difficult to say which family was the legitimate heir to that barren land, but Mogale took sides against my family. Muffled conspiratorial voices floated over the mmoto, the homestead mud boundary wall, loud enough to be heard by those who agreed with them but not by the enemy. Sympathisers came into our house to throw their weight behind my family.

"Madi a tla tshologa – blood shall spill," both families threatened. Blood and land were bound together by their sacredness.

Father planted four corner poles to indicate that the land was really his. The following day we found them uprooted and replaced by different poles. Blood boiled in my young veins. We uprooted their poles and re-erected ours. Overnight they did the same in a ding-dong battle.

Mother took the battle to new fronts. She filled barrels with water and placed them on the disputed site, a mark of ownership in that dry village. The water was spilled overnight and we found empty containers strewn around. Mother screamed obscenities at the perpetrators of that crime, plotting and counter-plotting in the neighbourhood. She concluded by threatening to bewitch all her adversaries.

"I, daughter of Moabelo, am not a novice in witchcraft," Mother shouted. "I sucked witchcraft from my mother's breasts. Time has now come to use it and I'm going to use it without mercy."

A few days later Mogalatjane was bitten in the hand by a rat. The hand swelled and for some days he was bedridden. The mischievous rat ended what could have been a bloody war: our adversaries retreated for fear of the all-conquering rodent.

— Chapter Two —

WHEN I WAS NINE YEARS OLD and in Standard Two, Father insisted that I be exposed to the life of looking after livestock. He said a boy was no boy and would not make a good man if he couldn't look after goats. He spoke from experience.

Father said when he was young, 'heathen' boys looked after the goats of the Christians. He had gone to the neighbouring Christian village of Maupaneng to herd the goats of an old man called Moses. During his stay there he was excluded from indulging in Christian luxuries like drinking tea and eating white bread. Instead he was given fresh goat milk and brown bread. He grew up resenting the crude treatment he had received at the hands of the Christians, but still believed looking after livestock was good for boys.

I was to be exiled to my maternal grandparents' village, Rosenkrantz, in GaMatlala' Thaba, to look after goats, sheep, donkeys and calves. Our family in Manaleng did not have livestock and only three families in the village had cattle and goats.

When I arrived in Rosenkrantz I found a world different from Manaleng. Through the bus windows, I saw that the land swarmed with life and was decorated with it. Trees of all kinds stood proud and beautiful against the lush green backdrop.

The houses were built wide apart and people in a house could shout at each other without their neighbours hearing what the acrimony was all about. Virtually every homestead had a cattle kraal. Some, like my grandfather's, had more than one.

It was late afternoon when I walked from the bus stop to my grandfather's. The animals were returning home, many of them to be milked. The smells of green vegetation, of animal dung, of milk – all invaded my nostrils. The mooing of cows, the bleating of sheep and the chirping of birds were all parts in the welcoming song.

Grandfather, Grandmother, aunts, uncles and cousins welcomed me warmly and the children my age giggled, mimicking my dialect.

I wandered to the kraal to join a boy named Mmonoa, who was milking the cows. He told me to use a stick to keep the calves away from the cows, and to let them out one at a time to suck for a while and soften the udders before he milked the cow. This was to be my role, that of mokotedi, in the milking; in the years I spent in Rosenkrantz, I never milked a cow myself.

We returned to the house and I found a feast waiting. There were fresh milk, whey, sour milk, morogo and game meat. As my aunts spread enamel plates to dish out the sumptuous meal, I planned how I was going to eat mine: I would start with porridge and meat, switch to porridge and sour milk, and then wash it down with fresh milk. I was disappointed though, because the children were told to choose only one protein food to add to the porridge. I quickly learnt that children could not enjoy more than one type of meat during a meal. That evening I chose porridge with fresh milk.

Grandfather's porridge was dished out in a mogopo, a wooden dish.

I thus joined a large family of uncles and aunts, cousins and others whose relationship with me was rather obscure. It was warm but I still missed the deep affection that I enjoyed back home. Here there was no Ntate to recite family praises whenever I pleased her and no one used my nicknames of Sputnik and Sony.

Looking after the goats was difficult. They ran helter-skelter with the bells round their necks ringing incessantly, and tried in vain to climb trees with their front hooves while teetering on their hind legs. They shifted from one tree to the next as if the untasted leaves were sweeter.

Sheep were not troublesome and the least worrying were the calves. Donkeys were restrained with leather straps tied round their front legs.

Talking about donkeys, I remember an incident one afternoon when a police van screeched to a halt in front of the house. A white policeman and his African colleague jumped out. The white instructed his colleague to untie the donkeys. As if his junior were too slow, Whitey joined in the work of setting the donkeys free.

Grandmother, short and stout, screamed, her squint eyes burning fury. She shouted to Grandfather for help.

"Ramotsejwa ke die mense" was Grandfather's nickname, which translates as "the one well known by the people." He was a fierce fighter, and a tough disciplinarian who sliced my bare back with a stick if goats came home late. I expected him to rush out of the hut and join Grandmother, at least in shouting at the intruders. He didn't. He remained glued to his stool, mumbling something meant to mean nothing.

The donkeys' freedom was short-lived, however. Grandfather, tall and subdued, emerged from the hut after the animal liberators had driven off and instructed me to hobble them again. That day Grandmother was my heroine.

For three years goats were my hell. I remember the day I jumped awake at the explosion – "Rata-tat-tat!" – as the sky was split by lightning and the earth heaved. The clouds were dark and intimidating, threatening to burst and flood the baked earth. I had dozed off in the shade of a mopipi tree. Now the whole world was covered by the shade cast by the brooding clouds.

There was no goat in sight.

I strained my ears to hear the bells they carried round their necks. Nothing. I ran around, searching. I prayed to the God of Abraham, Isaac and Jacob to help me find the goats. After a while I saw a jackal feasting on the carcass of a goat. It ran off as I approached.

In a panic I ran home to get a wheelbarrow to carry the carcass. As I was blindly running I saw the herd, which had fled when attacked by the jackal.

The physical beating I got from Grandfather was bad enough, but the worst punishment was the constant taunts and jeers about my abilities as a shepherd. We would be sitting around the fire and Grandfather would curse: "Ever since I've had you as a herdboy, I've lost a goat or a sheep every day!"

On his balance sheet, I was a liability. I couldn't milk cows, nor could I hold on to an ox-drawn plough. Grandmother would join in with her comments and my aunts would add their bits and I would squirm in shame.

Perhaps I slept on duty because I ate heavily before I went out to herd, often porridge and sour milk.

Herding livestock was not my only problem. While other boys combined good herding skills with hunting ones, I never brought home a hare that I had caught. I didn't even know how to trap birds – but one day I brought home a bird that "would extinguish a fire with its dripping fat". Everybody was surprised that I had trapped it.

"You're now becoming a boy," Aunt Phuti commended me.

The following day Mmonoa exposed my secret: I bought the bird from another boy for two cents. I was deeply humiliated.

This incident pushed me to learning how to trap birds. I set the traps, but when the time came to check whether there was a kill, I would invite one or two other people to accompany me as witnesses that I was not a cheat.

Another art that I learnt in those days was whistling. I drank lots of urine along the way because we believed that drinking cow's urine was a precondition to mastery.

Goats and sheep were not my only occupation. I also attended school.

Lamola, our principal at the Rosenkrantz Primary School, should have been pensioned off years before. Rumour had it that he rejected the Education Department's pension offer, arguing that pensioners always died a year after retirement. Lamola had taught Grandmother and Mother. I was now his pupil.

He was the darling of every pupil, but his teaching staff disliked him for the same reasons that we loved him: he allowed us to go home after the mid-morning break. He would be seated on a chair under a tree, half-drunk and fighting off sleep. He nodded his grey head at regular intervals, and it was up to the pupil to edge in his request to go home somewhere between the nods.

I was one of those who always left school at break. Something told me I was ruining my chances of passing at the end of the year, but I rationalised by telling myself that I didn't need much education to be a miner or a labourer. I had made up my mind about my future career.

I hated Thursday, the handwork day. Thursday is called Donderdag in Afrikaans, the day of beatings, and our teachers interpreted it literally. We always had the worst beatings on Thursdays. I always left the preparations for handwork for Wednesday evening, when I would run around collecting sisal and preparing the fibre for weaving. In the handwork class on Thursday I would pretend to be busy weaving. After school I would throw my crude efforts away, hoping to do something better in the remaining six days. This cycle worked until the teacher demanded that everyone bring his handwork to school for end of year marking. I had nothing that I had produced.

I stole Mmonoa's sisal basket. It was possibly the best in the school.

I was worried by its artistry and beauty, so I soiled my hands and rubbed them on it to make it dirty to suit me. The basket stubbornly refused to part with its magic. I hid it in a plastic bag till I was called to present my work. I dragged my feet towards the teacher at the table in front. When I uncovered the basket giggles swept across the room.

The teacher held the basket, looked at it and at me, and burst into uncontrollable laughter. The whole class joined her.

"Whose basket is this?" Miss Mamabolo asked.

The other pupils had not been asked that. It wasn't really a question but I answered, pretending to be confident: "It's mine, madam."

"Who wove it for you?"

"I wove it myself."

"Are you sure you wove it yourself?"

"Yes, madam."

"Children, is he telling the truth?"

There was a chorus of "No!" that nearly lifted the roof.

"You see, this can't be your work. Don't think I don't know you," she said. She called Caiphus Selomo, a pupil who lived near my home, and whispered something to him. He went out and came back with Mmonoa.

"Are you Mmonoa?" the teacher asked him.

"Yes, madam." '

"Do you see these baskets on the table?"

"Yes, mistress." '

"Can you pick yours?"

Without hesitation, Mmonoa picked up his basket and I wished the ground could swallow me.

"Shame." The word was murmured by many in the class, not with its usual English meaning but with the African connotation of sympathy. They knew what was in store for me on this Donderdag.

Miss Mamabolo called a male colleague of hers to come and administer the cruel caning, and she added a sermon on cheating.

End of year reports came and I had passed. I was the most surprised person because I had already resigned myself to repeating Standard Two. They even gave me marks for handwork. "What handwork?" I wondered quietly.

Awake and in my dreams, I was haunted by images of my home Ga-Mphahlele. Pictures of Manaleng, Magaseng, Manganeng, Molalaneng, Diraganeng, Maupaneng, Mamogoshudu, Maleka, Thabaneng and other villages in GaMphahlele flashed in front of me. I always looked southwards in the direction of GaMphahlele. The pictures I conjured were filled with play and fun and little work.

Then in December 1973 the pictures became real when I finally returned to Manaleng.

— Chapter Three —

THE BUS GINGERLY WENT down one steep bank of the Hlakaro River and up the other to get to Manaleng. Tears welled in my eyes: I had the habit of crying whenever I left or arrived home. It also happened when I arrived in Rosenkrantz but not when I left it. By the time the bus stopped I was sobbing uncontrollably.

My mind was shuttling between Rosenkrantz and Manaleng, between GaMatlala and GaMphahlele. I had spent three years away from home.

The place had changed and I liked some of the changes and disliked others. Mother had a fourth child, Malose; Tsokoane had died.

Manaleng boys had their own football club; my former classmates were a class ahead of me because I had failed Standard Three in Rosenkrantz. We now had a communal tap in the village and no longer had to draw water from springs or from the Hlakaro.

I had left Rosenkrantz with a reputation as a bad herdboy and an even worse pupil. Now my playmates in Manaleng laughed at me and mocked the way I spoke in the northern dialect of my mother. I would rehearse sentences in my mind before uttering them to avoid making a fool of myself. Still they would laugh. At school our teacher laughed at me too and oral tests were torture.

However, it didn't take me long to get my old dialect back and put my linguistic problems behind me. I took my place in the home and in the community.

In Manaleng I was not judged by my skills in herding goats or sheep: a child's worth was measured by his or her skills in hewing firewood, drawing water and cooking. I was at home here but not without silly lapses. One day I sliced tomatoes as Mohlolatlala and Nthabiseng looked on. This was my first step from the peripheral duties of cleaning pots and dishes to actually cooking. After slicing the tomatoes, I realised that I hadn't washed them. I tried to wash the pieces and my little brother and sister burst out laughing.

I also learnt how to make bricks using sand from the Hlakaro. I learnt to mix six wheelbarrow-loads of sand with one bag of cement and water to make about 50 bricks. These I used to build a toilet and other structures around the house.

I felt a little guilty taking the sand from the river. It made me feel as if I were a conspirator with the limping man who had established a brick-making firm, and drew tons of fine sand from the Hlakaro's rich belly every day. We gored holes into the dream river.

With my confidence restored, I was getting to be more and more useful around the house. I planted extra trees in the yard, and every afternoon I carried water in a bucket from the communal tap to water them. I built a rockery with stones picked from the Hlakaro. Father enthusiastically supported the tree planting and often brought home saplings. A few survived and flourished. Four jacaranda saplings that Father brought from town died because I forgot to plant them. I remembered that I had to plant them only when Father smiled contentedly during a thunderstorm and said: "With rain like this you need not water the jacarandas."

"What jacarandas?" I asked.

"The ones I brought you to plant. Where are they?"

"Oh, I forgot."

We raced to the door, Father kicking and insulting me in pursuit. He didn't follow me outside. I planted the trees. More rain came down and they were flooded. I sheltered in the shack in the yard till the storm passed. When Father went out for a drink, I went into the house to change clothes. Mother criticised me for forgetfulness and said I was lucky to have a tough father.

"He'll make you a man yet," she said.

On my return from Rosenkrantz I joined the Manaleng Hotbeans Football Club. Before I left for Rosenkrantz the most popular football club was Mooihoek, with most of its players from Manaleng, Manganeng and Magaseng. They were the local giants, clad in black and gold jerseys.

I now found that Hillside F.C. had ousted Mooihoek to become the iron-fisted tyrants of local soccer. It was composed largely of players from Thabaneng and students from outside GaMphahlele.

I joined Hotbeans simply because it was a Manaleng team. I was given the nickname Danger Sewalawala or sometimes The Great. Both were misnomers as there was nothing in my football that remotely resembled greatness or danger for the opposition. I later found out that I earned a place in the side as a reward for my punctuality and regular attendance at practice sessions. Latecomers were whipped on the buttocks. Anybody who used obscene language or fought in the football ground was also whipped.

I played in the B division, although frankly I don't believe I deserved a place even in the C division.

My younger brother Mohlolatlala played fairly well and could also keep goal. One day when he was the keeper during a practice session a miracle happened: I scored a goal, according to everyone but my brother. He argued it was not a goal. He said the ball passed close to the goalpost but outside. He appealed to me to tell the truth.

"It was a clear goal," I swore.

Truth is that my brother was right.

Back home I confessed that it was not a goal and pleaded with Mohlolatlala to understand that I couldn't let an opportunity like that slip through my fingers. He understood and forgave me.

It was almost impossible to 'eat' Hotbeans – the expression we used when one side beat another. And it was not because Hotbeans was a talented team but because when it became clear we were headed for defeat, the Manaleng lads would start a fist fight and the match would be abandoned.

Maredi 'Oshkosh' Sebake, a big lad, would chase the ball and hold it in his hands. When the referee judged for a handball, he argued and threatened violence. The decision had to be in his favour for the game to continue. No disciplinary action was taken against him, no matter what violation he committed. In retrospect, I think he would have been a star in rugby.

In the club he was responsible for whipping those who violated the rules. He loved it, played and fought for it.

Internal wrangling and poor attendance left Hotbeans cold and disgusting. By then I was club treasurer. Mother kept the money for me and often borrowed it to buy domestic items like salt or a tin of fish. When I stopped attending practice a delegation from the club descended on my home one afternoon to fetch their money. Fortunately

Mother had just replenished it so I gave them the five rand and the book corroborating the amount. They appeared surprised that it was all there. My ties with Hotbeans ended that afternoon.

Inspired by the national soccer legend Kaizer Motaung, I regrouped disillusioned members of Hotbeans and we founded Danger United. We cleared a piece of ground, erected goalposts and used it as our playing field. Before long we had money in excess of twenty rand, with which we bought a whistle and a standard football. We celebrated each victory with bread and achar, a mango pickle.

I dreamt of Danger United challenging and beating Kaizer Chiefs, a child's dream.

Sadly the club collapsed, never to rise again, because of poor attendance and because my attention was drawn away from football.

— Chapter Four —

THE PEOPLE OF GAMPHAHLELE call going to the mountain (going to the initiation school) koma, and every winter they chant: "koma ka dilete e a bogwa" – circumcision is celebrated by all nations.

Legend was that the practice of male circumcision was started in the distant and dim past by a man called Mohusoa. The foreskin of his penis was pierced by a stalk and he couldn't pull out a stubborn splinter. He had to cut off the skin to get relief. When the penis was healed it was unique and was envied by other men. They asked him to cut off their foreskins and thus the practice of male circumcision was born.

I've heard variations of this story in different parts of Africa. In Lesotho, for example, the originator, a herdboy called Ratladi, was trampled by a cow while he was at a cattle post and his penis was injured. The older men decided to cut off his foreskin.

Initiation is done in winter and always on the mountain. Traditionalists argue that it marks the transition from childhood to adulthood.

I was sceptical because I had seen initiated people stealing chickens or other items of insignificant value. I had seen them do things that self-respecting men wouldn't do. I expected people who had passed into adulthood to be more skilled and better equipped to face life's challenges. Apart from the cloak of superiority that they wrapped around themselves, they were ordinary.

That winter of 1975, Father told me that I was going to climb the mountain for initiation. Since he was away at work most of the time, he left an old man called Mahupe to be in charge of my initiation rites.

On the eve of my departure, Mother looked worried and perturbed. In her Bakone clan circumcision was taboo. Now she was witnessing her first-born take a leap into the dark.

After supper, Mother boiled sweet potatoes and persuaded me to eat a few.

"Eat, my child. I wonder what they eat on the mountain," she said, as if those sweet potatoes would satisfy my hunger for the duration of my initiation.

Ntate was happy beyond words that her grandson was on the verge of manhood.

Other boys my age were also preparing to go to the mountain. There were many circumcision schools and each boy was taken to the one preferred by his parents. I was to go to Mamagohle – which Father chose because it was reputed to be the toughest.

The regular academic schools had just closed for the winter, so the initiation wouldn't interfere with our formal schooling to a significant degree.

The following day Mahupe knocked on the door, clad in a coat and carrying a switch and a blanket.

"Where is the boy?" he asked in a businesslike manner.

I hastily dressed and joined him.

"Have a safe journey, my son," Mother said as we slipped into the darkness.

Mahupe was a man of few words, and we were quiet most of the way. He walked briskly, as if we were late.

Nature too was quiet, with only the shuffle of our urgent feet bruising the silence. Even the mountains were in deep slumber.

We crossed Hlakaro River, turned east and walked parallel to the river for some distance. Molongoane was now behind us. Before us loomed the silhouette of the larger and higher Maake Mountain. The night seemed to turn darker when we traversed the eucalyptus plantation at Maleka. In the plantation dry leaves and twigs crushed under our feet and a light breeze caressed the tree branches, defying the silence.

We walked through ploughed fields before starting the rocky climb up the mountain. The veil of the night was beginning to peel off and we stepped up the pace. We turned north and then climbed more steeply to the summit. As we descended on the other side, I became tenser and fear gripped me as I heard voices filling the mountain and echoing beyond.

"Are you afraid?" Mahupe asked.

"Yes."

"Invasion!" a man shouted when he saw us. Switches whistled and cracked and other men repeated the chant: "Invasion!"

Men wielding switches charged at us. I looked at Mahupe, wishing he would shout to me to run away, but the short man was unruffled. That comforted me.

He addressed them: "Hey, young men, I have no business with you. Where is Rabadia?" This is the name of the head of an initiation school.

"He's by the fireside," one answered. "We know you have no business with us but please lend us this young man."

"You can have him. He's yours." Thus I was detached from Mahupe's protection.

The men didn't beat me up – they just asked me my name and what village I came from.

"Invasion!" they shouted and turned their attention to other new arrivals. The numbers were swelling and the voices rising in volume. There was a large contingent of dogs and their barking, fighting and wailing added to the din.

Still more men "invaded" the mountain. I didn't have to see them: the cry of "invasion" and the whistling of switches signalled that somebody was entering the ancestral shrine.

At sunrise somebody broke into song and all men joined in. We the uninitiated were left out because we didn't know it. Men stamped their feet and waved their sticks, knobkieries and switches to the rhythm of the warrior song.

Some baditi, young instructors who have graduated from the initiation school, assembled the newcomers.

One of them said: "Listen carefully to this song. You'll never hear it again unless one of you dies during the initiation. It is the anthem of the mountain and we sing it only on the first day of camp or when somebody is dead."

I got to know that baditi did the cooking in the school, drew water, brought supplies from the village and did other chores besides mentoring us.

My mind could not settle on the song as we were herded away from the singing men. About 150 metres away we were ordered to queue according to the seniority of our families in the tribe: the son of the chief was at the head of the queue and I was somewhere in the middle.

The men we had left were still singing as they grouped themselves into three circles. We were ordered to go one at a time to the middle of the first circle. When my turn came, a mass of humanity opened and then surrounded me. One of the men cut my long trousers into short pants with a sharp knife. I had prized the trousers and my heart ached when I saw them reduced into shorts in this summary manner. The next circle opened to swallow me and I was ordered to take off my jersey, shirt and vest. As I unbuttoned the shirt, a firm hand grabbed its collar and pulled it off, ripping the buttons loose.

In the third circle I was ordered to take off my shoes, trousers and underpants. They were thrown on a big heap of other clothes, to be burned with everything else at the end of our stay.

I stepped into the open as the last circle closed behind me, and I was instructed to sit on a large rock. And so on that chilly morning I was made to bleed for my manhood.

It was a bloody and painful day during which we ate nothing. At sunset we were herded to the mphato, the open camp about 50 metres in diameter, surrounded by rocks and newly cut tree branches. We sat in a circle at the perimeter, according to the rank of our families. There was an inner circle of fire that had to burn unceasingly for the duration of our stay; in the centre were three pyramids of different sizes built of rocks. Rabadia ignited the fire in the ancient way of creating friction between two pieces of wood.

Rabadia and the baditi had smaller camps near the entrance to ours. Food was cooked at the baditi camp.

We were asked how we would like to have our porridge for dinner – with sour milk, kudu biltong or morogo. We were told we could have all three if we liked. But we were shocked when we found out what the foods were: different types of beatings. Kudu biltong, for example, was a slash with a switch on the bare back. We were told to imagine meat or milk as we devoured mountains of flat porridge.

We sat naked at the fireside, were taught songs and dances and sang till late at night. We slept in the open camp at our assigned places in the circle, each with a small blanket we had brought from home.

Early in the morning Rabadia gazed at the stars and worked out that it was time to wake up. For our morning bath, we had to smear ash from the fire all over our naked bodies – we were told this would keep us warm. We poured more ash on our hair so that when another part of the body lost it, we could replenish from this extra supply. We had porridge for breakfast and left the main camp to a stopover camp about 400 metres away. We were wearing the flimsy blankets around our waists and were armed with knobkieries.

At the stopover we were told that we were going hunting, and that those who were not well would be exempted and remain behind. About forty people said they were ill.

We were instructed in the craft of hunting. We were to hunt in a line curved like a horn. If anyone wanted to relieve himself, he had to run ahead of the formation and never remain behind. In that way he would not get lost.

At the command of "Take cover!" we had to fall flat on our bellies where we were, even on thorny shrubs or human excreta. At first, when we went down gingerly, selecting convenient spots, the baditi beat us with kierries and switches. They would also kick our backs if they were not flat. Before long we were braving thorns and human waste and we were commended for our mastery.

We took cover before we crossed roads, when a plane flew over us or when there was an unexpected sound.

That day we brought back a huge kill of springbok, hares and rock rabbits, but we ate none of the meat. It was the old men who enjoyed the game, and they gave the leftovers to the instructors.

Rabadia and the other old men asked us how the baditi had treated us when we were in the bush. They appeared concerned about our well-being. We were lulled by their fatherly concern and told them how we were assaulted and showed them our wounds. Those who were left at the stopover camp because they were ill were worse than we were. Suddenly the old men descended on us with switches, saying that if we had the audacity to reveal bush secrets nothing would stop us from revealing mountain secrets to women and the uncircumcised back home. They said a man, like a sheep, does not cry out.

Baditi again beat us, this time in front of the old men, for telling on them. Quickly we learnt to shut up about the ill-treatment by baditi, but the old men continued to ask us every evening what bad things the instructors had done to us.

There was no book or a pen to jot down notes; we were expected to commit our lessons on lore and poetry to memory and repeat them precisely whenever we were ordered to do so. We learnt new songs and dances.

The sadists tortured us in the name of tradition. Each mistake cost me a whipping.

Every day we went out hunting and collecting firewood under the supervision of the baditi. The old men would remain at the mphato, the camp.

Father visited the camp on weekends. He would sleep in Rabadia's camp and the following day come and instruct us like any of the other old men. He would not single me out as he went round the circle, but I was proud of him and his knowledge. He was happy beyond words to see me entering manhood.

On the eve of the closure of the school we kept vigil, singing all night.

In the morning we smeared our bodies with letsoku, a mixture of red ochre and fat, and put on our dihlaba, skin pants. Our hair was cut in the tradition of koma: the sides and back shaved, with a circular tuft left at the top.

We descended from the mountain, singing and brandishing our sticks to the rhythm. We were warned not to look back and therefore bowed our heads. The mphato behind us was set alight and black smoke rose till it was a menacing cloud. I could only imagine the long tongues of flames leaping up as the wood crackled beneath them. Initiates are not allowed to see the destruction of the mphato. The belief was that any newly circumcised person who dared to look backwards would be killed instantly by the spirits of the clan.

We arrived at Rabadia's home in Bolopa village and entered a big arena; women were ululating and blowing phalafala horns and men were reciting praise poems.

I could not identify any person I knew because my head was bowed, and I doubt if my mother or father could pick me out in sea of crimsoned humanity.

We sat on reed mats laid in a circle in the arena and wrapped ourselves in the new blankets that our families had brought along. Our families also brought us food, mainly porridge and meat. On the mountain we had been equal in deprivation, but on our graduation the quality of blanket and the quantity of food showed the initiate's family background. I'll never forget the sad sight of one of us eating mophane worms because that was all that his parents could afford. I wished I could give him some of my meat but I was not allowed to move from my mat.

Some time during the celebrations Rabadia announced the name of our regiment, Makgaloa. In the past African armies were deployed according to their mphato, or regiment.

That night Makgaloa slept in the kgoro – kraal – and the following day we dispersed to our respective villages.

Ululation and praises filled the air as we passed through the villages. Women provocatively shouted, "We'll have the warm one from the fire!" as they jokingly invited us to their beds. They cursed uncircumcised men and vowed never to marry cowards who feared to go to the mountain.

There were three of us from Manaleng – Thema, Maremele and I. We crossed the subdued Hlakaro and arrived home to excitement and jubilation. Even the winter sun extended a warm welcome to us. The children, extremely frightened by what they must have perceived to be people from some dark forest, wailed as they were brought to us and we smeared them with ochre. Goats were slaughtered for the feast and we were showered with gifts.

Thus the community declared us men.

The family formally gave me new names. Tradition demanded that we shed childhood names and assume manhood ones. I had to shed the name Letlapa and all women and uncircumcised men had to address me as Moroatshoge, my manhood name, or as Ngoato, my salutation name. Only my regiment or those who had been to the mountain before me could call me Letlapa. I, however, didn't like my manhood name, and told people at my school and in the village that I preferred to be called Letlapa. They thought I was strange, but gradually people around me accepted my choice.

As for me, I felt only relief that the rigours of the mountain had come to an end and I was returning to the normal life of a child in the village. The initiation appeared to be an episode I was glad to leave behind.

— Chapter Five —

AS THE YEAR 1975 drew to an end, I fell ill. I became so emaciated that my kneecaps slipped backwards painlessly. All day I slept under the morula tree in front of my home and brooded. Sometime I fell asleep while eating and I would wake up to find cold porridge crusted on my hands.

Mother said these symptoms were the results of the hard work she had long warned me against – moulding bricks, building the court-yard, sinking the toilet pit, fetching logs from the mountain and building a rockery.

She said in her home village, a man had worked so hard that he lost his mind. One evening as the men were drinking beer after the day's toil in the fields, the man looked up at the moon and said the sun was very hot. At first his friends thought he was joking, but when he started looking for shade under the tree, they saw it was serious. They realised he was ill when he tore his clothes off, claiming the sun was burning him.

I suspect it was not only my body that was exhausted; my mind was too. The world around me had suddenly changed, or so it seemed. I was at home yet I pined for an unknown 'home'. My yearning worsened when the sun set, and I prayed God to let me live till I was at least twenty-one. Fear of death and mental illness gripped me as I waited for God's final whistle. I feared both but preferred death to madness.

Father took me to a doctor in Pietersburg, but I found it difficult to explain my ailment to him. I told the doctor I saw things differently from how I used to see them. He asked if there was a problem with my eyes. He tested my eyes and found there was nothing wrong with them. How are things different? I couldn't explain. In the end he gave me some tablets and we left. Volumes of concern were still written on Father's face. Getting sick was bad but failing to explain it to the doctor was worse.

At night I would wake up to go and pass water outside. I would be surprised that children were still awake and singing in the festive mood of Christmas. It always told me that I had gone to bed early. The children's voices haunted me and reminded me of another place in another universe nobody knows. The lyrics of one song were very sad, telling of a child who asked where her father was and was shown his grave. I pitied the singers.

I would linger outside in the moonlight listening to the children.

I pitied Mother, whose son was on the brink of death or insanity. I imagined how she would look at my funeral, wailing uncontrollably as the wooden coffin descended into the grave. Father would be next to her, trying in vain to hold back his tears.

I restricted myself to the yard and no longer went out to play with other children. I went to the shop only after sunset.

On Christmas day Father took me to a female sangoma, a traditional doctor, in a village near ours. She exuded confidence, and looked at me as though to assure me that all my troubles would now be solved.

She told me to take my shoes off, and gave me a pouch full of bones to shake and then throw on the goatskin spread on the mud floor. I rattled the bones in the bag while Father looked on expectantly. Then I threw the bones on the mat. The sangoma read them and asked me to shake them again.

Then the words came out – from Tsokoane, my paternal great-grandmother, through the sangoma. Tsokoane was very angry at Father's house: since her departure to the land of spirits, all her material

33

relics had been desecrated. My sickness was an expression of her wrath. The sangoma said I was lucky to be alive.

However, it was not too late to mend our ways. All that Tsokoane wanted was that her great-grandson wear neck beads she left when she died. Everything would return to normal if we obeyed the command. Disobedience would be punished by death. The word of the dead should never be transgressed.

"'Now go home and look for the beads," the imperious sangoma ordered. "And you, young man, from today the beads will be part of you – you must never ever take them off, even when you're bathing. Tie them around your neck or waist, the choice is yours, but you must never take them off. If you do, you'll die."

Father nodded gratefully, as if I were healed already. He paid the sangoma – I didn't see how much – and we walked the stretch back home.

When we arrived Father told Mother about the ancestral commands, and she ransacked the house and found blue beads. She was certain they belonged to Tsokoane. I wore them around the neck.

The sangoma had not divined anything miraculous: all old women wore bead necklaces and they spent hours weaving beadwork.

I was ashamed of my baubles. That night I undressed in the dark so that my brother and sister wouldn't see my necklace.

I no longer worried about the illness but about the yoke around my neck. It enslaved me, curtailed my freedom. Even in the heat of the tropical sun I had to button up the shirt. The day after our visit to the sangoma, my cousin Hatata came to spend the night at my home. He spotted the beads and exclaimed. Then my brother and sister noticed them too.

The three said I was destined to be wealthy because Matane, a sangoma-cum-businessperson in our village, wore beads and was very rich. Matane owned cars and trucks, a restaurant and a coalyard.

I wasn't listening to them. Instead I was deeply worried that my cousin would go out blabbering about my imminent riches and girls would shy away from me, thinking I was a witch.

I felt humiliated. I had to choose between death, the end of my agonies and miseries, and the humiliation and torment of the beads. By New Year's Day I had made my choice. I went to Mother with the beads and a matchbox in my trembling hands and said: "I'm tired of these beads and I'm going to burn them now."

"Are you mad?" Mother asked.

"It's better to die or be mad than to walk around with these things."

She tried to grab me as I bolted out of the house to the nearby dump. She managed to retrieve the beads and wondered if the worst wasn't knocking on her door. Later my younger sister Mafokeng wore the beads until the string broke and they fell off bead by bead. The remaining beads were put in the toolbox.

On my side, I was relieved that I no longer wore the beads, which I had recently shifted from my neck to my waist. I was prepared to meet the gods head-on: if they were mad I would help them recover their sanity; if they decided to call me to their world, I'd join them and fight them in their territory.

Once I had thrown the beads off, I ventured out of the yard during daylight. I joined other boys and stopped being a loner, brooding under the morula tree. My mind stopped focusing on my health.

I read the Bible which Mother kept in the house and went to church on the first Sunday of the New Year. I went to the Methodist church at Diraganeng across the river.

Our family was torn between Christianity and the traditional way of life. Father, like his mother, did not go to any church but he would tell people he was Methodist.

I was not a foreigner in the church. Aunt Machuene and Mother had occasionally taken me there against my will. Every time I went, I would be bored and hungry and wish the priest would let us go home to eat. We could come back after the break, as we did at school.

On this Sunday, however, I was hungry for spiritual food. I had gone there to seek support in my battle with the gods. I immersed myself in the service, which ended too soon, while I was still enjoying it. I loved the sermon, the singing and the heavy sighs from the congregation. I felt great relief from my worries.

On my way home I passed by Madipowane's place. She was about two years older than I was and she used to defend me against bullies. Her mother, like mine, was not born in GaMphahlele and so they clung together in friendship. Madipowane was a born-again Christian, and a member of a group of Christians calling themselves Abazalwane. When I got to her home, our conversation turned to religion; she preached the gospel to me and I listened attentively. She told me that even people who went to church needed to be born again to get to heaven. Madipowane advised me to read the Bible as I'd never read it before and communicate constantly with God through prayer.

I took in every word she said. My spirits were revived and I felt light shed on my path. I arrived home late that afternoon and read the Bible. Every verse was loaded with inspiration. I shed my fear of the gods – in fact, I despised them. They were the gods of Manaleng, of the Amorites, destined for destruction in hellfire.

A few days later I went back to Madipowane in high spirits. We discussed the Bible and she told me it was time for me to be saved. I was to find a secret place to say my prayers and seek God's salvation.

That day I read the Bible till late at night. I wanted everyone to sleep before I went out to pray. Mother seemed to have vowed not to sleep before I did. She came at regular intervals to the kitchen to see if I was still reading. She found me absorbed in the Bible. Father, who had not said a word about the beads, also came in. He asked why I was not going to sleep and I told him I was still reading.

When I was satisfied that they were all sleeping, I gently opened the door and slipped out to the rain-soaked maize field to say my prayers for salvation.

Thus I joined the Abazalwane. Now armed with the Bible, I didn't only despise the ancestors, but also those who believed in them – Mother, Father and the family elders. I obeyed their earthly orders when the orders didn't contradict God's commandments. It was God who instructed that a child should obey its parents to earn the bonus of long life.

I bade farewell to the heathenish customs and rituals that the scriptures condemned. For example, a sangoma once visited my home on Father's invitation to 'strengthen' the house and protect us from evil spirits. Part of the ritual was to make cuts on our foreheads and the fronts and backs of our necks, and to rub medicine into the cuts. He wanted to begin with me, the firstborn, but I refused.

Mother begged me to cooperate, saying the medicine wouldn't be effective if we didn't all accept it.

I knew this was the devil himself speaking through Mother. I was like Jesus in the wilderness, tempted by Lucifer. I refused to bend.

The ritual started and ended without my participation. Inwardly I prayed for Mother, the family and the whole human race to repent before it was too late. Father did not comment on my stance against the sangoma.

By this time I had regained my weight, although I still pined for an unknown home. It had been a slow process of recovery that started after New Year's Day.

I drew deep spiritual satisfaction from the fact that I was on the side of the victorious God, who didn't demand offerings of goats, sheep and sorghum beer. God was not frivolous – he didn't smoke dagga, to translate the Sesotho saying.

I carried my Bible everywhere and at school read it at every opportunity. When we were not at school we went from house to house preaching the gospel. Madipowane and Mpobane, a talented preacher who could convert stones and trees with his emotional sermons, were zealous. I was not as enthusiastic because I was shy, and felt embarrassed when we went into people's homes to disrupt their schedules and tell them what they already knew, that the day of judgement was imminent.

I was also afraid of ridicule from other boys my age. When I passed by their gambling place, they would interrupt their dice game, laugh at me and shout: "Moruti (priest) – come and pray for us."

I would debate with myself whether to go preach to them or ignore them. Going to them might mean that I was falling into Lucifer's trap of wilfully disrupting my sacred mission. But what if there were potential converts among them? I would tell them to follow me if they were genuinely interested in the gospel.

I hated the house calls, but we the converted were obliged to preach in every house where we were welcomed. We spoke about the joy we felt now that we had accepted Jesus as our guardian, our path and light. We preached about how we had lost friends and relatives after we were saved, but how this only strengthened our faith.

Whenever it was my turn to preach, I felt like running away. I wished the earth would swallow me. I would tremble and my voice would quiver.

When we prayed, we all said our different prayers aloud. Some would say short prayers while others prolonged theirs as if there were a prize for the longest prayer. In the frenzy of prayer some would burst into strange sounds. They would shout and howl and sigh in the grip of the Holy Spirit. I would listen and silently question their authenticity. At the end of the service, Mpobane would interpret what had been said in tongues.

When Ntate died I was already a Christian. She knew my position pretty well. We had clashed over initiation, but before she died, Ntate asked Father never to force me to go to the mountain by enlisting the services of lehwete, a legion of initiated men who raided the uncircumcised and forcibly took them to the mountain.

In the tradition of the tribe, I still had to go through the second phase of my initiation, bogwera, which generally takes place a year after the first, bodikana.

I told the family that because I was now a Christian I was not going to the mountain again. Ntate was disappointed by this and asked me to think again, but I stuck to my guns. It hurt her deeply that her grandson would be a legaola, one who didn't take a second turn on the mountain. The stigma would be nearly as unbearable as having her grandson being a leshoboro, an uncircumcised man.

There was less stigma on an uninitiated woman, lethumasha.

The last time I visited her, she was lying on a legogwa, a reed mat, groaning in pain after a bout of fits. She was bracing herself for another attack. She looked at me but appeared to be distant. Her eyes seemed to say: "Your religion has pushed us apart, Ngwanangwanake (Grandson)."

Silently I accused her of being a servant of the ancestors who would always be far from the people who served the true God.

My father's brother, Uncle Seputule, found me with Ntate. He came from Johannesburg and was with a youthful sangoma. The sangoma gazed at the groaning Ntate and then said she would be on her two legs by the next day. Uncle was happy at the prediction while I found the satanic presence of the sangoma repulsive. I left to go home and that was the last time I saw Ntate. She died the following day.

As I was walking to Thabaneng to tell relatives about Ntate's death, I could hear the big bell at Moshate, the Great Place, tolling in mournful rhythms. The long, sorrowful intervals between the notes implied that somebody had just joined the world of the sleeping.

Since my childhood the tolling of the bell tormented and haunted me. I could never get used to it. If it rang while I was eating, I immediately lost my appetite. If it rang while I was on my way from fetching water, initially from the river but later from the communal tap, I would feel weak in my legs and the water from the bucket on my head would spatter as I shook with fear. If it tolled at night, I found it difficult to go back to sleep. I feared death. Even obituaries read on the radio scared me.

When Tsokoane died I was at Rosenkrantz, and this meant that I was encountering death first-hand for the first time with the death of Ntate.

Relatives came from near and far. I sullenly drew into myself as the family prepared to bury her. I thought their rites, like covering the mirrors, painting the windows with ash and bathing in the medicine of the sangoma, were heathen. I quoted passages from the Bible to defend myself.

They said they understood but it was essential that I co-operated to give Ntate's spirit peaceful passage into the world of the ancestors. They said her spirit would be restless if one of her grandsons did not perform the family rituals. I refused and we drifted further apart.

Ntate was buried at Manaleng Cemetery. I was not there. My religion was one reason I stayed away. The other was that I was scared of death and corpses. I had never seen a dead person before and I did not want to see Ntate's body.

After the funeral, Ntate's elder sister, Makgolo wa Dithabaneng (Grandmother from Dithabaneng) tried to shave my head. Other family members were already clean-shaven. She was ready with her razor blade. I brought out my Bible and read her verses in which God warned the trekking Israelites not to imitate the customs of the infidels, like shaving their heads when they were in mourning.

"I hear you, child of my child," she nodded wisely. "If you choose to follow the Christian God, stick to him and to him alone. Don't mix him with other gods. If you mix them you'll get mad and collect rubbish at the dump."

I suspect she told my relatives to leave me alone because after that conversation no one bothered me.

Stories of my faith spread wide in the villages of GaMphahlele. People looked at me with awe. Ordinary Christians were astonished by my zeal and I was proud of winning the battle against Satan.

The winter of 1976 dragged its feet but it finally arrived. Magaola, graduates of the first phase of initiation like myself, prepared themselves to go to the mountain for the final time. I was not preparing because I was not going anywhere.

Mahupe, the man who had taken me to the school the year before, kept reminding me that I had to be ready. I always told him I was not going.

Father didn't try to persuade me to go and his silence disturbed me. It was the menacing silence of a lion in its lair. I would have felt better if he had roared.

And it was during this silence that word spread: "Koma e tswele dithabeng – it's now time for the initiation school!"

Every winter the villages of GaMphahlele reverberated with these words. Songs echoed along mountain ranges well into the morning hours.

A few days rolled by and nothing happened. Then on the Sunday morning Father asked me to get into his friend's car. Father, his friend and I drove to Bolopa, where his friend lived. It was crystal clear that we were destined for Mamagohle, the circumcision school.

As the car meandered over the hilly landscape, Father vowed he was not going to have a son who was a legaola. His friend supported him and said he was surprised that, having gone through the toughest phase, I was now afraid of bogwera, a picnic in comparison. He said this time the initiates ate food from home cooked by women. He urged me to go and collect my last medal of manhood.

I was quiet all the way. I'd never even dreamt of converting Father into my new faith: he seemed to be beyond redemption.

When we arrived at the man's house, he and Father drank whisky and talked about the golden days of yore when customs were honoured voluntarily. In the background, Radio Lebowa played jazz, music that I didn't like. The presenter enthusiastically introduced each song, elaborately telling us about the composer and band and the soloists and the dates on which the music was recorded. Some was recorded during and before the Second World War, and for the first time I realised just how old jazz was. That day I came close to liking it.

In the afternoon Father bade us farewell and left for Pietersburg, Polokwane, where he worked. He had arranged that his friend take me to the mountain at cockcrow the following day.

I was up before the man and made my way back home. Mother nearly collapsed with shock when she saw me. She knew the consequence of defecting from the mountain – insanity. The spirits of the mountain haunted defectors to their graves.

Once a teacher from a Christian family was abducted to the mountain. His relatives reported the kidnapping to the police. The police descended on the village and threatened dire consequences if the man wasn't produced instantly. The man came down from the mountain.

The elders of the tribe were angry at this mockery of our traditions by the white man. They cursed in muffled tones and swore the man would never ever be normal again. The man became the village drunk.

Every time the elders looked at him, they were firmer in their beliefs that you don't turn your back on customs. I know it was alcohol that was responsible for his condition, nothing else.

Mother thought I had defected, but I had vowed to myself never to defect – not out of fear for myself but fear of insanity for Mother. When I related the whole story to her, that I had not even reached the mountain, she sighed with relief.

I took my Bible and left, intending never to return. I had nine cents in my pockets and could buy at least a quarter loaf of bread and achar, a popular diet in those days. God would take care of the rest.

I walked and walked. Occasionally I would stop under a tree to read and pray. Between Maralaleng and Dithabaneng, my stomach rumbled, reminding me that it was empty. I walked till I spotted a shop at Dithabaneng. I fumbled in my pockets – there was no money. I walked out of the shop to retrace my steps and search. There was no money.

What am I going to eat? Where am I going? Where will I sleep? Questions tumbled out. I prayed God the provider for answers. Unthinkingly I took the direction back home.

I lifted my thumb to hitch a lift but cars passed me, shovelling a pall of red dust in my face. My lips were parched.

It was already dark when a car finally stopped for me. I told the driver I was going to Seleteng. He nodded his head and I jumped in. I recognised him as Maisaka's father and hoped that he wouldn't recognise me. But he did, and immediately told me he sympathised with my cause. He said children had to be given the right to make their own choices on koma.

As the car cruised along I wished it would break down so we would have to sleep in it. But it rattled along the bumpy road till its owner's village of Molalaneng.

I thanked Maisaka's father and said good night. I walked past my home in Manaleng and crossed the river to Diraganeng. I didn't know where to go. I wandered until I found myself at Madipowane's home.

Her father spoke darkly about the deeds of the pagans while his wife, Mmago Rosy, prepared food for me. She gave me porridge and roasted meat. My throat was sore but I managed to finish the food.

I thanked them and bade them a good night. As I walked out I wondered where they thought I was going to sleep. I was on the run but I went straight home.

I had come back to reclaim my sleeping place, my birthright. I had been the prodigal son for less than twenty-four hours. I entered the house through the kitchen window, which had a wooden frame. I was the only one in my home who could open it from outside. I fetched blankets from the sitting room, where they were usually placed for the times I came home late from my preaching. No one knew I had left home for good. Even on that day I was expected home and so they had kept supper for me and put out my blankets for my return.

No matter how well I had eaten outside, I was always hungry for my home food. I ate as if I hadn't eaten only an hour earlier.

Before I slept Mother popped in and told me Father was around. This was unusual because it was a weekday. Mother told me that he had gone out. When I heard news of Father's presence I resigned myself to defeat. A million thoughts flashed through my mind till they merged into the greyness of sleep.

Then Father stormed into the kitchen where I was sleeping and stripped the blankets off my naked body. He slapped me hard across my drowsy face. Mother came in time to see Father tossing trousers to me to wear. I put them on. Mother sighed heavily and left the chaotic scene.

Father pushed me out of the house into a car waiting outside. Mohlompheng's father, Matsemela, was at the wheel. They sandwiched me between them as we sped off to the initiation school.

Everybody at the school seemed to be waiting for me. Baditi surrounded me, asking me if I had really said God didn't want me to be initiated. This was a golden opportunity to preach to them.

"Yes," I answered boldly, and yet I had never uttered the words attributed to me.

"Where did you meet God? Is he short or tall? Next time you see him, tell him he's a leshoboro and needs to be circumcised." They mocked and argued.

I earned the nickname Moruti, priest. I quoted extensively from the Bible during the three weeks of bogwera.

"Jesus himself was circumcised," one moditi countered.

"Yes, but he didn't go to bogwera to waste time on the mountain."

All visitors to our mphato wanted to see Moruti. I was a curiosity because I condemned their customs right at their source. Some dismissed me as mad; others called me a coward. But I was never singled out for harsh treatment, and I said my prayers regularly but silently.

We concluded our course, and in the eyes of our society became fully-fledged men. Ululations and praises greeted our return. I washed the ochre off my body and with it the humiliation I had suffered at the hands of heathens. I vowed to follow God with tenacity never seen before.

I soon realised that I was the most fanatical of all the Abazalwane. Other sisters and brothers did not clash with their families and clans in the way I did. Most of them didn't come to the night services because their parents disapproved. My parents had also tried to stop me, but for me the heavenly order prevailed over the earthly one.

I found that I was the only one meeting the obligation to tithe. We were bound by scripture to contribute a tenth of our possessions to the church, but I didn't see anyone else meeting this obligation.

One day I used one rand before subtracting the tithe. This haunted me, and in a prayer I promised God that the next time I received money, I'd contribute it all to the church no matter how large the amount. Thus when Uncle Caiphus sent me forty-five rand, I gave it all to our fiery preacher Mpobane in the presence of Madipowane. I confessed what I had done before. Mpobane murmured a short prayer in appreciation of the money and I felt an invisible hand cleansing my conscience.

When I was not at school, I divided my time between preaching and running my business – selling fruit, tablemats and soft goods, buying bones and empty bottles and taking photographs. Father encouraged me in business, bought stock for me and on occasion helped with transport to ferry bones and empty bottles to Pietersburg. I suspected Father's motive was largely to prise me out of a religion that had taken me away from my family. Father and son found common ground in the business.

I traversed the villages of GaMphahlele doing business and got to see the extent of the poverty in our land. I often came across naked children rummaging in the rubbish dumps for anything they could turn into toys. Their legs were emaciated and their bellies would be bloated like balloons. Around them poverty stretched to the horizon.

My customers were the better-off people, and I was hard-hearted in my dealings with them. Even if a customer was only one cent short of the price, I wouldn't part with an item. I believed that a million rand minus a cent was no longer a million.

When a person owed me money and told me to collect it on a particular day, I accepted no excuses. If he owed me five rand, I added one rand to compensate for my valuable time and energy, and if he was still unable to pay, I would take the item back and tell him he still owed me for wasting my time. Time was money. If he could not pay the premium for wasting my time I would threaten to take an item of furniture from his house.

When I went out to collect money, I took two or three tough-looking boys with me. One dark night four of us – Madimetja, Kotsenala, Shampo and I – were returning from Lebowakgomo and had just passed Mamaolo when a car blinded us with its headlamps. Our eyes were still adjusting to the darkness in the wake of the car when we heard the metallic click of an Okapi knife being opened. A short man stood in front of us, with his knife poised to stab.

We bolted in different directions. The man called us back, assuring us that he did not want to hurt us. He said he'd pulled the knife because he thought we were deliberately blocking his path. We told him we hadn't intended to provoke him, but the car lights had blinded us. He pocketed his knife and we shook hands.

The man boasted that he had been to see his girlfriend in Seleteng. Her parents were very strict, but he and the girl managed to pull wool over the parents' eyes to be able to meet as they had done that day. He mentioned her name – Lucy. Our Sister Lucy, my fellow Mzalwane. My friends didn't know her, and to them it was just another boy's ad-

43

venture story. To me it was a betrayal of what we believed in and preached. The scriptures barred us from romance before marriage.

In my fanaticism, I hadn't even bothered to ask if Christians could fall in love and have sex before marriage. I simply took it for granted that we were not supposed to fool around among ourselves, nor with unsaved people.

Now here was Sister Lucy fooling around with a knife-wielding tsotsi.

As we resumed our journey home, my friends spoke excitedly about the encounter. I was quiet, speaking only in response to a direct question. One thought whirled in my head – to terminate my membership of the church at the earliest opportunity. That "at the earliest opportunity" was too vague: "first thing tomorrow morning" was more like it.

I tried to pretend that my faith was put to the test by her betrayal, but deep down I knew I was jealous. If Sister Lucy wanted a lover, why hadn't she chosen me? I loved her; I loved her two sisters; and I loved Madipowane. I often thought of taking them to bed but I was afraid of telling them I loved them. It would have sounded unchristian.

I was at Madipowane's place first thing in the morning.

"From today, I'm no longer one of you," I told her.

"Are you serious?" Madipowane asked in astonishment.

"I'm not joking – it's some of you who are joking with Christianity when I'm serious."

In minute detail I related the story the man had told us about Sister Lucy. Madipowane tried to persuade me to continue in the church. I refused.

As we parted I felt like a bird that has just escaped from its cage. The story of Sister Lucy had come at a convenient time, when I was tired of the boring and unreal world of Moses, Joshua and Mary. Formal religion had suffocated me.

I told myself I was now going to pray to God when I chose. There would be no compulsory house-to-house preaching and humiliation. I would no longer have to speak in public.

In my prayers I asked God to understand that I needed freedom, and that I'd die or kill for it if necessary.

In my emotional turmoil I started to wonder about praying to the same God as John Vorster, the white ruler of our country. Was this God collaborating with our evil rulers? What did He have to say about the people of Manaleng, Magaseng, Manganeng and Lehlokoana, and the naked children rummaging through garbage dumps and finding nothing?

Did God know that somewhere in the giant shadows of the Kgoahlampa, villagers ate plain porridge and used salt grains as relish? Did He know about hairy Boers clad in safari suits roaming the villages and robbing poor people of their farms?

For the first time I found myself questioning God's very existence. I put the Bible in the drawer and looked for something else to stimulate my mind.

— Chapter Six —

I DISCOVERED HISTORY – but not that of Jan van Riebeeck nor of his successors, the 1820 Settlers. It was the history of the people in whose midst I lived. I asked the old people about our past.

I found it absurd that I had to learn about Napoleon, the village in which he was born, his parents' names and so on, when I hardly knew the origins of my own ancestors. I couldn't understand why my people's history had to be told only from the time the Europeans came to our land. It seemed that divorced from the Europeans, they had no story to tell.

Our real history thrilled me.

I learnt that Mphahlele had not always been Mphahlele, but that the clan was the product of a quarrel in the house of Maake. The old man Maake had many wives but loved his last and youngest wife most. The older wives hated the favourite. Maake decided that before he died he had to ensure the continuing safety of his young wife. He sent Kgoarane, his son by his favourite, to scout for a new home for his mother, brothers and sisters.

Kgoarane, a famous hunter, and his dogs set out into the wilderness. From the summit of Mount Mahlatji he sighted land with lush vegetation, rivers and mountains. He loved it and went back to report to his father.

The old man Maake arranged for their surreptitious departure at dead of night. To destroy their spoor, they ditched the name Maake and adopted the name Mphahlele. However, they retained the Maake clan name, Moroka.

The more sophisticated historians of the clan said we were originally Batonga from Lake Ngami in western Botswana. Over the ages Batonga became Baroka.

GaMphahlele ended up as home not only to the newcomers but also to other diverse clans – such as the original inhabitants of the area,

Swazis who carried the name Mazwi; Bakgalaka, who originated in Zimbabwe; Mathabathe, who came from Zululand; Ledwaba, who were Ndebele; and Mphafudi, who originally were Venda. We lived in peace and as one.

Source after source gave me their version of events, with some disturbing contradictions in parts. But inspiration was what I sought, not precision, and this I found among the grey-haired women and men. My pride was restored.

The rich stories inspired me to write a book, *Kgosi Letsatsi wa bodibeng le Bakgaga* (King Letsatsi of the deep pools and the Bakgaga). It was a narrative poem about King Letsatsi, who sent a bolt of lightning to strike the Bakgaga.

I sent the manuscript to a publishing house but it was sent back with a rejection slip. I tried again with an anthology of poems celebrating the achievements of eight people from GaMphahlele. I called it *Dioka Tsa Bakgaga*, the heroes of the Bakgaga. I travelled extensively to interview whom I thought were community heroes; but a measure of my political consciousness then was my inclusion of Cedric Phatudi, the discredited leader of the Lebowa Bantustan.

I was still working on the book when my life changed dramatically and my attention was diverted. My cousin Moses and I started a student union at the Ngwana-Mohube High School, where I was in Standard Eight. By this time, 1978, religion was behind me and my eyes were opened to what was happening around me.

The earth-shattering Soweto student uprising of 1976 had come and gone, and Black Consciousness founder and leader Steve Biko had died at the hands of the security police in September 1977. As my consciousness was raised, I thought school grounds were the terrain where the war for liberation would begin – but not where it would end.

The Union of Self Study (USS) was founded ostensibly to help students with their studies, but secretly we sought to participate in a world that was changing at an incredible speed around us.

The executive committee was drawn from Standard Eight pupils, and I was elected president. News of the formation of the union reached the school principal and he summarily banned it. Thoughts continued to buzz in my head, and they settled on one idea: I had to leave the country to study and to train as a soldier, and return to fight whites.

On Monday August 14, 1978, Father left me with one hundred and twenty rand to pay into his fixed deposit account at a building society in town. He was leaving for Johannesburg to fetch his employer from Jan Smuts Airport and would not have time to go to the bank.

I took the money, went to town that day and bought a bag, a shirt and toiletries. I returned home late at night and hid the new stuff in the toilet outside.

In the morning, I asked Mother if I could see Mmatlou, my month-old sister. I couldn't tell Mother that this would be my farewell peek at her. The baby was fast asleep, and I patted her soft cheeks and tried to open her eyelids. Mmatlou jerked away, and I wondered if she would ever get to know me.

I said goodbye to Mother, who believed I was on my way to Dr Machupe Mphahlele at Groothoek Hospital.

"O sepele gabotse – go well," Mother said, and put her head back on the pillow. The chairs, pots, doors, windows, floor and the sleepy figures of my sisters and brothers seemed to scream at me, trying to hold me back.

Outside I cast a last glance at the morula tree. It was deep in thought, meditating on the troubles that lay ahead of me. The breeze caressed its nude branches and whispered questions about my reckless decision. In the dawn Manaleng seemed united in its disapproval of my departure for foreign lands.

Only Father knew where I was going; but he did not know the whole story. I had lied to him that I had secured a scholarship abroad. He was thrilled by this and said he would give me a big farewell party, slaughtering a goat and brewing sorghum beer for the ancestors to clear the road of all obstacles. He'd said we would tell the family it was a routine sacrifice to the gods. We would whisper our prayers to the ancestors so that other members of the family wouldn't know I was leaving. The feast was scheduled for the following weekend.

I wasn't waiting for the ancestors to bless me. I had long declared them dead.

At Mamaolo I boarded a bus bound for Germiston. I did not use the bus stop near my home to avoid inquisitive people asking me where I was going.

The monster rolled thunderously on the dirt road. Through the window I saw the weather-beaten bushes by the roadside and felt sad. As we went through village after village, spewing some passengers and swallowing others, my heart ached.

The bus arrived in Germiston. I had chosen Germiston because at school I had learnt it was the largest railway junction in the country. For the first time in my life, I saw a passenger train. In Polokwane, Pietersburg, I had seen only goods trains. A ticket examiner told me I had to go to Johannesburg Station to get a train to Botswana.

I saw a passenger train crawling away and another one whizzing to a stop. I ran into the one that stopped.

"Se ya kae setimela se – where is this train going?" I asked the people packed around me.

"Where are you going?" some boys about my age or a little older asked me. Their shirts were hanging loose, they wore takkies and their caps over their eyes. They were obviously tsotsis, young hoodlums.

"Park Station."

"We are also going to Park Station," they said and offered to carry my bag.

I refused their help.

"My child, this train is going to Pretoria," an old woman with a parcel of vegetables clutched to her huge bosom told me. I thanked her and got out. The boys stretched their arms to force me back into the train, but I summoned every fibre of my strength and set myself free.

I went back to the ticket examiner at the platform entrance and he promised to tell me when the right train came.

It came. Its doors were congested with thrusting, shuffling and impatient humanity. I spotted the window, threw the bag through it and jumped in after it.

When I arrived at Park Station I asked a ticket examiner where I would find a train to Botswana. He answered in Zulu, a language I didn't know, but I caught the crucial words "platform 13 and 14".

After wandering around and going up and down stairs, I saw platform 13 and 14 flashing a broad smile at me. I rushed into the third-class section of the train, and it pulled off as if it had been waiting for me. I was in a moving bedroom that was remarkably different from the beer hall I rode from Germiston to Park Station.

Through the window, the Egoli lights were a colourful galaxy. Back home in Manaleng, we talked about Egoli as "Gauteng Maboneng, a matala le a mahwibidu" – Gauteng, the city of green and red lights.

We thought a visit to Egoli was a precious privilege, especially if you survived to tell the story. Survivors told us of murder and injury, of daylight robbery and rape. They described money-crazy undertakers who hired killers to go out mowing down people to boost their businesses. They told us of women who loved men as long as they worked and brought money home at the end of each month; then ditched the men when they fell ill or got old. The survivors told us about Zulus who wiped out whole clans in retaliation for minor injury to one of them. They told us of the blanket-clad Basotho called Russians, who were fearless and unforgiving when provoked. I believed the stories because quite a number of bodies of people murdered in Egoli lay in graves in the Manaleng Cemetery. I was always fascinated by these stories of brave men killing each other and always asked myself why this energy was not put into fighting our white oppressors, who had been lording it over us for centuries. Our people found it easier to kill their brothers and sisters and eat into themselves.

The train wormed its way into the belly of the night. As the Gauteng lights receded, I tried to sleep; but I was too excited. It wasn't easy to sleep on a moving bed. Just as I was dozing off, two men with door keys dangling on their necks and carrying an unmistakable air of authority entered the compartment. They asked if any of us were going to Botswana. Two of us raised our hands. They asked for our passports and I gave them my passport and my dompas. The other man held a Botswana passport. The two men cursorily looked at his passport and then focused their attention on me.

"What's the purpose of your visit to Botswana?" they asked in menacing voices, their bulky bodies dwarfing mine.

"I'm visiting my relatives."

"Are you not a student?"

"I am."

"Do you have a permit to be out of school?"

"Yes, I do."

"Let's see it."

"It's in the passbook."

They paged through the passbook. I moved closer to help them find the school stamp and the principal's signature. Suddenly and inexplicably, the men turned angry and threatened to lock me up if I didn't tell them the truth.

"We know all about you, silly boy. Now tell us before we hurt you."

"You can hurt me if you want to but there's no other truth besides what I've told you."

Just as suddenly as they had lost their tempers, they calmed down and became concerned uncles. They said they feared for my safety in terrorist-infested Botswana. They warned me against the communists who would poison my little innocent mind. The terrorists and the communists were likely to persuade me not to come back and they would turn me into one of them.

"Au! Are there terrorists in Botswana?"

"Yes, thousands of them," one of the men answered.

"What is the Botswana government doing about them?" I asked with a feigned concern.

Their unpredictable tempers flared up again. At first I was shaken but later I got to enjoy the drama without showing it. I guess everybody in the compartment was fascinated by the scene.

"Look here, young man, one day you'll be seated with us in the waarheidkamer (truth room) and we'll remind you who we are and who you are. We'll remind you of this conversation, that we told you that you were not telling us the truth about your visit to Botswana. Then you will tell us the truth, like it or not."

They wrote down my particulars in their pocket notebooks and left the compartment.

The two had not asked us for our tickets and therefore were not ticket examiners. A woman travelling to Zeerust said they were security policemen.

Their constant mention of the word "terrorist" had reminded me of the white official in Lebowakgomo who issued me with the passport. He too had warned me against the evil terrorists who had made Botswana their haven.

I assured him I'd never become a terrorist's tool. He had flashed a condescending grin and gave me the passport. I grinned meekly and said, "Baie dankie, baas." (Many thanks, boss.)

I had acquired a passbook and the passport in quick succession, without my parents' knowledge. I broke my vow never to carry a pass because I wanted to leave the country without hassles. I chose a 'legal' exit because skipping across the border was dangerous. Somebody had told me that the fence between South Africa and Botswana was electrified, and was patrolled day and night by heavily armed soldiers. He told me that if one eluded the soldiers and the electric fence, nature would catch up with the fugitive. He said corpses of hundreds of youths who had tried to cross into Botswana lay frozen in the snow-carpeted mountains between the two countries.

From my geography classes I knew there was no snow between the two countries, but I had the nagging fear that the Boers, providers of distorted education, might have kept these facts and features from our syllabus.

I wasn't prepared to take the risky route. I would consider it only if all chances of getting a passport were closed.

With valid documents in my pocket, I feared no one. When the train stopped at the Ramatlabama border post in the afternoon, I was relaxed. We alighted and took our passports to the immigration office. After a while, an immigration officer asked us to keep quiet as he called out our names and handed back the passports. A Kilimanjaro of passports was reduced to an anthill. Then they were reduced to about ten . . . five . . . still my name wasn't called. About ten of us were straining our ears for our names as if it were the Day of Judgement.

The image of the two bad-tempered men in the train flashed through my mind. The twin devils must have alerted the immigration authorities that I was coming. When the passports on the table came down to two my anxiety turned into fear and panic. Finally my name was called. I took the passport and got back into the train.

Those whose names were not called were bundled into a police van and driven back to Mafikeng. Among them was the Motswana boy who had shown the security police his passport during the trip from Park Station to Mafikeng.

Just when I thought I had cleared the last hurdle, an immigration officer came into the train to distribute forms to be filled. Where it asked for the address of my host in Botswana, I wrote "Princess Marina Hospital, Private Bag X05, Gaborone". I concocted the address. I had learnt of the Princess Marina Hospital in Gaborone and the Queen Elizabeth II in Maseru from conversations with Dr Machupe Mphahlele, and the private bag was his address in Chuenespoort.

Even after we had given back the forms, the train did not move. My anxiety was renewed when a hefty, hairy Boer clad in military fatigues came aboard and moved from coach to coach, checking passengers' passports. When he came into our compartment, pistol holstered on his bulky waist, I was unnerved.

He symbolised our oppression, tough and invincible-looking. I thought if this was the type of beast we had to fight to regain our land, perhaps I should think again. I told myself that the same tough Boers had been killed like flies by the Cubans in Angola. I imagined the Cubans to be as small as their island home and felt reassured that they could give the Boers a bloody hiding in the bushes of Africa, where the Boers have been causing trouble for three centuries.

My plan was that after academic studies in America or England, I would go to Cuba or Russia for military training. I would then return home to fight this man and his kind. My fear of the Boer soldier gave way to utter contempt for him. He inspected my passport, scribbled something on it and stamped it. Without saying a word, he returned it and left the compartment. I pitied him. I had a picture of him cut down in a hail of bullets.

The train jerked its massive body and crawled into Botswana.

— Chapter Seven —

I HUNG OUT of the open window and inhaled the air deeply. Was this really Botswana?

Patchily thatched houses stood solemnly in the fading light of the sinking sun. The inhabitants were probably worse off than the people of Manaleng: their houses were far apart, and they could therefore not shout over the mmoto to ask for a few spoons of sugar, for instance, from their neighbours to sweeten their tea.

When the train arrived in Lobatse it was already night. I looked outside, searching for the town, but all I could see were a few dark houses. I didn't see any of the glittering lights of a town.

The train pulled off, headed for Gaborone. It stopped at several sidings before it reached the capital of Botswana. When we arrived, I took a taxi to Princess Marina Hospital hoping to find someone who knew Dr Machupe Mphahlele. Such a person would probably help me with accommodation for the night. Nobody knew him.

Disappointed, I left the hospital and wandered around the town with its thick bushes on undeveloped land. Gaborone did not have a single traffic light, and for me traffic lights determined whether a place was a town or not.

I walked towards my marker, the towering red light at the station. To get to it I went through a bushy area where the American Embassy is situated today. I crossed the rails and walked deeper into the bush. I stopped where the Gaborone West residential area is today and decided to sleep there. I curled up on my bag, using it as a mattress. The moon overhead was shining and I wondered if somebody in Manaleng or Seleteng was looking at it. If it were Mother, Father or Moses, we would be linked through the moon.

It was cold as my mind rewound the cassette of my life. Where did Mother think I was? She was expecting me back home that same day. How would she cope with my absence? I had told the immigration officer that I would be in Botswana for seven days. This was only my first. So I still had a chance to go back home to Mother. No, never: I had cut my moorings.

I slept fitfully that night.

Early in the morning I shook dirt from my clothes and headed for town. Thoughts of Mother, Father, brothers and sisters and my cousin Moses whirled in my head.

I was the first customer for the day at the Botswana Book Centre, and I stayed longest. I moved from shelf to shelf, reading titles, prefaces and introductions. I wanted to read all the volumes in the bookshop but I ended up buying Alan Paton's *Cry The Beloved Country*. I then looked for a comfortable place to read it.

I had expected to hear the whizz of flying missiles and to smell gunpowder in the book, but all I found were a Bible and a pulpit. I was greatly disappointed.

The winter sun was racing to sleep, a sad time for those who had no place to spend the night. People clutching their belongings walked purposefully out of the town centre. They knew where they were going. I just walked aimlessly and finally trailed behind those heading back to town, mostly watchmen and cinema patrons. The chill eventually cleared the streets.

Where to now?

I would not go back to where I'd slept the night before, so I boarded a train to Francistown. I would get a chance to compare Francistown with Lobatse and Gaborone.

I thought that because it had an English name, Francistown would dwarf the towns with African names. This train, bound for Rhodesia (now Zimbabwe), roared through the night.

I expected the passengers to speak Setswana, but these spoke and sang in a language I didn't understand. They sang and danced, and the names Nkomo, Mugabe and Smith popped up in virtually every song. These were certainly not hymns. From the movements of their tough, muscular bodies, I could tell they were war songs and dances.

In Manaleng I had heard stories of Rhodesians eating humans and I now got scared. But I also remembered our mathematics teacher Lawrence Morasui telling us that Rhodesians were on the verge of attaining independence, thanks to the struggle they had waged to liberate themselves. Without putting it in so many words, he had urged us to emulate them. My fear of my fellow passengers gave way to admiration. These must be the people Morasui had spoken about.

They sang about Zimbabwe and not Rhodesia. I loved the name I had first heard from Morasui, and in that train vowed never again to call that country Rhodesia.

When the train pulled into Francistown in the morning, about two-thirds of us alighted. I was even more disappointed by this 'town'. There were a few shops and then shantytowns called Somerset East and Somerset West. It was worse than Lobatse and Gaborone and the natives called it 'The Ghetto'. While I was wandering around, I decided to phone Dr Machupe Mphahlele at Groothoek Hospital back home.

He told me that my parents were worried about me and advised me to go back home. I said no. He suggested that I contact a certain Moabelo working at a bookshop in Gaborone. The same evening I was in a train back to Gaborone.

Moabelo received me warmly. He had been expecting me, as Machupe had phoned him after our conversation. He sent me to a house in New England suburb, where I would meet Mrs Modise, the younger sister of the Chief Minister of the Lebowa homeland, Dr CN Phatudi.

I had hastened to dismiss Gaborone as a bush town. But there was another side to the town: New England reminded me of white suburbs in South Africa. The houses were big and the lawns were manicured.

The dignified Mrs Modise came to the gate but didn't open it. Still standing outside the yard, I introduced myself and she listened patiently. I expected her to let me in and to talk about GaMphahlele, which she had not seen for many years; but instead she asked: "What can I do for you?"

"Nothing," I said and bade her good-bye, irritated by her reception.

I went back to roaming the streets, stopping at intervals to read. At nightfall I went to the charge office of the Gaborone Central Police Station and told the police that I had run away from the Boers in South Africa. I told them that if I had not run away, I would have been executed. The police seemed too busy to listen to a brat who had left his caring parents under the pretext of running away from apartheid. Later I established that these policemen had listened to numerous exaggerations like mine and had reached the point where they paid no attention.

I sat on the bench and leaned on my now battered looking bag. Virtually every policeman reporting for duty asked what my problem was, but they didn't wait for me to finish the story.

"Just wait – we'll attend to you later," all of them promised, and did nothing.

A tall, dark-complexioned, stooping policeman in the clumsy shorts of Botswana policemen woke me up as if the charge office were on fire. At first I was disorientated as he harshly asked me: "Monna, leina la'ago ke mang – you, what's your name?"

He didn't give me a chance to answer as he shot a barrage of questions: Where do you come from? What nationality are you? What do you want in Botswana? Whom do you know in Gaborone? Are you a spy sent by the Boers?

"Sergeant, bring me the keys to lock this thing up," he concluded, and strode away as if he was going to fetch the cell keys.

I hated him for calling me a Boer spy. He didn't come back and I went back to my bench and slept.

This drama was repeated on every one of the four nights I spent in the charge office. Sometimes this funny policeman Sitambi would wake me twice or thrice in one night. At first I feared him but later I found him amusing.

The only time I went out of the charge office was to buy food and newspapers. I would then return to my new 'home'.

"How long do you think you'll stay in this place?" a policeman asked me. At long last somebody was paying attention.

"As long as you want me to be here," I said.

"Which political organisation do you belong to?"

"None."

"Which one would you like to join?"

"I don't know them. You can help me by calling their representatives to come and explain their organisations' policies to me."

"That's impossible," he said with an air of finality. "I can call the ANC people because I know where they stay. They are here in Gaborone. But it'd take us three days to reach PAC people. I would need a special car because they are in the Kalahari Desert. It would take us another three days to come back. And then there's a student organisation, but they are not serious people."

"I can't join an organisation I don't know."

"We can't keep you here forever either," he said, losing his temper.

"I prefer not to join any organisation. I need to study them first."

"Where do you think you'll study them? Here? You must be joking. You can leave this place only when you tell us the political organisation you belong to. We have to release you into the hands of an organisation."

"I don't know what to do. You know better. Which political movement should I join?"

"The ANC. If you're serious join the ANC."

"Okay, from now I'm ANC."

He was as excited as if he were himself ANC. He brought me forms and helped me fill them out. He told me he had already phoned the ANC office and they were on their way to fetch me.

He also said that while I was waiting for the ANC people, I should go and complete forms at the Ministry of Home Affairs and at the Botswana Council for Refugees. He gave me directions and I went there on my own. For a change there was progress and I was delighted.

At the BCR I found refugees from Lesotho, Namibia, Angola, South Africa and Zimbabwe. The Zimbabweans were the overwhelming majority. I was accosted by a youth who introduced himself as Tom Nkoana. He said his instincts told him I was a fellow South African.

"What organisation do you belong to?" he asked sympathetically.

"The ANC," I said.

"When did you join it?"

"I've just joined it at the police station."

"How can you join a political organisation at the police station? Who recruited you?"

"A policeman."

"I see," he sighed. "These police are corrupt. They are paid by the ANC to recruit for it. Did he tell you what the organisation stands for?"

"No."

Anger rose to his eyes. He looked at my papers and shook his head. He said the PAC and the ANC were two sharks that swallowed up ignorant people like me. He said the ANC would send me to Angola, train me as a soldier and thereafter keep me on a leash and not allow me to go home to fight the Boers. If I rebelled and insisted on going to fight, they would kill me. He said the PAC was no better. They would send me to Tanzania and dump me in a camp without food. Moreover, the organisation was undergoing a serious leadership crisis. Tom said the two sharks were also very tribalistic, favouring the Xhosa.

Throughout this analysis Tom did not utter a word about his own organisation. I didn't believe everything he said, but I was frightened by the prospect of leaving Botswana before I was sure of my choices. If conditions in Botswana proved unbearable, I could jump the fence back to South Africa. If Tom were right and I found myself stranded in Angola, it would be impossible to get back.

I felt helpless as Tom castigated my organisation, the ANC. It was my duty to defend it but I didn't know it. He knew it. On the other hand, it would be the height of madness to join an organisation and leave it on the same day. In fact, in this case it would be within the same hour. I was not prepared to leave the ANC before I got to know it.

"I hear you, but unfortunately I'm already a member of the ANC," I said.

Tom retorted: "The ANC you talk about doesn't even know you. Even if they did, you have the right to leave them if you decide to."

"Look." I showed him my papers. "It says here that I am ANC. If I leave it I'll be arrested. The policeman who recruited me will give evidence against me."

Tom laughed and said if I left the ANC he would go with me to the police station to fetch my bag.

"If I left the ANC, which organisation would I join?" I asked.

"None. You would have time to study the organisations and make your pick."

These words dissolved my doubts. I was not prepared to be anybody's captive. Compulsory affiliation to a liberation movement was a negation of liberation itself. I wanted to be myself and chart my own course, unfettered by organisational resolutions adopted without me.

I was hugely relieved. Tom helped me jump the queue and fill in the forms at the BCR. I walked with him to Bontleng suburb. We entered a big grey house and were enthusiastically welcomed by youths my age and others a little older. They shook my hand, calling me comrade or camarada. This was the first time I had shaken hands with so many people at one time.

Tom too got pats on the back. "Jy's 'n tier – you're a tiger."

I didn't understand why they were praising Tom, and wondered if I had made the right decision.

We ate lunch, porridge and gravy with bones, and after that I went with Mahlomola, one of the young people in the house, to fetch my bag from the police station. When we returned to the house, called Lagos, it felt good to have my first bath since Manaleng.

Lagos, named after the former capital of Nigeria, housed members of the Soweto Student Representative Council (SSRC), which had led the student uprisings in South Africa on June 16, 1976. It was named Lagos because the SSRC and its leader Tsietsi Mashinini had cordial relations with General Olusegun Obasanjo's Nigeria. The house as well as a farm in Lobatse were said to have been bought for the SSRC by Nigeria.

The SSRC were creating 'a third force', an alternative to the ANC and PAC that had failed to sustain the armed struggle in South Africa. I was told that all that the older organisations could manage was to claim credit for things they knew nothing about. Where were they when the youth of Soweto took the lion by the mane in 1976? They were now claiming credit for the uprisings at a time when the ordinary South African had even forgotten they existed.

Nigeria, flush with naira because of its booming oil industry, was the sponsor of the third force.

According to my new friends, Tsietsi Mashinini ranked among the top heroes of Azania: his name shared glory with immortals like Shaka, Moshoeshoe, Makhanda, Bambata, Lutuli, Mandela, Sobukwe, Biko and Tiro.

The day Mashinini asked me to go for a walk with him I felt honoured. I listened attentively as he spoke with a confidence that bordered on arrogance. He predicted that South Africa would see the bloodiest liberation war ever on the continent, and he would be commanding the liberation forces. He said Western countries would side with the South African regime but his forces would be victorious.

His right hand man, Khotso Seatlholo, was small in build and looked fragile, but he was brilliant and articulate. The two young men, Tsietsi and Khotso, were the pillars on which the fledgling SSRC rested.

Masilo, affectionately called Silos, would tell me: "We are going to prove the great Karl Marx wrong. He said students could start the revolution but couldn't sustain it. We shall prove him wrong."

In the mornings we had political classes and the evenings were devoted to cultural activities. We sang, beat drums and danced till the front of our yard was packed with admiring neighbours and passers-by. Poetry was woven into our singing and dancing. When a poet took centre stage, the singers hummed a tune under his words, the drums softening their beat as his voice rose to the sky. When the poet's voice came down, the singers' voices and the drums climbed to fill the vacuum.

Some of us attended school but education wasn't always the objective. Many attended for the allowances, free meals and accommodation. Some went to the Resource Centre, the learning institute designated exclusively for the refugees. One could enrol there for a class any time of the year, and most South African refugees used it to while away time and meet friends. They renamed it the 'Re-nuisance Centre', arguing that the quality of its education was worse than that of the Bantu Education they had escaped in South Africa.

Those who didn't study asserted that the education programmes were sponsored by the American CIA to drain the liberation movement of its lifeblood, the youth. They campaigned vigorously against school. Some of them had turned down offers to study in Botswana, Nigeria or overseas. Others had returned from those places venomously castigating the 'imperialists' for emasculating our legitimate struggle by dispersing the warriors throughout the world's colleges. They didn't tell us whether they had passed or failed their courses. Instead, they spoke incessantly about the beauty of airhostesses, the ecstasy of flying above the clouds and the high esteem in which South Africans, especially Sowetans, were held.

I didn't go to the Resource Centre but chose to read on my own at the Botswana National Library. As my knowledge of Gaborone increased, I used the American and the British libraries in the town.

Thus the days rolled by.

One evening in my third month in Lagos, Joe Maphunye confronted me: "Comrade, what do you say? Are you joining us or not?"

"Give me some more time, comrade. I'm still thinking about it."

"How many times have we given you more time, comrade? You have to decide today. We can't live for so long with someone who is not a member of the organisation."

Joe was right: I had deferred the matter many times. I told him: "I want to join you out of commitment and not because it is the convenient thing to do."

"Do you think that if you join us today, in future you won't be able to get out if you want to? You can join us today and leave tomorrow if you feel that way. There's nothing that ties you forever to us, but for security reasons, comrade, we just can't live with a person who is not a member."

"In that case, no problem. I'm a member from now on," I said.

Joe's freckled face beamed with triumph but a tinge of guilt pierced my conscience. I was joining the SSRC out of convenience and not commitment. Fear of losing accommodation had influenced my decision. But Joe didn't give me forms to fill out and did not ask me to take an oath of allegiance. This eased my conscience.

Living in Lagos had provided me with an opportunity to study the various political organisations and compare them. I read the ANC's Freedom Charter and the speeches of Mangaliso Sobukwe, the founding president of the PAC. I made up my mind that the PAC was my home.

As I read Sobukwe's speeches I felt as if I had co-authored them. I identified with his views on the question of land, on mental liberation, non-racialism, education, African unity and the history of Europeans in Africa. He placed land at the centre of the liberation struggle, believing that true liberation would come when Africa and her wealth were restored to the indigenous people of the continent.

According to him, the oppressed had to be liberated mentally first. When he launched the PAC's Status Campaign, he told the nation: "We are reminding our people that acceptance of any indignity, any insult, any humiliation, is acceptance of inferiority. They must first think of themselves as men and women before they can demand to be treated as such. The campaign will free the mind of the African – and once the mind is free, the body will soon be free."

He said the Status Campaign was an unfolding and expanding one, involving the political, economic and social status of the African. The campaign grew into the PAC's 1960 anti-pass campaign that led to the Sharpeville massacre.

Sobukwe left a plum job at the University of the Witwatersrand to lead the anti-pass campaign. He called on all men to leave the "distinctive badge of slavery and humiliation – the pass" at home, and surrender themselves for arrest at the nearest police station for refusing to carry it.

The police at Sharpeville panicked when they saw thousands of men and women marching to the police station and shot at them, killing sixty-nine and wounding hundreds.

The campaign was a watershed in South African history and catapulted the liberation struggle from peaceful protest to armed struggle.

On the issue of race, Sobukwe said there was only one race to which all belonged, the human race. He said that in the vocabulary of the PAC the word race as applied to man had no plural form.

"We do, however, admit the existence of observable physical differences between various groups of people. But these differences are the result of a number of factors, chief of which has been geographical isolation."

He said that the myths of race and racial superiority or inferiority had been propagated by European colonial powers in order to justify robbing Africans of their land and exploiting them.

Sobukwe's dream was the creation of a United States of Africa under one government. It would serve as an effective shield against foreign domination and domestic tribalists bent on tearing the continent apart. He urged Africans to reserve their first loyalty to Africa and not to ethnic groups. He believed a divided and disjointed Africa would always be easy prey for greedy foreign powers.

Sobukwe had the solution to Azania's ills.

What was in his writings had been lying in my subconscious being and running through my veins. Even as I was telling Joe I was joining the SSRC, I knew my home was in the PAC. Physically I was SSRC but spiritually I was Poqo (another name for the PAC, adopted from the Xhosa word for 'pure' by its insurgents in the Transkei in the early 1960s). It was only the infighting within the PAC that kept me from joining the organisation then.

In the meantime I clashed often with the leaders of the SSRC and those close to them. They didn't, for example, respect the cooking roster that they had drawn up. They found all sorts of excuses not to do domestic chores. They came home late and drunk, breaking the curfew that they themselves had imposed.

One day I raided their cushioned heaven, the room in which Amanda, a mountain of a woman, slept. She lay leisurely on the bed, reading a novel. I greeted her and then took all the dishes of food that she had been keeping for the leaders who had not yet come back. She protested, telling me that the food was for Khotso and company.

"And where are they?" I asked her. I was shaking with anger.

"They've gone to the cinema," she answered.

"If they have money to go to the cinema, surely they'll have money to buy food. Right now there are hungry people in the house. First come, first served – I'm taking this food to them." There was seldom enough food for all the people in the house.

"Okay, you'll answer to Khotso when they come back."

That night I was violently shaken awake and angry voices demanded their food.

"I gave it to the comrades who hadn't had supper. By the way, it's not your food – it's our food. Who do you think you are? The gods of this place? They came before you and were hungry."

I was just short of insulting them when Khotso, an intelligent reader of moods, ordered everyone to leave me alone. They filed out and he followed them.

From that day the eating pattern changed: it became first come, first served. For me the struggle for freedom starts with the small, daily things.

Hunger made us blind to some of the things that we did to undermine our noble ideals.

For example, as we left on our nocturnal expeditions, one of us would say: "Comrade Amanda, please stay to boil the water. We're coming back."

"Okay, comrades," she would say as she swung her imposing hips into action – the hips that were said to have left Nigerian men exclaiming in admiration when she was a student in West Africa.

In a few minutes' time we would be back with a chicken or two stolen from the neighbourhood. The chickens in Bontleng, New Canada and Extension Four and the owners of gas cylinders had peace only at month-end, when refugees got thirty pula each from the United Nations High Commissioner for Refugees (UNHCR). We were expected to live on this amount for the whole month.

Each resident of Lagos contributed twenty-one pulas of this to the communal coffers, so that for about two weeks we could afford to buy groceries. For the rest of the month we scrounged around and thus stole chickens.

I left lagos after an SSRC conference decided to rename the organisation the South African Youth Revolutionary Council (SAYRCO) and to form an armed wing, the Tactics and Strategy Unit (TSU). I didn't want the new name because the organisation would still be bowing to the oppressors by using their name for our country. Kaizer Rantsho and I found new accommodation in a house run by the International University Exchange Fund (IUEF).

Kaizer agreed with me in my dispute with SAYRCO. He was light complexioned, short and stocky. His body and speech exuded life. I'd get tired of counting his push-ups before he got tired of the exercise. He laughed thunderously at the slightest joke and he himself told plenty of them.

He complained about my gait and the way I carried my body. He told me I had to pump more life into it. I did, but just for the moment after the criticism; then I would return to my natural state, a bundle of clumsy bone and muscle.

I didn't know how deeply he loved me till a speeding car knocked me down. The only thing I remember was the car thundering down the road; then a blackout. The next moment I heard Kaizer shaking me and calling my name. I came to and when I tried to stand, wobbled like a drunkard. The driver hadn't stopped after hitting me.

We went to a house nearby, that of Drake Koka, a fellow refugee from South Africa.

Before Mrs Koka could greet us, Kaizer was saying: "Ke bone lefu ka mahlo – I've seen death with naked eyes."

MaKoka drove me to hospital. I didn't have any broken bones, only minor bruises. She took us home and laughed at us, calling Kaizer "Lefu" – Death.

Early in 1980 Kaizer left our new home to go and study at St Joseph's College in Kgale, just outside Gaborone. I was undecided about my future.

— Chapter Eight —

A FEW DAYS after Kaizer's departure I decided to join the PAC and its military wing Apla. Central committee member and senior Apla commander Enoch Zulu was having lunch when I entered the flat where he stayed in Gaborone. He gave me a spoon and I shared his dish of porridge and meat. I was hungry.

Zulu impressed me with his generosity and straight talk: "Comrade, you can apply in writing for membership of the PAC but not for membership of Apla. Once you're in the PAC, the organisation will decide where to deploy you, taking your gifts and talents into account."

I returned the following day to hand in my letter of application. Zulu was not there but he had told me to hand it to Elias Ntloedibe, the PAC's chief representative in Botswana.

A week later I went back to find out about my membership, but Ntloedibe had forgotten about me.

After I'd reminded him about the letter, he exclaimed: "Oh, it's you, comrade. Your application has been accepted. You are now a fully-fledged member of the PAC."

I was shocked. How could the PAC accept my application without calling me to explain the controversial remarks I'd made in it? I had said I reserved my loyalty for the revolutionary leadership of the organisation, and rejected all the reactionaries and sell-outs. If I found the leadership of the PAC reactionary, I would still want to be a member, but would reject that leadership. I believed that blind loyalty was dangerous because one could be loyal to a gang leader, a dictator or even a mad man masquerading as leader of a party or a nation.

I hadn't thought the PAC would accept my application without calling on me to explain the parts on loyalty. I doubted that Ntloedibe had read my application. It all left me with the impression that the PAC was not a serious organisation, or at least the person who represented it in Botswana was not. But the speeches of Sobukwe that I had read in Lagos, the carriage of Enoch Zulu at our first meeting and the impressive Apla cadres who had visited us in Lagos made me overlook Ntloedibe's ineptitude. I resolved to stay in the PAC.

A week after I joined the PAC the Botswana government ordered all refugees who were not attending school and were not employed to move into the Dukwe Refugee Camp, 130 km north-west of Francistown. The camp had housed thousands of Zimbabweans who had returned to their country in preparation for independence.

I and about fifty others steadfastly defied the order, fearing that if we were in the camp we would be sitting ducks for Boer commando raids. I didn't know the PAC's official position on the matter, but voiced my anger in the presence of a PAC member, Raymond Johnson, and he didn't call me to order. If he had said I should go to Dukwe, I would have defied him.

Thousands of refugees in Mozambique and Zambia had been slaughtered in their camps by the Boers and Ian Smith's killers. The world could only look on helplessly and "condemn in the strongest possible terms".

We had underestimated the resolve of the Botswana government. I was woken up one morning before dawn by loud knocking at my window and shouts of "Open up!"

When I tried to peep through the window, I looked into the muzzles of guns and flashing torches. Botswana Defence Force (BDF) soldiers were rounding up all the recalcitrants.

We were taken to the Botswana Police College, and those who had been caught up in the sweep by mistake were released there. The rest of us were addressed by Botswana cabinet minister Daniel Kwelagobe, who gave us the choice of resettlement in Dukwe or deportation back to South Africa.

We chose Dukwe. It was a journey of about 600 km from Gaborone. Each of us was given a loaf of bread, a tin of corned beef and a pint of milk for the road. About thirty of us and our luggage were crammed into the back of an army truck, which was escorted by five Landrovers carrying soldiers armed with machine guns and rifles. The headlamps of the vehicles were switched on.

"Do you know what refugees eat in Dukwe?" asked fat Valiant, who walked with a limp, as the truck rolled noisily northwards on the tarred road under the burning afternoon sun. The truck fluttered its canvas covering as it tore through the still air.

"If you know, tell us," Komane answered.

"They eat one meal of sour porridge, ting, and pigeon."

"How is the pigeon cooked?" somebody asked.

"They dish out the ting and hand out slings, show you the bush and tell you to go and shoot the pigeons for your meat," Valiant answered amid laughter.

I laughed too, even though my heart was heavy with pain. I felt like a captured beast and the soldiers were herding us towards the slaughterhouse. I had heard first-hand accounts from Zimbabweans about raids by Rhodesian commandos on their camps, and I had seen horrific pictures of mutilated bodies strewn on the grounds of the refugee camps after the attacks.

It was night when the convoy reached Francistown; then it changed direction and headed north-west towards the Botswana-Zambia border post of Kasane. The convoy slowed down, left the tarred road and turned left. A kilometre from the main road the vehicles stopped and cut their engines.

"Borra, loeto lo felela fa – gentlemen, this is the end of the journey," one soldier said as he opened the tailgate of the truck.

"You make it sound like a pleasant journey," Valiant burst out. "You Batswana, wait till South Africa is free. I'll be an immigration officer and I'll teach you a lesson."

"Did you say immigration officer?" another soldier asked and laughed. Valiant and his crutches struggled to get out of the truck.

At the administration centre, some South Africans who had arrived at the camp before us had come to welcome us. They had heard from the radio that we were on our way. They told me that although there were two PAC people in the camp, there was no formal PAC structure there. SAYRCO members offered to look after me till my organisation established itself. The settlement was demarcated into plots, and I walked with the five SAYRCO members to Plot Five. I smelt the night heat and green vegetation.

We reached our destination, a cluster of huts that had been built by the Zimbabweans. My companions told me that the camp covered about five square km and once housed twenty thousand Zimbabwean refugees. All but a few hundred had gone back to Zimbabwe after the Smith government, the British government and the Zimbabwean liberation movements had signed the Lancaster Agreement, paving the way to democracy in their country. Their huts were now empty.

John and Morena showed me the hut that was to be mine. They helped me clean the hut and gave me a candle, a box of matches, three blankets and a sponge mattress. They warned me about snakes and scorpions and said that they had killed a big snake near their huts that very day.

After they left, I had a restless night under the cloudless and starlit African sky. The buzzing and stinging mosquitoes kept me awake. There was an earthy smell from the mud floor and walls and the thatched roof. I did not cover my body as it was hot and dry.

I woke up at sunrise and surveyed my new surroundings. There was bush all around us, with lots of thick mophane trees (that sustain mophane worms). The mud huts of Dukwe were built in clusters. Some refugees used blue tents supplied by the United Nations. Next to our cluster, the SAYRCO cluster, there was a soccer field and beyond it were the ANC huts and tents. From every cluster of huts, curled smoke mushroomed lazily upwards and then thinned out. Men, women and children struggled with creaking red wheelbarrows loaded with water barrels, firewood and an assortment of other items.

My new friends had breakfast of bread and tea, which I couldn't eat because I don't drink tea or coffee and I could not eat the plain bread.

Two comrades accompanied me to the administration centre to fetch my fortnightly ration of maize meal, a cup of rough salt, two cups of white sugar, two tins of mackerel fish, a bar of blue soap, five litres of cooking oil and a razor blade. I was also given two silvery pots of different sizes, a spoon, three blankets and a sponge mattress. We pushed the stuff on a wheelbarrow.

Once a week we were given meat and twice a week we had rations of bread. Our monthly allowance was reduced from the thirty pula a month we had received in Gaborone to five pula a month per refugee. We were told that the difference was used to buy the supplies. We knew that the mackerel was donated by the Republic of Ireland and the cooking oil was a gift from the people of the United States of America, and that millions of dollars were donated to four million African refugees through the UNHCR. Somebody along the line was getting rich from working with refugees.

We also knew and resented that European refugees were each given more than a hundred times what an African refugee got. We knew that the United Nations still favoured people of European descent. There was no equality and justice among nations and peoples and continents.

It was also interesting to us that the ANC refugees in the camp were all indigenous Africans: none of their white members landed in Dukwe.

I stayed in the SAYRCO cluster for two months and then left to join the PAC members in Plot Four. There were also Zimbabwean stragglers and refugees from Lesotho in this cluster.

Dukwe ieelele
Ke tshaba Dukwe ieelele
Ke tshaba Maburu a tla mpolaya
Dukwe ieelele.

(I'm afraid of Dukwe
I'm afraid the Boers will kill me here.)

The Basotho men lifted this song to the sky, their bodies soaked in the sweat of a dance they learnt in South African mines in days gone by. I joined them because music is infectious: it both begs for and demands your ears. It wounds when it's summoned to heal. It urges us to forget at the same time that it tickles the memory awake. It fills the air, flows through the bloodstream and carries the singer and his audience to the edge of the universe, where only imagination can reach. It abandons them there, lost and enjoying their new state.

We sang after every football match, whether we had won or lost. I played for the Basotho club, the weakest in the Dukwe league. Other PAC members played for the Black Consciousness Movement of Azania (BCMA) because there were too few of us to form our own club. Other sides were SAYRCO, ANC, Angola, Zimbabwe, Namibia and the Botswana Police Eleven. The Namibians were the strongest side.

My team, the Lesotho outfit, was a colossal joke. In age we ranged from nine to sixty-five years. Our goalkeeper Masiu was the oldest player in the league, and the only ball that didn't get past him was one that hit his huge and clumsy body. Lekomola brought his nine-year-old son to play. Given this set of players it was no wonder I was a regular in the side.

Surprisingly, the best fullback in Dukwe was in our team. He was a hulking man who was previously a soldier in the Lesotho army and was popularly known as Lesole la Leabua – Leabua's soldier, after the Prime Minister of that country.

Every club that played us was assured of a wide goal margin and two points. The only two points we salvaged were in the match against Angola, a side made up of tough and fast players. They failed to turn up for our match against them and the referee awarded us the two points.

When SAYRCO played us, they knew and we knew they were going to win. The first minute into the play in our first match against them, SAYRCO players decided not to mark us. We drove the ball towards their goalposts with primitive and inaccurate passes and they didn't make the slightest effort to stop us. Pat Ledwaba, their acrobatic keeper, looked on contemptuously as the ball passed him into the goal-mouth.

We celebrated our first ever goal with dancing and whistling. Ma-Lekomola, our only female fan, ululated victoriously on the sideline. I shared the excitement but knew it wouldn't last long. Our strong opponents would unleash their fury in the second half.

In the first half SAYRCO dribbled stylishly and there was huge laughter, applause and cheering from the entertained spectators. Our opponents would dribble past our keeper but instead of scoring, they would pass the ball backwards. They demonstrated their grace and artistry.

About ten minutes from the last whistle, SAYRCO did the expected. They played with purpose and targeted our goal-mouth. Lesole la Leabua stood like Colossus at the back, thwarting all their efforts. We helped him by kicking the ball out at every opportunity. We kicked it far over the wood fence and infuriated our opponents. The minutes ticked away.

SAYRCO players lost their confidence and started panicking. Ernest Mokgakala of the combustible temper shouted orders like a defeated general testing whether his troops still respected his authority. That authority was challenged and his side disintegrated as each player made efforts to redeem his name. The laughter and applause, this time for the underdogs, intensified.

And the referee blew his whistle three times and the game ended. The scene changed into a festival for us and mourning for our opponents. We sang and danced till late at night.

Soccer provided rare moments of joy and healing, but it also reminded us painfully that we were a divided people. This was clearly shown when BCMA played ANC. The BC, who were militant on and off the field, said the match was between Azanians and South Africans: they represented Azania and the ANC represented Suid-Afrika. On the field were two nations fighting it out with deep animosity.

Still fresh in my memory is the rough manner in which an ANC player tackled a Black Consciousness one. A BC member among the spectators said the tackle "was not unexpected". He had hardly said that when a player avenged the rough tackle. The game degenerated into rough play and insults until the spectators were relieved when the match ended.

Football also created a bond between us the refugees and the local Basarwa (Khoisan) community. Although I don't remember ever seeing them coming to watch a soccer game in Dukwe, I remember a Dukwe picked team visiting Nata, about 60 km from the camp on the way to Zambia, to play them. I went along as a spectator.

When the eleven Basarwa players trooped onto the very sandy and uneven football pitch, they were barefoot and wore torn shirts and pants that were far from a football kit. They looked like hunters on the trail of wounded game rather than footballers. Their thin legs seemed to have been designed to track animals and not to kick a ball. They had parched light skin and unkempt kinky hair.

We wondered what formation this motley crowd was going to play. We didn't have long to wait for our first shock: within ten minutes of the kick-off the Basarwa scored a goal. They moved nimbly while our players panted and huffed as the sand bogged them down. From time to time the Dukwe players would take off their boots and empty them of sand.

Shortly before half time, the Basarwa scored what to me seemed a legitimate goal. Initially the referee accepted it as a goal but after the Dukwe side objected, he reversed his decision. He was from Dukwe too. The game ended with the score at 2-1 and we had won – a hollow victory.

As our truck negotiated the sands out of Nata towards Dukwe, Ali Phosa summed up our attitude to the game and to our opponents: "Comrades, we couldn't let the Bushmen beat us."

We looked down on Basarwa as inferior. We did not see the irony in our attitude: we, the victims of racism, had false notions of racial superiority over fellow Africans.

Back in Dukwe, soccer continued to bind us together. It made us forget our political whimpering. In the bushes of Angola, ANC cadres and Savimbi's UNITA forces were locked in mortal combat, but in Dukwe they kicked the pig's skin together in joy and harmony. Soccer was a unifier in this politically diverse community.

One day a man and two women arrived with a letter from Ntloedibe addressed to me. In the letter he asked me to receive the three comrades who were members of the PAC in good standing. The man introduced himself as Ngcobo from the eNgcobo district in the Transkei. The older of the two women was his lover and the other was her sister. He said they had come from Zimbabwe and had skipped the border at Plumtree.

Ngcobo had one eye, was in his mid-40s, tough looking, of medium height and light complexioned. He said he and five other PAC members left South Africa in 1965 after they were ordered by the organisation's leaders to go to the PAC's external headquarters in Lusaka in Zambia. However they were intercepted and arrested in Rhodesia. He said they were convicted of treason and sentenced to life imprisonment. It didn't occur to us to ask him how a foreigner could be convicted of treason in any country.

Ngcobo said they were released from prison only in 1980 when a general amnesty was declared at Zimbabwe's independence. On their release, his five colleagues took out Zimbabwean citizenship. He went to live in Harare with a family that adopted him. His lover was a member of that family.

Although he enjoyed life in Zimbabwe, his conscience nagged him to continue with the struggle. He decided to leave Zimbabwe to rejoin the PAC. The two women refused to remain behind and said they would go with him, even if he was going to war. They found the PAC office in Gaborone, and after Ntloedibe had listened to their story he sent them to me.

It was a touching story.

After Ngcobo and his two women settled in the Dukwe community, we realised that he was a dagga addict. He smoked the stuff with
Mafu, Oupa and Ali. When he was high Ngcobo would tell the people
who shared the zol with him that he had a BSc degree from the University of Addis Ababa in Ethiopia. He had graduated in 1973 – a year
when he was supposedly in a Rhodesian prison.

He would tell graphic stories about the way Rhodesian security
forces used to track down and kill Zimbabwean freedom fighters. He
said the anti-terrorist skills of the Selous Scouts were unsurpassed in
Africa. He rated them on par with the British Special Air Service.

As if realising that he had gone too far in praising Ian Smith's soldiers, he would try to make up for it by praising the freedom fighters.
He would praise Mugabe's Gugurahundi – the Year of Great Storms,
1979 – as decisive in taking Zimbabwe to people's power in 1980.

One day Mafu and Ali visited my hut and asked me what I thought
of Ngcobo. I told them they should know him better because they
smoked dagga with him. Mafu got angry at this, and fished out two
photos from his shirt pocket.

In both photos, Ngcobo's women were wearing boots, military
green trousers and T-shirts inscribed with the words 'Ziso Revanhu', a
Shona phrase meaning 'the eye of the people', and 'Pfumo Revanhu',
'the spear of the people'. These were the auxiliary forces of Bishop
Abel Muzorewa, who was installed as premier of Zimbabwe-Rhodesia
before Zimbabwe attained its real independence. In both photos they
had posed with their rifles.

"So we've been living with soldiers among us," I said when I recovered from the surprise and the shock. "How did you get these?"

Ali told me that they had searched Ngcobo's bags while the three
were out of their hut doing laundry in the bush. Mafu, Ali and I
agreed that we had to act swiftly. The following morning I boarded the
truck to Francistown to inform Solly Ndlovu, an old member of the
organisation from Alexandra Township. The two of us went to the
Special Branch office and related the story but Mr Manyaneng, the
head of the Special Branch in Francistown and a former member of
the South African Police, was not convinced.

"How far did you go in school?" he asked me.

"I went as far as Standard Seven."

"There you are. This is not a security matter. You are jealous of educated people. I know in politics the uneducated people accuse the educated of being sell-outs. It's irrelevant whether Mr Ngcobo obtained his

BSc from the Randse Afrikaanse Universiteit or Addis Ababa. What matters is that he is more educated than you are. By the way, are you still at school?"

"No."

"There you are, Mr Ndlovu. Here is a Standard Seven with all the doors of learning opened for him but he chooses to live in the bush and call other people enemy agents. Just go to school and leave security matters to us."

As we left, Ndlovu shook his head in disbelief.

The Dukwe-bound truck would leave late in the afternoon and arrive at night. I did not wait for it because I was in a hurry to report back to my comrades. Ndlovu gave me some money and I hitched a ride back to the camp.

When I arrived at Plot Four, the comrades told me the police had taken Ngcobo and the two women to the police station at the administration centre. I asked if the three had taken their belongings with them.

"No," Elijah, a black belt karateka from Daveyton, answered.

I was worried that they had left their stuff behind, but we waited to see developments. About an hour later Ali found me brooding in my hut. He told me the threesome had come back and Ngcobo had asked for a general meeting. I told Ali to go ahead to the meeting and I would follow him. I stole out of Plot Four and headed to the administration centre. Somebody must have seen me and reported to Ngcobo, because I suddenly heard footsteps behind me. When I looked back Mafu, Elijah and Ali were actually chasing after me and shouting. I stopped.

Mafu grabbed my arm and said: "We've got you today." He asked me why I was leaving when I knew there was a general meeting.

"Comrades, the convenor of this meeting is Ngcobo, an enemy agent," I said.

"This is a PAC meeting, not Ngcobo's. Let's go and answer for the lies you spread among us."

"But, comrades . . ."

"Shut up," Mafu interrupted me, his bloodshot eyes flickering with hatred and his stout body smelling of dagga. "This is not the meeting. You'll speak in the meeting."

"Do you think we are small children? Let's go," Elijah said as he held my other arm tightly.

"Please MaAfrika, please comrades, don't beat him up," Ali pleaded with the two as they dragged me along.

Another refugee, Komane, saw them dragging me and followed us. He too pleaded with Mafu and Elijah not to beat me up. I was taken to Ngcobo's hut where I found five people in a meeting chaired by Ngcobo. His two women were with Oupa Moorosi and his wife Nombali.

"Who's this one?" Ngcobo asked, pointing a contemptuous finger at Komane.

"I'm Komi and I'm here to ensure that you don't assault Letlapa," Komane said as he squatted on the mud floor.

"Komi, this is a PAC meeting, not a neighbourhood meeting."

Komi stood up and left.

I protested but Mafu slapped me hard in the face. Ngcobo stood up and came to where I was squatting and punched me in the ribs.

He warned me: "There will be order in this house. If you want to speak, you first raise your hand and you may speak only after the chair has granted you permission."

Mafu slapped me again and a rain of blows and kicks followed. I screamed. Ali threw himself between my assailants and me and shouted for help from the neighbours.

"Please, don't beat him up, MaAfrika," Ali yelled.

The three women shouted obscenities and emptied two buckets of water on me. The floor turned muddy and slippery and their shoes spattered dirt in all directions.

"Stop now, comrades," Ngcobo's voice boomed above the din. "Comrade Letlapa, we are doing this out of love not hatred. We love you. You are a young promising man who needs guidance. Your problem is your tongue. You are a liar and a thief who steals other people's property. You stole these two ladies' album, removed two photos and took them to the Special Branch in Francistown. You stole my five hundred pula. I've just come from the police station, where I laid a charge. At least there is evidence that some of the stolen property was found in your possession.

"Tell this house what political objective you hoped to achieve when you told me that Oupa and Nombali's child Tshepo was actually fathered by another man in Selibe-Phikwe, and the wool was pulled over Oupa's eyes?

"You also told me that Nomsi's husband Mfundo killed David Sibeko. You are a liar. Comrades, I must congratulate you for your resoluteness in dealing with this snake among us. I declare the meeting closed."

I limped out of Ngcobo's hut. My whole body ached and my voice was hoarse from screaming. Komane and his girlfriend Pinky came to see me. After they left I lay down and wept. The dagga solidarity had triumphed over the bond of ideology.

Early the next morning I packed my things and bade farewell to Ali, Komi, Pinky, Masiu and Lekomola and his family. I told them I was going to Francistown for good and that whoever wanted to occupy my hut could do so.

"It's painful to part with you in this manner," Mrs Lekomola said, and wished me a safe journey.

At the administration centre I saw Khupe, the man who was responsible for refugee movements in and out of the camp. He saw me carrying a bag and asked me where I was going, because I was not on his list of people going to Francistown that day. I told him I had come to say goodbye as I was leaving the camp for good. When he asked if I had a police permit to leave the camp, I told him I didn't need one, and that I was not going to ask for permission from the police who protected infiltrators. He forbade me to board the truck, and threatened to tell the police to stop me from going to Francistown; but I replied that I was actually going to the police station to bid farewell.

I entered the charge office and asked for the station commander. I told him I was leaving Dukwe for good and that I didn't need a police permit. He countered by saying they would arrest me if I broke the laws of Botswana. I waved my hand and walked out.

I got a lift in a truck from Zambia on its way to a South African harbour.

In Francistown I lived with Ndlovu in the suburb of White City. For a living Ndlovu sold live chickens, meat and beer, and I helped him with his business. I rode a bicycle with a front carrier loaded with cow's heads and hooves to deliver in Somerset East.

I left Botswana for Tanzania in February 1981. Ndlovu drove me to Francistown Airport. He shook my hand and said: "Isina muva liya-bukwa – the last dancer gets the loudest applause. Go abroad and learn fighting skills. Today the world accuses us of not fighting, but the day we start it will want us to stop."

Two years later I learnt that Ndlovu had died of cancer.

— Chapter Nine —

THREE DAYS AFTER I ARRIVED in Dar es Salaam, Mike Muendane, a member of the PAC's central committee, asked me to be Vusi Make's bodyguard when he went to court to testify about the killing of David Sibeko, the organisation's co-leader and secretary for foreign affairs. Me! A bodyguard? I'd never dreamt of being one.

Mike knew I had not had military training and that I had just arrived in Dar. I didn't want to remind him of my obvious shortcomings and I agreed to guard Make, then a fading star in the PAC's constellation.

John Nyathi Pokela, a much brighter star, had just taken over as chairman of the PAC. He had arrived in Dar a week before me. Make was now vice-chairman.

Make sat in the back and I was in the passenger seat next to Muendane as he drove to court. When we got to court, I squeezed into the packed public gallery and listened as Thobile Gola gave evidence. Six PAC members were accused of murdering Sibeko.

Defence counsel grilled Gola, a shy-looking man reputed in PAC circles to be an efficient administrator. He had hitchhiked from the Mbeya Camp to Dar es Salaam to warn the leadership about the assassination plot, but had arrived too late to save Sibeko.

I pitied him as counsel asked him what I considered silly questions, for example: "Are you a Marxist or a Christian?" Hesitantly Thobile answered that he was a Christian. A barrage of intimidating questions followed. Why didn't he oppose the plan to kill Sibeko? It was a democratic meeting allowing for all views, was it not? Was he disloyal to his comrades at the camp? Was he loyal to the leadership of the PAC?

Then 'Baby Elephant' Make took the stand. He was not fazed by the court. He explained that he had been with Sibeko in a house in the suburb of Oyster Bay in Dar when the six arrived, accused them of selling out and shot at them. Sibeko was hit while he (Make) ran and hid in the pantry. When the shooting stopped, he came out of the pantry to find Sibeko lying in his blood.

The defence lawyer, a short man of Indian origin, cross-examined Make: "The accused will say you and the deceased led lives of luxury, globetrotting and sleeping in expensive hotels. Is that true?"

"Given the chance, who wouldn't?" Make boomed back with his powerful voice, amid giggles from the public gallery. To this day some PAC members invoke Make's words when they're caught indulging in extravagances.

The defence couldn't understand why the smaller Sibeko was hit while the bigger Make escaped to hide in the pantry. It therefore asked the court to go and inspect the house. I joined the entourage to the seaside house in Oyster Bay, more as a curious spectator than as bodyguard. The whole thing was exciting for me.

After pointing out the various significant spots, Make struggled to squeeze into the pantry where he said he had hidden; but I assumed that with fear spurring him on, he had found it easier to slip into it on the day of the murder.

I rooted for the accused simply because exile is pain and imprisonment for a person in exile is multiplying the pain several times. I also knew that the assassination of Sibeko could not be justified in any way. Instead of repairing the PAC it ruined it.

The case eventually ended with the six getting long jail terms.

The day after I had been Make's bodyguard, I visited the National Library instead of going to the PAC offices – breaking with the PAC members' habit of flocking to the organisation's office every morning for no reason. I had never seen a library as big as that in my life: both the size of the building and the number of books were enormous. By special arrangement I was granted membership on the day I applied instead of waiting the usual two weeks. The old woman of European origin who helped me spoke Swahili and consciously avoided English. I was flattered by the way the people in the land of Nyerere held freedom fighters from the south in high esteem. I was doubly impressed because I was from a country where whites were rulers and not servants.

I used the library to while away time.

It was during this period that I met Pokela, or simply Poks. He came to visit our house with Joe Mkhwanazi, who later became the PAC's only member of the KwaZulu-Natal Legislature. After we had exchanged greetings, he asked how old I was.

"Only twenty!" he exclaimed after my reply. "Do you know in what year I joined the struggle?"

"No, I don't know."

"Nineteen forty-four."

"Nineteen forty-four!" I echoed, more in appreciation than surprise.

"Nineteen forty-four," Mkhwanazi repeated in his deep, gravelly voice. "Where were you then? You were not even in your mother's head."

My trips to the library were cut short when I was sent to Bagamoyo, the transit camp outside Dar for PAC cadres waiting to go either to school or for military training.

Morale in the camp was high because of Pokela's arrival in Dar and his immediate ascendancy to the organisation's helm. It was boosted further by the arrival of about thirty recruits who came via Lesotho. Groups that had been trained in Lebanon, Sudan, Nigeria and Guinea also arrived. A group from Tabora, west of Dar, joined us and was reintegrated into the PAC after a spell in the political wilderness – they had now disbanded their short-lived Azanian People's Revolutionary Party, formed when they were expelled from the PAC. Another group had come from the Itumbi Camp in Mbeya.

Bagas, our name for the camp, hummed. Each group had a story to tell, and had stories told about it.

The group from Nigeria included people like Raymond Fihla and Willie Nkonyeni, who had both studied aviation.

The Guinea group told us about the poverty and hunger ravaging the West African country.

The group from Sudan was noisy. They would imitate their Sudanese instructors, who were crazy about physical fitness and endurance. The cadres who came from Sudan would point at one another, reminding each other of breaking down during their training. We split our sides laughing at jokes about men malingering and weeping because of the bone-crushing training in the Sahara Desert. Jan 'Goebbels' Shoba, an extroverted and tough former boxer, was the noisiest in the group. He was also a fitness fanatic.

The group from Lebanon talked only about war. We envied their experience of the war in West Asia – what is sometimes arrogantly called the Middle East by Europeans, who describe the world with themselves at the centre. They told us of the incessant barking of gunfire as the Palestinians, Lebanese, Syrians and a wide variety of militia on one side, and the Zionist Israelis on the other, were locked in the war for land. Theirs had been a tough mixture of theory and practice.

The group from Mbeya was supposed to be the core of the Azanian People's Liberation Army. They were a difficult and rebellious crowd and refused to participate in some of the camp programmes like physical training. They looked down on members of the camp administration as 'abomafik'izolo' – Johnny-come-latelies.

The Mbeya group strongly resented Vusi Make's leadership, accusing him of ordering the shooting that resulted in the death of four people in the camp. Make denied this.

The group from Cambodia, which had had military training earlier than the others, had a long story to tell. The twenty-one cadres had left Tanzania in June 1977 for Khmer Rouge-ruled Cambodia, led by Ezrom Mokgakala: PAC policy then was that every group going for training had to be led by a member of the Central Committee.

The group had a two weeks' stopover in China where they met top Chinese leaders like Deng Xiaoping and the visiting Japanese premier. They toured several Chinese provinces by plane, bus and train.

They also toured Tiananmen Square, the Great Wall of China and places that saw fierce fighting during the Chinese War of Liberation.

Before they flew from Beijing to Phnom Penh, the Chinese warned them to brace themselves for hard times in Cambodia because life would be different. The group's deputy leader S'gubu Dube told us that when they landed in Phnom Penh they were struck by the extent of the devastation: burnt-out warplanes, the carcasses of tanks, gutted buildings and roads with gaping bomb holes. Although the war between Cambodia and the USA had ended in 1975, Phnom Penh looked like a city still hosting a merciless war.

The money they had brought into Cambodia had no use, not because it was foreign currency but because the Pol Pot government had abolished money in 1975. Cambodia had reverted to the barter system. Banks and shops were demolished because they epitomised evil – money. Television transmitters and TV sets had been destroyed. Four million city dwellers had been uprooted and forcibly taken to the countryside to work in the rice fields.

The PAC group had to learn the Cambodian language before they commenced their training. They joined the Cambodian peasants in the fields, and tended pigs, goats and rabbits. The Cambodians worked seven days a week but the PAC cadres were allowed two days of rest. The only holiday was the national day celebrated in May. On this day in 1978, they were part of the multitude that went to listen to Pol Pot reaffirming the Khmer Rouge's resolve to make Cambodia a classless society.

As part of this classless Cambodia, the youths from Azania had shed their clothes and wore the national uniform of black trousers and shirts, green caps, red scarves and rubber sandals. However in this classless Cambodia, government officials dressed differently: their trousers were grey and their shirts white.

The training was interrupted after a year when Vietnam invaded Cambodia. The invasion came at the height of tensions between the Soviet Union and the USA and between the Soviets and China. The reason advanced by Vietnam was the need to create a federation of South-East Asian States. Vietnam had already pocketed Laos and been in skirmishes with China over boundaries. The Vietnamese were bankrolled by the Soviet Union in their wars against their neighbours.

The PAC cadres joined hundreds of thousands of Cambodians fleeing to Thailand in the north-west. Vietnamese planes rained bombs on the fleeing columns of marchers. All along the way there were skirmishes between the Cambodians and the Vietnamese. In their march they breasted many mountains and crossed many rivers, including the Mekong River.

The early days of the march were bearable since there was food. As soon as the food supplies ran out, death and disease reigned. The refugees turned to a diet of black spiders, frogs and bamboo shoots as they marched through the dense forests and monsoon rains. The poison was removed from the spiders before they were roasted. The group from Azania, now reduced to twenty because Mokgakala had been recalled to Dar to attend a PAC conference, was given priority when the meagre food was shared.

People died of hunger and the bombing, and were buried in shallow graves with body parts protruding from the ground. The gravediggers were sapped of energy and couldn't dig deep. The Vietnamese pursuit didn't abate.

Relief came only when they crossed the border into Thailand. The PAC men remained in the refugee camp for a month before they flew back to Tanzania via Pakistan. Most of the members of this group had not recovered fully from their Cambodian experience.

Cultural activities temporarily concealed the cracks as we united in the common joy derived from song, dance and soccer. We sang and danced in the hall and played soccer on the open ground called the Mothopeng Stadium, after PAC veteran Zephaniah Mothopeng, who was imprisoned on Robben Island.

When Pokela came to Bagas, he liked watching football at the stadium. He told us he had played soccer on Robben Island: he had been imprisoned there for thirteen years after being kidnapped from Lesotho by the South African Police.

"And there's still a lot of soccer left in me," he said.

Pokela did the unexpected, at least from a person of his standing. One day I was heading down to the river when I saw a diminutive figure half submerged in the water. It was Pokela, bathing like the rest of us. Other leaders bathed privately in their makeshift bathrooms and used hot water. He bathed where we bathed. I hesitated, wondering whether to go forward or turn back and wait until he was through. I went into the river and bathed side by side with him, and he chatted with me as if I enjoyed equal status.

Pokela had been in Tanzania for less than a month, but he had already scored a spectacular goal with the disbanding of the Azanian People's Revolutionary Party (APRP) and its reintegration back into the PAC.

Pokela divided his mission into three tasks: to unite the PAC, to orientate every PAC member in exile homewards, and to establish a permanent link between the exile wing and the home front. He stated this mission at every opportunity, with his voice pitched high and his forefinger waving in the air.

The year 1981 saw far-reaching changes in the PAC and in its army. Pokela steadied a PAC that had been wobbling along. A Task Force was formed to recreate the High Command and reorganise the army. It performed the functions of the High Command, since there was none.

The ageing Edwin Makoti was relieved of his post as Secretary for Defence and replaced by the youthful Sabelo Phama.

Sabs, as we affectionately called him, had infiltrated back into South Africa in 1978 as part of Operation Curtain Raiser. He braved police roadblocks and border patrols till he reached the Transkei, where he was arrested. But his revolutionary spirit didn't wilt in prison: after his release, he continued where he had left off and went back into exile. He inspired me.

On a lazy afternoon in Bagamoyo, the parade bell rang and we ran to the grounds. Bassie Mabusela, the camp commander, dismissed the trained cadres, saying the parade was for those who had not had military training. He told us the precious moment we had all waited for had finally arrived: we would be going for training. Forty of us would go to the West African state of Guinea and thirty to Yugoslavia.

The two lists of names were read out and I was put in the group going to Guinea. The group bound for Yugoslavia was happy while ours was subdued.

Members of the Task Force sensed our unhappiness and called us to the camp hall the following morning. They told us Guinea was poor and there wasn't enough food in the country. Drugs and other medicines were hard to get and life in Guinea was difficult. But difficult conditions were part of quality training.

Chris Mokgopa, a tall, hefty, jet-black man with squint eyes who was nicknamed Russian Tank, told us: "MaAfrika, we are not sending you to Guinea to study cooking or nutrition. We expect you to come back as tough soldiers."

When he later defected to the Boers in 1984, we changed his nickname to American Tank.

Bassie, who had recently completed his further training in the Sudan, supported Chris. He said we could not call ourselves Pan Africanists if we were unhappy about being sent to some parts of our continent.

We drove by truck from Bagamoyo to Dar es Salaam. After a few days in the capital, we boarded a plane to West Africa. As we flew over Mount Kilimanjaro, the crew pointed it out to us and the plane circled this beauty of nature. The crown of the African landscape was topped with snow, defying the furnace of the equator burning a short distance away.

— Chapter Ten —

WE WERE BOOKED for an overnight stopover in the Grand Hotel in Abidjan in Ivory Coast. One man in our group took one look at it and concluded it was a five-star hotel. Others nodded in agreement. I looked at every conceivable part of the hotel, hoping to see five stars or words engraved on some part of it to confirm my comrades' assertions. There was nothing.

The hotel and the rest of Abidjan were sheer beauty. The sea embracing the city lent it a touch of dream. That was the Abidjan we saw. The tough porters with frighteningly scarred faces we encountered at the airport surely lived in an Abidjan we didn't see, conveniently tucked away from the tourists' inquisitive lenses.

Some of us chose the people with whom to share their rooms, while others like me, who had no particular friends, left the decision to the commanders. They paired me with Harari Mlamleli, a short and muscular young man my age.

"Oh, I was told there was one comrade from Botswana – is it you?" Harari asked, opening a conversation that would keep us awake into the following day.

"Yes, it's me."

"But I was told his name was S'khulu."

I laughed and explained how I earned the name in Bagamoyo.

"Do you know Fezile and S'gubu?" I asked and he nodded. "They and I called each other S'khul' sam – my lord. Surprisingly that name stuck to me."

I told Harari the story of my life.

Homesickness is like the sea. It attacks in waves, alternately flowing and ebbing away. With me it reached the high tide when I was ill, especially when I suffered from malaria. It was at its ebb when I was involved in action pointing to the home front.

I became homesick for my family, my school and my village. I missed Mother and her endearing names of Sony and Sputnik. I pined for the songs – endless song forever renewing itself in the evening lit by glow-worms. In those days, no major event happened without a song being composed to immortalise it. We were a village of composers, singers and dancers. We even composed a song in praise of Neil Armstrong's moon landing.

I pined for song and the drumbeat of malopo – the spirit mediums – tearing and shredding the night. For centuries this beat has been a salve to Africa's bruised soul. To this day no African village is complete without a drumbeat.

I pined for the popular village lullaby:

> *Child of mother, keep quiet*
> *I'll throw you in the backyard*
> *And strap a reed on my back*
> *The reed that doesn't cry*
> *That comes during the season of rain*
> *The season of rain and wind.*

In Botswana I would assemble young girls and boys and teach them these songs to alleviate the homesickness. They sang after school and left for home at sunset. But their voices lacked the magic of Manaleng on a starlit tropical night.

In the military camps our songs were meant to prepare us for war. Serious stuff. Songs all the same. A booster of morale.

We were fighting a war that uprooted us from our land, a war that should have been fought and won by our grandfathers and grandmothers. We were thousands of miles from our homes, our families and from the war theatre. Forever drifting away and losing the pulse of our people. Always being reminded by our hosts, in unsavoury terms, that we were barely tolerated guests who didn't know when they would be leaving.

Had I made the right choice by leaving South Africa? I always asked myself this question when I was homesick.

Sharing my story with Harari assuaged the homesickness. Then it was Harari's turn to talk and I listened.

He spoke of the revolution and the need to draw more workers and peasants into it, as they were its foundation and pillars. Harari's voice was no longer mild: it was as loud as that of a preacher at a night vigil in a forsaken village. He was throwing his arms in the air and shaking his head angrily.

Harari exuded knowledge as he strode through anthropology and political science and history and medicine. I regretted that I had spent so much time in barren Botswana, instead of imbibing from the calabash of knowledge that Harari had tasted. Like me, he left South Africa in 1978 but he was a decade ahead of me.

We slept in the morning.

A powerful knock shook the door and woke us up. My immediate thought was that someone must have forgotten his room number and was knocking on every door trying to find it. That person was probably drunk.

"Comrades! Comrades!" The voice was unmistakably that of the group commander, Sam Motau, a teetotaller and a stickler to discipline. I rushed to the door and flung it open. "Comrades, are you still sleeping at this time? The whole group has already left for the airport. We've been looking for you all over the place. Forget about washing – let's go. Now!" He bolted out with some of our luggage.

We got away with a hasty shower. When we ran downstairs we met Sam on his way up to carry us out of the room. He was with two other comrades who had remained behind to help him find us.

Sam showed us our breakfast. "And I give you one minute to finish."

I was relieved to see him negotiating in English with a French-speaking taxi operator. The language barrier gave us ample time to exceed the one-minute limit. When they finally reached agreement through the medium of gestures, we boarded the taxi to the airport.

Those who were early at the airport were impatiently waiting for us, because our passports were always kept by the commander. They cursed Harari and me for oversleeping, as if we were sleeping in a hotel for the first time. They didn't know that for me it *was* the first time.

The plane was waiting for us and had to wait longer as Sam was sorting out the passports and other travel documents, half of which had been clumsily forged. The immigration officials were impatient in the din they and our group created. Other travellers looked on in amazement, wondering what the hell was going on.

Some asked who we were, and they got different answers depending on who responded: we were a football team from Lesotho, from Swaziland, from Botswana, from Tanzania; we were tourists; or we were students going or coming from school.

Finally Sam abandoned his methodical approach and handed every member of the group a passport or travel document, regardless of whether it was his or not. I had a valid passport, which was handed to somebody else, and I ended up with a travel document bearing the photo of a bald, old man. The immigration official stamped it without saying a word and returned it.

We thought there would be forty seats waiting for us in the plane – after all, we had booked for this flight before we even left Tanzania. To our surprise, three of us couldn't get seats. We had to leave them in Abidjan and they joined us in Guinea the next day. Fihla was not surprised. "This is West Africa, my friend," he said. "We are very lucky to get as many as thirty-seven on board. I would not have been surprised if none of us got seats. Here you have to bribe even after your booking has been confirmed. And if you have the money you can bribe your way into the plane, even without booking."

Fihla knew West Africa well because he had spent several years in Nigeria studying civil aviation.

We arrived in Conakry on July 6, 1981. We were fresh from the glitter of Abidjan, so Conakry looked antiquated, with dilapidated buildings and potholes and battered cars in the streets. Poverty hung like a pall over a country that had obtained its independence from France in 1958.

When the French left, they uprooted telephone poles, emptied offices of furniture and important project files and stationery, removed windowpanes from buildings, took all the money they could lay their hands on, and shipped the stuff off to Europe. In their wake they left a poor but proud nation.

Poverty did not deter Guinea from helping the oppressed on the continent and beyond.

The Centre National Kwame Nkrumah (CNKN), where most of our training took place, was located 36 km north of Conakry, in the Dubreka Prefecture. It was built on rocky land and was surrounded by dark green kankilibanyi bush.

The Guinean instructors beamed with smiles as they welcomed us. We returned their smiles, even though we could understand only a few words – like 'revolution', 'liberation', 'impérialisme' and 'camarade'.

We were served a mixture of rice and sweet potatoes in enamel plates. With hotel and airline delicacies still lingering on our palates, we merely nibbled at the food and threw it away on the garbage dump. We lived to remember that food: it turned out to be our mightiest feast in twelve months' stay in Guinea.

The instructors gave each one of us a mosquito net and a pair of new yellow sheets. The climate in Guinea was not meant for blankets and duvets. Guinea has only two seasons, the dry and the rainy – both equally warm.

We were warned never to experiment with using paper in their toilets because the sewerage pipes were very narrow and designed to carry waterborne waste and nothing more. In place of toilet paper, we had to use water. In the early days we spent hours washing our hands with soap and sand and rubbing them against the concrete slabs to erase the stubborn smell. We laughed hilariously and consoled ourselves that what we were going through was part of the training.

One day as we were washing, Sakhiwo noticed something wrong with me: my efforts were concentrated on soaping and rubbing my right hand.

He exclaimed and asked: "S'khulu, which hand do you use in the toilet?"

"The one I use when I use toilet paper, the right hand," I answered amid uproarious laughter. It turned out that my comrades were using their left hands. From that day I switched to the left hand, which I found difficult as water spattered all over the place. After a while we got used to washing and soap alone sufficed.

We slept on bunk beds. After a short stay in a small dormitory, we were moved to a large one called Robert Sobukwe. It was one of about ten of its size and was named after the PAC's founding president.

Every dormitory or facility in the centre was named after a revolutionary of one shade or another. Among other greats whose names were emblazoned on the walls were Patrice Lumumba and Ho Chi Minh, the man who led the Vietnamese assault first against France and then against the USA in the struggle to liberate and unify his country.

There was Salvador Allende, the Chilean revolutionary; a medical doctor by profession, he made history by leading a communist party to electoral victory in an election in 1970 monitored by the West. This didn't go down well with the USA, and in 1973 Washington ousted him from power and installed General Pinochet.

The huge hall was named after Fidel Castro, the Cuban revolutionary who liberated his country from the oppressive regime of Batista. Mao Tse-tung of China and Che Guevara of Argentina were also among the giants who were revered at CNKN.

Every dormitory had its own set of toilets, showers, taps and concrete washing basins.

Our course was clearly defined – six months of infantry and three months of specialist training. We dreaded the thought of having to spend so much time in this starving country, but there was no alternative.

The instructors' attendance was very erratic. The two PAC members who had been left behind by the previous group to act as our interpreters, and who lived in the city, also paid very irregular visits to the camp. We spent days and sometimes weeks loitering around – our dull schedule interrupted only by Abu, the giant-sized cook, calling us to meals. He would stand in front of the dining hall, his black and white hat as conspicuous as the rest of his imposing frame, and shout "Le manger!" – food! – while his cupped hand made deft movements to the mouth. We knew we would get a few more grains of rice and a little more fish because he was in the kitchen. We all liked Abu, or Oshi, as we fondly called him. He had a habit of lifting his huge shoulders and shouting "Oshi!" as if roaring the war cry of one of the thousand tribes in West Africa.

We were aware that Abu, like the people in the stores, helped himself to food meant for us, but we loved him for making a difference when it was his turn to cook and for being jolly all the time.

He alternated with a tiny old man whose real name I never knew, nor cared to know. We called him Pourquois, French for 'why'. He never let a person finish a sentence without barking an unfriendly "Pourquois?" He hated us and we also loathed him, and suspected that he deliberately cooked badly. He stirred the mixture of rice and fish with the same shovel he used to clean the gutter where scum, mucus and phlegm floated repulsively. West Africans were always chewing kola-nuts and spitting after cleaning their teeth with sticks. Dead flies were common in the food Pourquois gave us.

Our breakfast was a small piece of French bread and tea made from kankilibanyi leaves. When there was no bread, we were fed soft porridge made from rice. Fihla boycotted breakfast, saying it made him hungrier instead of filling him. He gave his share away and used breakfast time to condemn Sekou Toure's economic policies and the corruption afflicting the country. I on the other hand started drinking the tea because I was hungry.

Our instructors offered us kola, which they ate with relish as if it were delicious. I found it unpalatable and none of us developed a liking for it. Moreover, it was a small nut, which didn't alleviate the pangs of hunger.

Height, the physical training instructor we had heard stories about while we were still in Tanzania, came to the camp. Somebody saw him from a distance and alerted the whole group, shouting "Height!"

In a flash we assembled in the Parade Square, and he looked impressed by our pace. He instructed us to fetch our full equipment. We ran into the dormitory and brought out our helmets, MP44 rifles, trench-digging spades, gas masks and water bottles. Height inspected us and nodded his head in satisfaction.

This was his second visit to the camp, having earlier welcomed us to CNKN. On that occasion he was in a gay mood. This time he meant business. He was of medium height and slender and not the giant I had imagined him to be. His eyes darted around menacingly like those of a snake poised to strike.

He ordered us to run and we ran to where only Height knew. He loved the toyi-toyi, a rhythmic jog with the thighs raised to at least parallel to the ground, accompanied by a chant. It was the tonic for long-distance runs. PAC cadres had learnt the toyi-toyi from Zimbabwe African People's Union (ZAPU) combatants in Libya. We sometimes called it 'The Slogan'.

Each time we passed through a village Height instructed us to toyi-toyi. A mighty roar lifted the sky and echoed in the agitated village. Boots pounded the dusty ground and the villagers lined the road and ululated. Their cheers revived our weary bodies and souls.

Height always appeared unexpectedly, when we lay leisurely in bed thinking the next programme would be only on the following day. One afternoon he pounced.

"Height!" The whole camp rose from siesta. He led us to the artificial obstacle terrain and gracefully demonstrated a tumble on the hard ground, which was covered in sharp pointed stones. He ordered us to follow his example. All my comrades, except my embarrassed self and Rufus Zonyane, tumbled. Height exempted Zonyane because he was old: he had left South Africa in 1962, but only managed to go for training now, with our group.

I had previously failed to fall on a surface cushioned with sawdust. In fact, as a child I gave up the struggle to learn tumbling on the white sands of Hlakaro. During tumbling sessions I used to perch myself on a rock and watch my playmates performing all types of somersaults. It was voluntary then and there was no Height watching us.

My comrades were concerned about me attempting a tumble. I heard Qesh Ndonyana, one of the group's medicos, whispering to Sam: "Please chief, tell Height that S'khulu has a backache and can't perform the exercise. If S'khulu tumbles on these rocks we'll carry him back paralysed. You know the spinal cord is very sensitive."

Sam didn't know what to do. Much as I appreciated the comrades' concern, I didn't want to get special attention from Height.

Khaya, one of the older members of the group, looked at me mischievously and said: "Don't worry, S'khulu, this is a hard surface and everyone, including yourself, will tumble very well."

Two images flashed through my mind: one, tumbling well as Khaya had anticipated; and the other, being carried to the dispensary paralysed.

Sam, who was always the first in the group to act, tumbled extremely well. "Bon!" Height shouted in satisfaction, clapping his nut-tough hands and summoning the next person to follow. When a cadre didn't perform well but was adequate enough to avoid repeating the exercise, Height withheld his "Bon" and simply kept quiet.

My turn came.

I was scared that in a few seconds I would be taken away on a stretcher. I pumped confidence into my legs and trotted like someone who was about to make the tumble of the day. Cheers followed. I don't know if Height did say "Bon"; even if he had, it would have been drowned in the jubilation generated by my tumble. It was to be my last.

After the exercise we assembled. We were standing at ease when Height barked in my direction, his eyes flickering and striking terror.

I told the cadre next to me that Height was angry with him. He whispered back that I was the culprit. He was right. Height pointed a finger at me and shouted furiously in French. I looked this way and that and asked myself what sin had I committed. Height only got angrier.

"Numero!" he roared, demanding my number with his pen ready to write in his pocket book.

"Numero for what?" I asked.

"Order, comrade," my friends warned me against questioning the orders of the instructor. Elias, one of our two interpreters, said I had moved my body and head when I was supposed to be standing at ease, and that was what had angered Height.

"Numcro!"

"Ha ka shukuma – I didn't move," I protested. I didn't know whether to speak English, French, Sesotho, Xhosa or Afrikaans to convince Height that I hadn't moved. My colleagues said even as I was protesting my innocence in a mixture of Sotho and Xhosa, I was moving my head.

"Numero!" Height was now charging forward.

"Zero soixante six!" – I shouted my number and stood still, cursing myself for being a bundle of nerves. We immediately broke parade. Height didn't call me to mete out the expected punishment. But for a while I carried the stigma of "Numero!", which echoed around the camp, wounding my pride.

Our Political Commissar, George Moletsane, ran political classes for us. In addition to these classes I also read a lot of philosophical literature. Harari helped me as I grappled with new and fascinating thoughts.

I found the argument of the materialists compelling: I embraced atheism and stopped my secret and silent praying. My deep doubts about religion had started back at home in Manaleng, but because I had no alternative to religion I had clung to the god imported from Israel, contemptuously rejecting the indigenous worship of my ancestors. Materialism kicked both the African and the Christian drugs out of me and I was liberated.

— Chapter Eleven —

MONT KAKOULIMA. When the instructors mentioned these two words, I was gripped by fear – as they intended. The mountain maintained its ancient and majestic posture. It appeared to be looking forward to our long-awaited arrival and its revenge for the humiliation we had inflicted on it, spraying it with anti-aircraft artillery fire.

We were going into guerrilla manoeuvres in the terrain around the mountain; the climax would be the toughest of all exercises, a march to the summit. Everyone who has been on Mont Kakoulima tells you that you need strong bones to carry you to the top.

We strengthened our knees with tough exercises and were ready when the day dawned. We packed our rations of rice and large quantities of dried fish – its stench wriggled our noses.

During the exercise we slept in our hammocks with wet and muddy boots on, ready for any call to action. We constantly moved camp, sometimes just when sleep was starting to massage our tired bodies.

The weakness in this exercise was that we were barred from using blank ammunition, which would have made it almost real. The ban was in place because of another one of Guinea's endless coup alerts.

On one occasion a flare alerted our sub-group of an approaching 'enemy'. Our unit commander Sakhiwo ordered retreat and we moved swiftly. The flare landed in a planted field and started a fire among the crops. Some of us argued with Sakhiwo, suggesting that we postpone the retreat and go back to put out the fire.

"The enemy will be on us," Sakhiwo shouted. "Retreat!"

He moved to the front to set a faster pace.

"But Saks, this is not a real enemy," Babes argued as he picked up his pace to trot next to his commander. "This is just an exercise. We shouldn't leave people's crops burning because we are running away from a mock enemy."

"I've given you my order. Let's move."

Grudgingly the unit followed Sakhiwo. I agreed with him, because in earlier incidents we had been punished for lack of vigilance against the same 'enemy'. Now we could hardly distinguish the real enemy from the imaginary one. The flare was a signal for us to retreat, and we were doing exactly that. Nothing in the training had prepared us for the accidental burning of the fields of poor peasants. Part of me sympathised with them, but another wanted the instructors to reap the fruits of turning us into mindless, thoughtless robots.

One instructor called Elbrando came running after us, calling us back to extinguish the blaze. Sakhiwo ordered us to return at high speed. We fought the roaring fire with large tree branches while Elbrando shouted angry obscenities at us, wondering if we – and Sakhiwo in particular – were sane.

As a punishment he ordered us to continue carrying the branches after we had put out the fire. We walked uphill.

After a while, I realised I was the only person with a branch on his shoulder. My comrades had discarded theirs. I reasoned it wouldn't be wrong to discard mine too, even though Elbrando hadn't given the order. He appeared to have forgotten about the punishment. I was just in front of him when I threw the branch away. He ordered me to pick it up and shoulder it till he told me to discard it. I obeyed.

For years Babes, who had been urging me to throw away the branch, laughed at me when he recalled the incident. He would say: "S'khulu, one day you'll die because of your discipline. You spent nights at the sentry post when everyone else had gone to sleep. We, the undisciplined, move freely. When will you learn that these instructors are mad?"

That night I marched with the branch on my shoulder. I wasn't prepared to throw it away without orders. I accepted that I was dealing with madness – my madness, for which I wanted to punish myself. It is madness to try to be rational in an irrational world.

When we completed our training, the director of the centre, Aguibou Thiam, arranged an audience with President Ahmed Sekou Toure for us. Toure was visiting the USA and we impatiently waited for his return. We closely followed his itinerary as he moved from one city to another and from one state to another. A day in the USA for him was an eternity to us in Guinea.

Guinea had been a time of hard training and learning. Now as we waited, we also laughed and cried.

Night crawled slowly on as we lay in our beds covered with mosquito nets. We were laughing at Shoeshoe's jokes when the unexpected appearance of an officer silenced us. He was short and stout and his bulging tummy was restrained from spilling out by an untidily buttoned shirt. He beckoned us to stand around him.

He needed an interpreter but spurned Buti, our best interpreter. Instead he chose another, who was less fluent. The officer told us how deeply he loved us, his brothers. He said above all of us, he had singled out Buti as his special friend and had taken him to his house in the nearby village of Kasogna. He had shared the little comforts his house could afford with Buti.

"But, but . . ." The officer broke into tears. "But in turn Buti took my wife. He went with her to Kindiya without my knowledge. This is something a friend doesn't do to a friend, a brother doesn't do this to a brother."

The officer was greatly tormented and he didn't wait for our response. He left and silence fell on the dormitory. It was broken by the scratching of matches and the shout of "Skuif!" (give me a puff from your cigarette).

"Buti, mfan' akithi, udl'umfazi we ofisa?" – Buti, my brother, did you sleep with the officer's wife? – Shoeshoe broached the subject, and there was volcanic laughter from the rest of us now that the question was in the open.

Someone commented on the woman's youth and good looks. She was the officer's third, fourth or even fifth wife. All acknowledged her beauty. I wished I were Buti, gifted in the art of making friends, but the tears I had seen on the Guinean officer's plump cheeks made me question the wisdom of my wishes.

Toure's luggage was barely unpacked when he declared himself ready to see us. We wore new black shoes and brown safari suits, which were specially tailored for the occasion. At State House, we were joined by the PAC chief representative in the country, Vusi Nomadolo. We were ushered into what seemed to be a conference room, with plenty of chairs and a lofty podium. I was still taking in the splendour of the room when a voice ordered us to stand up.

Toure was wearing flowing robes and he walked tall.

He sat in the middle chair, flanked by his senior ministers. After the formal introductions, Nomadolo spoke and Toure responded. He spoke of his visit to the US and said that among other things, he spoke about the plight of the victims of apartheid. He said that every time he travelled abroad, he sensitised his hosts to the oppression in Azania and the need to support the oppressed. He said Guinea, with her meagre resources, was always ready to sacrifice for the cause of Africa, which was also her cause.

"When you are in Guinea, you are Guineans," he said. "You are entitled to the rights afforded to the citizens of this country. You are not refugees. How can an African be a refugee in Africa? When Azania is liberated, Guinea is not going to appoint an ambassador to Azania. You will be Guinea's ambassadors to Azania just as we are the Azanian ambassadors to Guinea. Pour la revolution!" he shouted his famous slogan – for the revolution!

"Prêt!" – ready! – we shouted in response, and applauded thunderously when he sat down.

The officials gave each of us a gift from Toure, a high quality wristwatch bearing his photo. It was the first watch I'd ever owned.

The following day we left Guinea after a year and three days.

We had a two-week stopover in Lagos, Nigeria, because it was the hectic month of Ramadan and airlines were ferrying faithful Muslims to Mecca for the hajj. The PAC chief representative in that country, Theo Bidi, found accommodation for us in the government guesthouse in the suburb of Surulere. I had heard horrifying stories about Nigeria so I confined myself to the guesthouse. Some comrades invited me to go to town with them but I refused. I wasn't prepared to be a juju for a million and one ritual killers roaming the streets of Lagos.

The longer the hajj lasted, the better for us. We had been in a hurry to leave Guinea, but we were not in a hurry to reach Tanzania. We had TV sets in our rooms and we followed the soccer World Cup in Spain. Finally and reluctantly we did leave Nigeria, a land of myths, legends, lunatics and truly gifted writers.

— Chapter Twelve —

WE FINALLY REACHED our new home, the Apla camp in the district of Mbeya in southern Tanzania. It was variously called the College, Itumbi, Mbeya or the Camp. It was called the College because people who were illiterate when they arrived at the place could read and write when they left it. Those who were literate when they arrived became crude intellectuals, and those who were already intellectuals generally kept away from Mbeya.

Humans survived in Mbeya but the story was different for some animals. No matter how healthy dogs and domestic pigs were when they arrived, they would get sick and die within weeks. The dogs wailed hauntingly, as if communicating some evil message, before they died.

But the dog-loving cadres never tired of bringing the pets to the camp and to their miserable end.

Only wild pigs thrived in this wild place.

An imposing double-storey, red-brick structure we called the Carlton Centre was the hive of camp activity. Its ground floor housed the camp press, the dispensary and the storeroom. The first floor rooms accommodated cadres, and a few tents were pitched near the Carlton to alleviate the overcrowding. The parade ground unfurled in front of the Carlton. This was also used for volleyball games and soccer, even though there was a soccer field just outside the camp.

The leaders' quarters, on the edge of the forest about 200 metres from the Carlton, were called Shanghai. This was where members of the central committee stayed when they visited the camp. The camp commander and his immediate juniors also lived there. There were others who saw themselves as the future leaders of the PAC who insinuated themselves into Shanghai.

There was no noticeable difference between Shanghai residents and the rest of us. We ate from the same pot, sometimes from the same dish with them. The cooking roster roped everyone in, including members of the High Command.

The kitchen was separated from the Carlton Centre by a narrow passage, and next to it was a water tap. A few metres from the kitchen we had an ever-growing mountain of firewood, enough to last a normal household for decades.

A few steps from the fowl run stood an old tree we called the Historic Tree (I still don't know why); under it we held meetings and listened to lessons in many disciplines. The benches and tables under the tree were made of logs split lengthways.

I shared meals with Babes. Food was served to individuals, but people grouped to combine and share their meals. A group eating from one dish was called a chama, a Swahili name for party. Babes was a valuable partner. On meat days, he was not ashamed to queue half an hour before the cooks rang the bell for mealtime. The cooks dished out the rice, the staple food. We helped ourselves to the meat, with each person entitled to one piece. Babes, always the first in the queue, would fork the two biggest chunks, usually ox knees.

Babes had the appetite of a bird, especially on Mondays when he nursed a hangover from the weekend's booze binge. This suited my giant appetite well.

Work was allocated according to the individual's physique. The strong ones fetched wood from the bush and called themselves the commandos; the weaker ones like me repaired the road into the camp; and the old and the sickly worked in the maize and groundnut fields.

The road team was called Kajima, after a Japanese road construction company in Tanzania. We loaded a truck with crushed stone from a heap near a disused mine about six km from the camp and filled holes in the road with it. Where the road was badly damaged, we laid down large wet logs and big stones before covering them over with the crushed stone. When we needed to do this, we asked the commandos to help us carry long, freshly cut tree trunks still dripping with sticky resin. The commandos were used to lifting small, dry and relatively lighter wood, so they heaved and cursed under the weight of the logs.

Rice was another area of great labour. All the camp irrespective of age or status participated in cleaning it, separating rice grains from the stones. It was irksome work, particularly when white stones masqueraded as rice. One cadre named Mpumelelo refused to go on rice duty, saying he valued his eyesight and he didn't want to damage it before he fought the Boers. But he did eat the rice with us till he defected to the Boers via Malawi.

Beans – what the Tanzanians call maharage in Swahili – were part of the diet we had to stomach. On lean days we ate beans without oil or fat, and when there was a salt crisis in Tanzania, we ate them without salt. Those were the tough days of magendo, the black market, when sellers hoarded retail goods and sold them exorbitantly on the black market. The beans were dark brown and big and tasted as if they had been cooked in hellfire by Lucifer. They took at least five hours on the fire to cook and gave us heartburn.

The beans also caused stirrings and rumblings and roaring in out stomachs. Frequently when we were jogging, a runner would break off from the formation and unleash a salvo of mighty farts amid cries of "Ngubo!" – blanket! I never got a satisfactory explanation of the meaning of the cry. Did it mean, "Get a blanket to smother the noises and the smell"? Whoever started it did us a service, because the cry of "Ngubo" removed the opprobrium from farting, and we felt free to rid our bowels of dangerous gases.

We drew water from the nearby pool only when the water-pumping machine had no diesel or its propelling belt was worn out. We were not the only users of the pool – we shared it with an elephant that obviously abused it. He came at night, ate and destroyed banana trees, splashed in the pool and left it muddy. Early risers often saw him lumbering away.

One evening as we were lost in song and tottering on the edge of nostalgia, somebody spotted the elephant. The singing stopped and we ran helter-skelter, trying to get into the nearest available door. One cadre shouted that elephants were not aggressive and we needn't be running away in a panic. He explained that noise irritates elephants and rouses their aggression. He said the one time when elephants are really unforgiving is when you bump into them during their mating season. Our expert allayed our fears and we went out to watch his majesty, the kind ruler of the wild. He looked far bigger than the elephants that Father once showed me as they grazed next to a circus tent in Polokwane. I didn't believe Father's elephants were worthy of the name elephants – why were they dancing to the music of the humans? The elephant in the Itumbi moonlit night was magical. It stood coolly as if posing for a photo, or affording those who had never seen his kind before ample time to stare.

Somebody suggested we see who could move closest to him. He would be our hero. Radebe, in his late thirties or early forties and a teacher before he left Azania, had slipped to a few steps from the monster when it flapped its ears, trumpeted sharply and charged at him. No one waited to see Radi's fate.

The elephant didn't harm him: he played hide and seek with it till late into the night.

If the elephant's shrill trumpet betrays its massive size, the lion's roar exaggerates its modest built. Occasionally a pride of lions lurked around the camp, coming as near as the football field. The roar in the middle of the night was frightening. It carried the magic of the wild. When it sounded, we cut our urinating short and rushed back into the house. Those who had been preparing to go out simply endured their overloaded bladders.

One day in broad daylight, the camp commander, Jan 'Goebbels' Shoba and Thabo Bodibe sighted a pride of lions relaxing and yawning on the path ahead. Goebbels ordered his soldier not to run away. Thabo obeyed the order and moved next to his lion-hearted commander. An earth-shaking roar from the pride filled the air, and, forgetting to change his orders, Goebbels sprinted. He outran Thabo to the point where Thabo lost sight of him.

Their story was a scoop for the Itumbi News Daily, where I was deputy editor. I interviewed the two. Thabo gave a detailed account of their experience. Goebbels was reluctant to talk but relented later. He insisted he issued the order to retreat, which Thabo might not have heard because he was too frightened. The story was the subject of conversation in the camp for days.

It was a repetition of an earlier story: Vuyo Fetsha once ordered his unit not to run when they sighted a herd of elephant. When the elephants charged, Vuyo, an accomplished sprinter, outran all the people in the unit. In the stampede, one cadre fell and the flying boots didn't give him a chance to stand up. He only managed to rise after everybody else had flown over him. He lost his axe in the incident, and that gave spice to the news pages. I interviewed each member of Vuyo's unit and marvelled at their contradictory accounts. They were unanimous on one issue only, that Vuyo had run away without issuing an order to run. Vuyo on the other hand laughed heartily and explained: "Sis'denge sodwa esingafun' ukuxelelwa ukuba ukufa kufikile – only a fool would expect to be formally told that death has arrived. They accuse me of not giving them the order to run away – why then did they run? Didn't the one and only order I issued say they shouldn't run away? I'm going to punish them for disobedience." Vuyo's tough, muscular body rocked with mirth, exposing the gaps in his teeth.

The following day's headline screamed: "Weapons Unaccounted For In A Hasty Retreat."

Among our readers were the twelve Tanzanian Special Defence Unit (SDU) soldiers stationed in the camp to protect us.

I learnt that captivating headlines drew readers into our newspaper. When Indian troops attacked the Sikh's holiest shrine, I gave the story the headline "Indian Army Storms Heaven!". Sikh fighters had taken refuge in the shrine in the naïve belief that the holiness of the place would keep away Indira Gandhi's forces. I told myself that the headline ranked among the best, at least by bush standards.

As time went by, journalism was included in the camp curriculum. I was excited and read journalism literature extensively. The editor of our newspaper, Molapo 'Professor' Molefe, conducted the lessons. The diminutive, light-complexioned and slow-speaking Prof had incredible stamina for work. He laced his speech with bombastic terms and would devote time to defining them.

"Dereliction of duty," Molefe said, as he reprimanded one or other of us in the newsroom. "I first came across that term in my passbook. My Boer employer wrote it in the column where he had to explain why he had fired me. I wondered what it meant, so I consulted my lexicon. Do you know what the phrase means or do you just enjoy its music ringing in your ears?" He paused and looked challengingly at his audience. "All I see here is mammoth dereliction of duty," he concluded.

One day he instructed me, without looking up, to go and call Eddie, whose copy he was editing. When Eddie came into the newsroom, those who knew Molefe's running battles with him positioned ourselves to listen.

"Comrade Eddie, how are you?" Molefe enquired, his head bowed in feigned concentration on the papers on the table.

"I'm okay."

"Comrade Eddie, in my capacity as the editor of Itumbi News Daily, I hereby officially inform you that your services are no longer required. The department of publicity can and will do better without you."

He lifted his head and his eyes focused on Eddie's.

The ever-smiling Eddie accepted his fate, and then shook hands with all of us in farewell. Molefe also stood up to shake Eddie's hand. "You're free to visit the newsroom if you so wish," Molefe said.

I had plotted the dismissal of Eddie 'Operations' Maseko, my dear friend, who is now dead. I complained to Prof about his poor work, and persuaded him that the solution was to relieve Eddie of his duties in a way that wouldn't hurt his pride. Prof sagely nodded his approval and said I should leave it all to him. He took a long time before he fired Eddie, who showed no bitterness whatsoever. In fact, Eddie joked about it.

That evening during supper under the Historic Tree, I told him about my role in his dismissal. The problem was the brevity of his stories. He'd listen to the radio all day – radio was our main source of news – and then give us a miserly two sentences for the newspaper. It was immaterial to him that the story was about a conflict that had claimed the lives of five hundred people and forced the UN Security Council to hold an emergency session: he would give us a few lines only. When I edited his copy, I would have to pad his bare facts with many unnecessary words. With his departure, the newspaper improved.

Eddie was however a great footballer and all-round sportsman, and it was as sports correspondent that he returned to the Department of Publicity. This time he performed very well.

One afternoon Goebbels summoned everybody to the parade ground. He ordered the cooks, the medical staff and the publicity personnel to leave their work; even the sick dragged themselves to the parade.

Goebbels's message was precise, short and haunting. "Comrades, from today we are turning this civilian establishment into a military camp," he said through clenched jaws. "You've become soft civilians, and I'll be failing in my duty as camp commander if I don't make soldiers out of you." His eyes flickered with deadly resolve. "Do you seriously expect to defeat the Boers when you still do old-age-home exercises? Boer commandos train till they collapse from dehydration. If we are to defeat them, we have to do more than that. No more civilian life in this camp. From now it's going to be tough-a-rough-rough and rough and rough!"

His last "rough" was grunted menacingly as he dismissed the parade.

Tough-a-rough echoed in my ears the rest of the day. I felt guilty that I was one of the civilians Goebbels was condemning. My performance during training was very poor. I couldn't run long distances.

The sceptics said it was impossible for Goebbels to implement his plan and transform the camp. I found solace knowing that among the sceptics were the camp's fitness fanatics. "Can you imagine running over thirty km on the first day, and increasing it to a hundred within a week? Impossible," they said as they discussed Goebbels's plan.

The next morning Goebbels rang the bell himself. I had already heard that bell so many times that night and had run many km and collapsed – all in my dreams. This time it was real.

As he struck the bell, Goebbels chanted:

Vuka phezu 'komdlezana …
Ndingu Nyerere mna, ndikhululekile andivuki!
Ub'usiyaphi emva kwa marhumsh' oShoba?
Ekuseni baya gula, entambama baya phila
Savumelana.

(Stop making love to the new mother …
I Nyerere am free and don't need to wake up!
What made you follow con men like Shoba?
In the morning they malinger and are healthy again at nightfall
You've bound yourself to the army now!)

Excited voices joined Goebbels's. Vuyo lifted his arms to transform them into the horns of a bull and pawed the ground with his boots, straining to be let loose.

I enjoyed the spectacle very much but I did not join in. To me it was a premature celebration much more appropriate to the end of the exercise.

Shoba led us as we trotted out of the camp in the darkness. He used a torch to light the way. Shoba chanted, whistled and pranced about like a child with a fascinating toy. I wished the darkness would envelop and slow us down until our return. Sadly dawn arrived and the sun poked its nose into human affairs. We stepped up the pace. Those who could not keep up were left behind. Somehow I coped.

As we neared the village of Matundasi, 16 km from the camp, we slowed down to allow those lagging behind to catch up. It was their voices more than anything else we needed. When we were all together, we entered the village dancing and chanting a toyi-toyi that the village will never forget. The villagers cheered and ululated. Just past the village, we turned and ran back to the camp.

When we left the village behind and faced the forest again, I was still in the front group. We ran. Only five remained in this group and I was the fifth. I was exhausted and found it difficult to keep up. I screamed and covered my eyes, pretending the elephant grass had cut me. Vuyo stopped to see what was wrong and the other three also slowed down.

"V-man," I whispered to Vuyo, "I'm not injured – just tired. Please go."

Vuyo joined Shoba, Babes and Ndumiso and they disappeared from sight. I followed.

I walked grimly on. Though I had performed below Goebbels's expectations, I was consoled by knowing that only four out of about fifty cadres were ahead of me. I made sure that none of the stragglers would overtake me.

About seven km from the camp I saw Goebbels sitting under a tree, cutting a pathetic figure. His lips were parched and he drummed his chest with his fist. When I stopped to help, he mumbled: "Yis'fuba – it's my chest, otherwise I'm fit."

"When did it start troubling you?" I asked sympathetically.

"Don't you know that I've got chest problems?"

"No. I didn't know."

He stood up, staggered and sat down again.

"Yinyongo – bile. I feel dizzy."

After a while, he stood up and we walked together to the camp. Most of our comrades overtook us.

Those who hadn't participated in tough-a-rough on that day regretted it for a long time because it was not repeated. Goebbels never again organised it.

One day Sam Motau announced: "Comrades, tomorrow we're all leaving this camp. Pack your things properly and get ready for the journey." Chichi – camp jargon for rumours – that we would be leaving the camp had been circulating for while.

Sam had succeeded Goebbels as the camp commander after Goebbels had been deployed to 'the front', either fighting in Azania or working in the countries around Azania.

We woke up early the next morning to load our belongings into troop carriers. We then found out that two cadres, Motsamai and Nkokheli, were missing. They had not slept in the camp that night. We guessed that they had gone to Matundasi, where most cadres had lovers, to bid their loved ones farewell.

Sam's body and voice shook with anger.

When the two arrived, Sam punished them by ordering them to do various exercises on the parade ground. Nkokheli, a Poqo veteran who had gone into exile in the early sixties, performed exercises that even I couldn't do. He tumbled with the agility of a leopard – a surprise considering his age and that he never participated in the camp's exercises. In the sixties and seventies, his generation used to run to Matundasi in the morning and walk the same distance to go and socialise in the afternoon. The fitness he had acquired in those days had lain dormant somewhere in the reserves of his body, emerging then when the need arose.

We stood watching the three-man drama in awe, some of our belongings still clutched in our hands. I both admired and sympathised with Nkokheli. He out-performed Motsamai, who was in his thirties.

Sam couldn't understand why Motsamai couldn't do as well as Nkokheli. In his fury, he sent for a whip and lashed out at Motsamai, who didn't flinch. He didn't even increase his pace in response to the beating. Sam strengthened his lashes and cracked Motsamai's back. Motsamai neither cried nor faltered in his stride.

Our attention shifted from Nkokheli to Motsamai. His courage and endurance were admirable. Our condemnation of his ill-discipline and sympathy for him merged into one as we wished every lash to be the last. But Sam was no longer beating him to punish him: he seemed to trying to extract a cry for mercy. The punishment ended without a peep from Motsamai.

A dark cloud of gloom engulfed us as we climbed onto the trucks to Mgagao in Iringa. We carried that gloom to the new camp.

— Chapter Thirteen —

"MWESI WA SABA, LA! LA! LA! – The seventh month, la! la! la!" the villagers around our camp in Mgagao exclaimed in Swahili.

We mimicked them: "Mwesi wa saba kuna baridi sana – the seventh month is very cold." We had arrived at our new camp early in 1983, and it was exceedingly cold. The villagers advised us to reserve our hasty comments till we had lived through the seventh month – the worst of the cold weather. We were not warmly dressed but relished the cold because it relieved us from mosquito bites and from the dreaded malaria. However we had to face the new terror of the jigger flea. When it bit it deposited a worm under the victim's skin.

Compared to Itumbi, Mgagao was a city. There were six spacious dormitories, a large administration complex, a large storeroom, a large kitchen, a shelter for firewood, flush toilets and showers. Most of the toilets and showers were out of order. Here firewood was a problem because the sprawling villages had denuded the area of every dry branch.

We had hardly settled in when the PAC Administrative Secretary, Joe Mkhwanazi, visited us. At the usual meeting that always accompanied such a visit, he conveyed Pokela's good wishes and the promise that he would soon visit the camp. In his gravelly, fatherly voice, Mkhwanazi advised us to dress warmly.

"It doesn't pay to hoard clothes for special occasions when you're dying of cold," Khwani said. "You'll die and we'll bury you and share your clothes among ourselves. It would be better to die in Azania fighting Boers."

Khwani's chilly warning prompted me to unpack my bag and retrieve clothes I had vowed to wear only when I left the camp.

"Now, lalelani kahle MaAfrika – listen carefully, dear Africans," he said, generating a new interest in what he was saying. "This is very important. Comrade Chairman said I should state it in no uncertain terms. Never ever stray into the village and make love to a Wahehe woman. Do you understand what I'm saying? Never ever."

We laughed, because Khwani was telling us what had been drummed into our ears since we arrived in Mgagao. It had become monotonous.

"Look," he said, "never take this as a joke. There is nothing in this world that a Wahehe man treasures more than his lover. One Member of Parliament had an affair with a married Wahehe woman. He's lying in his grave after being chopped with an axe, stabbed and stoned by the Wahehe community here in Iringa. He was not an ordinary person, mind you, but a prominent MP. The MPLA and ZANU have lost cadres because they wouldn't listen. Take my word, MaAfrika – forewarned is forearmed."

There were whispers of dissatisfaction against the rule banning us from the village. Some cadres went to the extent of calling the new place a concentration camp, a prison or solitary confinement. Some cadres, including members of the administration, sneaked into the village at night. There were also Houdinis who went into the village during the day without being detected. They would buy homebrewed beer and conceal it near the camp. The person would arm himself with a hoe or a spade and a newspaper and disappear, creating the impression he was 'going to the front', camp euphemism for going to the toilet. As the hours went by, he'd get tipsy and then smother his beer-smelling breath under a mighty song and dance.

Sam loved singing and drifted to any group that started up; but then he'd find the drunks leading the singing, and curse.

A general meeting was called to discuss the rule with Sam and to protest against corporal punishment, but he was unmoved.

About three months later there was another meeting, of greater importance. Enoch Zulu, a member of the High Command, the Military Commission and the Central Committee came to address us. He briefed us on developments in the organisation and the frontline states like Zimbabwe, Botswana, Lesotho and Swaziland, and on the home front – Azania itself. He told us we had to intensify our training if we hoped to defeat the Boers. He stressed that we should ground ourselves in sound political theory because politics is supreme over the gun. He said a soldier without a clear political orientation was dangerous even to his commander.

Zulu was a battle-hardened veteran speaking from practical experience. He had been involved in the 1961 Poqo insurgency in the Western and Eastern Cape, in the battle of Villa Perry in Mozambique in 1968 and in battles in Ingwavuma in northern Natal in the early seventies.

But again, all that was on the cadres' minds was the rule banning them from the village, and corporal punishment. This meeting ended on a sour-sweet note. Zulu agreed that we could now visit the village on weekends, but we had to be back in the camp by 6 p.m. Corporal punishment was to stay.

And life went on.

The garden thrived. We had abnormally large cabbages, beetroots, onions and carrots. The vast shamba, the ploughing field, was green with maize. We ploughed with a tractor, so our toughest manual work was weeding the fields. We called the maize field nguvu kazi – Swahili for 'hard work'. We reared a flock of pigs and slaughtered them for meat. Yugoslavia also sent us a large quantity of tinned food that drastically changed our diet. We shipped bags full of cabbage to Iringa town to sell. We were already anticipating a time not far off when we would be liberated from handouts from the OAU's Liberation Committee.

We aimed high.

But a few days after a visit by Pokela, we were agitated as we tried to analyse his speech. Our restlessness brought the camp to a standstill. We refused to do any work and demanded that Pokela return to clarify his comment that, as far as the programme of infiltration into Azania was concerned, the ball was firmly in our court. We believed that an inept leadership was delaying this programme. Sam tried to explain what Pokela had meant, but we insisted that Pokela, not Sam, come and explain. Sam sent an urgent message to Dar es Salaam and Pokela and his entourage did come back.

Pokela listened to our gripes for eight long days. It was a meeting where everyone wanted to go on record as having spoken. He sat through it all with the patience of a sage, like a rock in a stormy sea. The tides rise and slap it hard on the face, sometimes submerging it – but it reappears unperturbed. Behind the spectacles, Pokela's vigilant eyes were as penetrating as ever, moving from position to position, depending on where the speaker stood.

Bassie asked the house to sing before Pokela stood up to speak.

Siyahlupheka, Pokela
Wee Bawo
Sikhokhele, Pokela
O Viva Wee, Apla
Viva PAC.

(We are suffering, Pokela
Dear father
Lead us, Pokela
Viva Apla
Viva PAC.)

As we sang with gusto, I tried to figure out what Pokela was thinking as he sang about himself. What was he thinking about each one of us? What was he thinking about the APRP, which was worming its way into the bowels of the PAC? Singaye (a code name for the APRP) was as real as the air we breathed.

Unlike his angry colleagues and followers, Poks commenced calmly. He told us about his visit to China where he had met hardened communist revolutionaries – "not the quacks I've just been listening to – quacks!"

The Chinese had told him that from experience accumulated over long years of their revolution, they could tell a soldier's potential during his or her training. They could tell while he was still at the rear, before he was plunged into the front.

"After they trained Joe Gqabi – the ANC's chief representative in Zimbabwe, who was assassinated by Boers in Harare – the Chinese recommended to the ANC that he should never be appointed a commander.

"They said he was the type of person who would move forward regardless of what lay ahead – and a person like that must never be given a command. If he's a good soldier, he must remain one; but not be elevated to commander. We have such a person right her in our midst – Letlapa."

The sound of my name was like lightning. Eyes were turned to me for a moment. Without elaborating Pokela switched to another topic, leaving Gqabi's story of bravado hanging for any imaginative mind to interpret. My heart pounded.

Pokela warmed to the mood of the meeting. His voice rose to a shrill pitch and he punctuated his speech with the shout of "quacks!"

He condemned those who didn't want to outgrow the APRP. "We shall brook no factionalism." He warned those who promoted factionalism to stop before it was too late, quoting: "Revolutions is the goddess of the unmerciful. She devours both her enemies and her own children."

Pokela also warned about the dangers of people taking notes during PAC meetings. He said he'd observed people jotting things down, and had silently asked himself if he was really in a PAC meeting. He told us that during his Poqo days, a person would be killed if he was found taking notes in a meeting. "From now on, no one must write during meetings." Pens and papers disappeared into pockets. From that time to the time when I left the camp, I did not see anybody jotting down notes in a PAC meeting.

Pokela spoke for a long time.

The next day he was at the camp parade, clad in military gear and standing at the back of the officers in front of us, a position reserved for the highest-ranking person in the army. He was the ultimate authority and no one could displace him, unless they removed him from the chairmanship of the PAC. We were all in green fatigues and performed our drill to the best of our ability.

This Pokela was different from the one who had been breathing fire the previous day. He was conciliatory and appealed for peace. "Ntwa ke ya madula mmoho," he said – it is usually those who live together who quarrel.

After the marathon meeting, camp programmes resumed and we went about our business.

When Molefe left to study journalism formally in Dar es Salaam, I became editor of *Mgagao People's Daily*. In addition to informing the camp community, we also campaigned against ignorance, malingering and smoking.

In the fight against ignorance, we randomly interviewed members, from the commander down, on current events. We published the answers verbatim. If they were incorrect, we provided the right answers alongside and the person interviewed would be the butt of jokes in the camp.

I found people in the Publicity Department just as ignorant. They complained and asked to be exempted but I refused, arguing that no one had the right to be ignorant.

Sam was by far the keenest follower of current affairs and always scored a hundred percent. On parade he encouraged the cadres to read the papers. People actually started reading to avoid embarrassment. The Publicity Department provided a translator for those who couldn't read English.

The fight against smoking was not very successful among the smokers, but we grabbed and popularised Sam's slogan, "If you don't smoke, don't start." Only one cadre successfully kicked the habit as a result of our campaign, and we paraded him as a campaign victory.

The third campaign, against malingering, didn't last long. With the help of the medical staff, we singled out the malingerers and they were soon on the straight and narrow.

We established ties with the Iringa representative of the Tanzanian news agency Juhata. Cheche proved valuable: we asked for his comments on some of our material, and he provided us with journals on journalism.

One morning after parade, the army Chief Political Commissar, Dan Mofokeng, accosted me: "Where were you last night? I looked all over for you. In any case, a soldier should always be ready. Pack your things. You're coming with us now."

I shook hands with the comrades who were remaining, and then joined Sabelo and Dan in the car. Sabelo drove from Mgagao to Dar es Salaam and the following day I was above the clouds, flying to Gaborone, Botswana.

— Chapter Fourteen —

NOMINALLY I WENT to Botswana to be the PAC's Assistant Chief Representative. In fact I was on an Apla assignment to strengthen links with the underground across the border in Azania, and the posting was a good cover. Nyembezi Rodwell Mzotane was the Chief Representative.

As Assistant Chief Representative, I was invited to the Libyan People's Bureau – the Libyans call their embassies around the world People's Bureaux, and their ambassadors Secretaries of the Bureaux.

"Although you're a Christian, my brother, you have qualities of a Muslim," Brother Salem, the Secretary of the Bureau, said to me. "Can you please do something for me? In fact, you'll be doing it for the revolution. Could you list all South African, eh . . . Azanian . . . tribes for me? Show on a map how they are dispersed across the country and their numerical strengths? That's all I need, my brother."

"Only that?" I asked.

"Yes, my brother, when you've finished we'll see what next you can do for us."

"Okay. I will need marking pens, pencils, large sheets of paper, a ruler and crayons. My brother, I need to be thorough with the assignment. I'll need money for these items."

Brother Salem gave me the stationery that was available in the embassy and thirty pula to buy the rest. I gave the money to Mzo, as Mzotane was called by PAC members, and told him about the assignment. He laughed.

"Even our Arab friends can't think of African communities without slicing them into tribes," I said as I joined in the laughter.

My dear brothers in the Libyan embassy didn't know I was an atheist. To them, things were either black or white: those who were not Muslims had to be Christians. I often asked myself if these gentlemen were mullahs or diplomats, as they talked about Islam in most conversations I had with them. They told me they recognised Christ only as one of the prophets but not as the Son of God. They said Christianity was a version of arithmetic where three, the Trinity, was equal to one. They argued that Allah was one and indivisible and was neither a man nor a woman; personal pronouns like He and His could not be used for Allah.

I listened to their arguments and nodded silently. I was there as a PAC envoy and had to place the organisation's interests above my own. I also doubt if my own interests would have been better served by declaring my atheism.

"Now, my brother, I thank you," Brother Salem beamed when I gave him the colourful sheets illustrating 'the tribes' of South Africa.

I seized the psychological moment and said: "My brother, the PAC is a poor organisation. We are not supported by any superpower. Like Brother Colonel Muammar Gaddafi, we don't bow to Moscow or to Reagan. Can the People's Bureau help us with some money?"

Brother Salem said even though he was the Secretary of the People's Bureau, he could not decide on his own. He was a member of a committee of three that met to take decisions. He lectured me on how the People's Committees in Libya operate and presented me with Gaddafi's Green Book. He said after I had read it I should come back to talk about it.

I quickly put in a second request: "My brother, can't you help us transport arms in your diplomatic cars? Lately, the Botswana police and soldiers mount roadblocks, and you know what happens when they arrest us – five years' imprisonment if we're lucky."

"You don't know, my brother, even our cars are searched at the roadblocks," he said.

"What does diplomatic immunity mean, my brother?"

"My brother, it means I can park my car even where parking is forbidden and when the traffic police come, they don't give me a ticket. They fine the Botswana ministry of foreign affairs instead."

"Is that all that diplomatic immunity means, my brother?"

"Wait, it also means that you are now in Libya. No one can come here and search, not even the Botswana police. This is Libya, my brother," he flashed a big smile.

"Can Libya allow us to store arms on its soil, my brother?"

"My brother, you know we are diplomats. It's not possible to keep your arms . . . eh . . . what type of arms and how many do you need us to keep for you?" he switched his line in mid-sentence, his eyes dilating with interest.

"You see, my brother, I have to consult with my comrades about the quantity and types of arms. It is a very important decision and I can't take it alone," I echoed his earlier words in frustration.

We shook hands and I headed towards the exit, silently cursing the barren brotherhood and vowing never again to set foot in the Libyan embassy. However, Brother Salem called me back. He gave me three hundred pula in cash and said that was all he could afford at the time.

"Please brother," he pleaded, "read that book of Brother Gaddafi today. You must also read the Koran. It's a very good book."

"I'll read them, brother – today." I wondered if Brother Salem believed me.

I used to accompany Mzo to other embassies and government offices. Our language and mode of address varied from one embassy to the other. Some envoys preferred to be addressed as comrades, others as brothers and yet others simply as misters. We frequented the Libyan and the Chinese embassies – sometimes at their invitation but often off our own bat. The Chinese now seemed uncomfortable when called comrades. They eschewed discussions about socialism and were unhappy at the mere mention of Mao Tse Tung. They were irritated by what they termed the PAC's racist policies of excluding whites from membership.

Some embassies just didn't like us. The Zambians, for instance, had long wiped the PAC out of existence and didn't want to hear a thing from us. We tried in vain to meet them.

The Soviets, the sponsors of our rival the ANC and the rest of the so-called Authentic Six (Swapo of Namibia, the MPLA of Angola, ZAPU of Zimbabwe, Frelimo of Mozambique and the PAIGC of Guinea-Bissau and Cape Verde) also rebuffed us. However, I continued to visit their embassy in search of literature. Their receptionists wore masks of stone. Each time I went there, I'd tease them by asking something trivial about Russia: "How is the weather in Russia? I understand your country is very cold."

"Look, mister, we are not Russians," one would answer, her face tomato red with anger. "We don't know anything about Russian weather. We are the Soviets."

"Oh, is Russia different from the Soviet Union?" I feigned surprise.

"Read those books and you'll know the difference," she said with the air of finality, and picked up the phone and dialled.

The Soviet ambassador, however, had a surprise for us. He invited the PAC to the celebration of the sixty-eighth anniversary of the October Revolution. Mzo immediately made an appointment to see him. I don't remember what transpired at their meeting, but all I know is that our relations with the Soviets didn't go beyond a toast to a revolution that had long lost its bearings.

In one gathering of diplomats, I met the Nigerian High Commissioner. I praised his country for having produced giants who put Africa firmly on the literary landscape of the world. He invited me to visit him, but to telephone first. I never visited my newly acquired friend because a few hours after our meeting, the government he represented in Botswana was toppled in a coup.

Mzo longed for his wife, Nontato, and their three children, who were in Lesotho. He spoke about them incessantly. Every time he asked Dar es Salaam to let him visit them, he was promised an air ticket. Nothing happened. Mzo resorted to writing letters to them and sending them verbal messages. He was angry as he saw some people given money to travel to as far away as London to visit their families. His request to fly from Gaborone to Maseru would be so much cheaper.

The leadership of the PAC was being unfair, Mzotane said. The PAC condemned the South African migrant labour system because it tore families, the very foundations of our society, apart.

"What the PAC is doing is no different," he said. "At least the labourer in the mines knows that at the end of his six months' or one year's contract, he will go back to his family. In my case, this is the third year I haven't seen my family. I wonder if my boy Sizwe will still recognise me."

I sympathised with him because I had seen families ruined on the barren fields of exile.

One of the people I met frequently was Ace Mgxashe, who was employed as a reporter on the *Botswana Guardian* newspaper. The high and powerful in Botswana were the butts of his menacing pen. Once, for example, he wrote that the wife of Adolf Hirschfeld, the head of the Special Branch, was "so drunk at a party she couldn't stand on her hooves". Readers generally loved it, but not Hirshfeldt and the country's top brass.

Ace exposed the rigging of elections by the ruling Botswana Democratic Party (BDP) in the Gaborone South constituency. After his story, the High Court ordered another ballot and the opposition won.

On June 14, 1985 South African soldiers raided ANC houses in Gaborone and killed fourteen people. Ace wrote a scathing article, demanding to know why the Botswana Defence Force had not repelled the attack. He rejected the excuse that spikes strewn across the road had prevented any pursuit of the raiders, and asked why the soldiers had not used aircraft.

Sales of the *Guardian* skyrocketed. Ace became a celebrity. The government reacted by withdrawing his work permit and declaring him a prohibited immigrant. Not cowed, he knocked at embassy doors searching for a country that would grant him asylum. Many within the Masire government were angry that he was allowed to walk the streets of Gaborone. They wanted him to go to jail like all other prohibited immigrants and wait there for a sympathetic country. This faction won and Ace was arrested. He left the cells only when he was on his way to the airport, bound for the USA.

Life in Gaborone returned to 'normal'.

Good as well as bad news from Tanzania came through to us. We were saddened by the deaths of Harari and Makhubalo in an accident. Makhubalo, the Mgagao camp driver, was driving over a narrow wooden bridge when the truck slipped into the raging Uhimbo River. Besides our two comrades, three locals who had asked for a lift on the truck also died. Makhubalo's decomposing body was recovered a few days after the accident and Harari's was never found. It now lies somewhere in the vast expanse of Africa, its dream sacrificed at the altar of the angry river god, as the African myth goes.

Comrades in transit from Tanzania back to Azania told me that the goddess of the unmerciful had begun to devour her own children even before they faced the enemy. They said Mncedisi Sabatana had been killed in Zambia or Tanzania. The killers had told some PAC members that they had been ordered by the leadership to kill him, because he was still promoting the APRP within the PAC.

Mncedisi left the Mgagao camp when he was told that he was going to the front overland. On the morning of his departure he shook hands with his comrades. A group of them were slaughtering a hog. When Babes shook hands with Mncedisi, he warned: "Comrade Mncedisi, this is our last handshake because we'll never meet again. These people are going to kill you just as we are slaughtering this pig."

Mncedisi was unruffled, and he responded: "If they will save the revolution by killing me, let it be."

The killers later said Mncedisi didn't attempt to run away when they accosted him, and he didn't beg for mercy. Instead he asked: "Bafowethu, niyandibulala na?" – brothers, are you killing me?

The words unnerved the killers, but they shot him nonetheless.

The goddess went on to devour Mahoyi Mpondo, another former member of the APRP, and George Moletsane. Reports were that Mahoyi was stabbed to death in Tanzania while George was shot in Zambia or Zimbabwe.

Somewhere in the warm soil of Africa lie the bodies of the youths whose dreams were quashed by sheer madness parading as revolution.

More bad news came from other quarters, and the carrier was Mzotane: "My friend, you and I are no longer welcome in Botswana, especially you. The Botswana government says I must arrange for your immediate departure."

Mzo said he had been summoned to the President's Office. There he had found Hirschfeld, who told him the Boers had given Botswana a list of people they wanted deported from Botswana, and that we were on that list.

We were not given a deadline, so we had ample time to hand over to our successors. I showed them where we had hidden our arms and briefed them on our infiltration routes and vital contacts in Azania.

During my last days in Botswana I met Thembi Niezel. I was driving in a van in Gaborone when I saw a girl, young and innocent-looking. I stopped and greeted her and she responded. I told her I had stopped to appreciate her beauty. She gave me her address and I visited her on a Saturday.

At sunset we went to watch a boxing fight between South Africans Arthur Mayisela and Harold Volbrecht on TV at Mzotane's flat. Fights between an African and a white man always divided the fans on racial lines.

"Who do you think is going to win tonight's fight?" I asked Thembi.

"Volbrecht," she said.

"Volbrecht!" I exclaimed. "Do you know that he is a white man?"

"I know and I root for him," she said.

I told Thembi that since we were going to watch TV in a house full of South African refugees, all of whom will be rooting for Mayisela, it would be imprudent of her to openly support Volbrecht. I respected her choice but I didn't want her to suffer hostility and suspicion in the house.

She was quiet throughout the fight, which generated a lot of noise among the rest of us. Every blow that Mayisela delivered got us to our feet, and we ululated when we saw an ugly cut on Volbrecht's temple. The ululating and whistling and jumping rose when the referee stopped the fight to save Volbrecht from Mayisela's ferocious charge. Our joy was short-lived. The referee declared the fight a technical draw. He later said the cut on Volbrecht was a result of Mayisela's head butting. None of us had heard of a technical draw before. We damned a white man for yet again inventing a term that would spare him from a sure defeat.

Just as we were fuming and insulting the referee for denying us victory, we heard an agitated knock on the door. Odirile Moalafi had run to tell us that he had just heard that the Boers were going to raid Botswana that night. Within seconds we evacuated the flat. The unwritten rule prohibited anyone from asking another where he or she was going to hide.

Thembi offered to accommodate me overnight. It's one thing to be killed by Boers, but to be shot dead by an angry father or a jealous lover would scandalise my memory; nonetheless, I went with Thembi.

Indeed, she had the whole house to herself. She said her elder sister and her sister's ex-husband, a white man from South Africa, were fighting in the courts over the house. The couple had left the South African town of Vryburg to escape the Immorality Act, which forbade sex across the colour line.

I told her I wouldn't be long with her, because I had just secured a scholarship in Zimbabwe. I left the house on Sunday morning, and returned in the afternoon when we went for a drive. We parked and sat on the big boulders near the Gaborone Showgrounds.

She had her cassette player and a lot of tapes. Her music celebrated love. To this day when it plays, I relive that winter afternoon. She gave me her postal address in South Africa, and asked that we take photos of us together, since we had only a few days before I left Botswana for 'school'. At dusk we drove to Tlokweng, just outside Gaborone, to fetch a camera from her sister's ex-husband.

Thembi entered the house and I remained in the car a short way from the gate. After a while she came back with a middle-aged white man who greeted me in Setswana. After parting from the man, Thembi told me that he was her sister's ex-husband.

I spent another night with Thembi. We woke up early Monday morning and Thembi prepared breakfast with plenty of game meat. We were enjoying the meal and preparing to go to the shop and buy film when we heard violent banging at the steel gate. Thembi dashed out to unlock it.

The white man I had seen the previous evening stormed in with Thembi in tow. He was cursing in Afrikaans. He ordered me to leave and said Thembi was his wife. Thembi threw her slender figure between me and the raging man, shouting: "Jy lieg! Ek is nie jou vrou nie. Jy is Nontutuzelo se man!" – You are lying! I'm not your wife. You are Nontutuzelo's husband!

I remained calm and continued to chew the meat, though it had lost its taste. The man quietened down and said in English: "Please get out of my house."

I stood up and left, pretending I hadn't understood his earlier Afrikaans. When I saw Thembi later that day she apologised, and maintained the man was not her husband. That was the last time I saw her. I did write to her once from Zimbabwe and she replied.

Later, when I returned to Botswana, I rigidly adhered to the underground golden rule of not renewing old contacts if wanted by the police. However, I kept on enquiring about her from my comrades. Years later I learnt that Miss Thembi Niezel was now Mrs Liebenberg, married to the man who once chucked me out of his house.

Such is the life of a fugitive: starved of family warmth and other meaningful relationships. I always had to hide part of me from the person I loved, lest she found out too much and compromised a mission. Analysing every question she asked and watching every step she took. Lying about my profession. Knowing that tomorrow I would wake up in another country with a different name and surname.

— Chapter Fifteen —

IT TOOK ME about a month to travel from Gaborone to Harare, with spells in the cells in Plumtree and Bulawayo. After illegally jumping the border fence into Zimbabwe, I voluntarily surrendered at the police station in Plumtree; but the police suspected me of being a Zimbabwean dissident and locked me up.

The Central Intelligence Organisation (CIO) came frequently to question me. The officers gave me a mountain of paper on which to write my story. What I wrote was mostly fiction. They made me write it many times over and it was a miracle that I didn't contradict myself. I made sure my family background, my standard of education, the first names of my parents and the date of my birth were all factual.

On the evening they locked me up I told them I had left South Africa that very morning and had come through Botswana. I said I'd never been outside South Africa before.

It was winter and it seemed the person who designed the cells hadn't taken the changes in seasons into account. The cells smelled like a polecat's lair. The stench drove me into the courtyard, where I found welcome fresh air but had to suffer the cold. Nights were eternally long.

A week after I was first locked up I was transferred to Bulawayo and told I was detained under the state of emergency regulations. I shared a cell with another detainee.

Here we were saved from the monotonous diet of badly cooked porridge and beans. We were given bread and tea for breakfast, and porridge and offal for lunch and supper. We kept the cell clean and washed our hands before eating.

From Friday night to Monday morning, the story changed as the cell became a pigsty. Over forty prisoners, some bleeding from wounds they had sustained in drunken brawls, packed the cell, shouting, singing, vomiting, pissing on the walls and stripping us of blankets. As state of emergency detainees, we were entitled to more blankets than common-law offenders were, but these drunkards didn't know and didn't care about the regulations.

At meal times, you would have to lick your own hands for dinner if you wasted time washing them. People with blood and dirt crusted on their hands would simply plunge them into the cold porridge, leaving nothing for those who went to wash before eating. Each of us, with our dirty hands, would dig our fingers into the sections of the porridge that had not been touched yet. To our relief, on Mondays the riotous inmates would get bail and leave the two of us behind.

After three weeks, the CIO drove me to Harare. From a distance I saw the city's lights sprinkled beautifully on the belly of the dark night. We were three in the car. The driver, who seemed to be the senior, told me I had been booked into a five-star hotel. I already knew what 'hotel' meant – a police cell.

However, the next day I was handed over to PAC officials. They had learnt only that day that I was alive and in Zimbabwe. Matabeleland then was a field of death, what with the Fifth Brigade trained by the North Koreans killing and maiming 'dissidents'. My comrades thought I had been killed in the crossfire.

"Rraetsho – sir," Dan Mofokeng said excitedly as he gave me a warm bear hug, "we could hardly eat, worrying about you. We thought it was amen with you. I'm so happy to see you in one piece." Dan was using the name Romero.

I was taken to the home of the PAC's chief representative in Zimbabwe, Waters Toboti.

After I'd been in Harare for some months, Toboti spoke to me in a lowered voice: "This is between you and me. I know you – you're not going to tell anybody. You've been appointed PAC chief representative in Uganda. Sabelo will tell you formally before long."

Toboti was happy and he congratulated me. He saw this as a step forward for me, but I viewed it as a step backward: my dreams of going to fight in Azania were shattered. Later I learnt that the Ugandan leader, Yoweri Museveni, had turned down my appointment, saying he'd accept no one but Templeton Ntantala as the organisation's representative in Kampala. He insisted that he wanted somebody who would not only represent the PAC, but who would also help him rebuild Uganda after the ravages of wars stretching from the days of Idi Amin. Museveni had lived for years with Ntantala when they were both exiles in Tanzania. I was relieved, and his decision not to accept me is one I'll always respect Museveni for.

Two months later, Toboti again came to me to say: "This is between you and me – you're now a member of the High Command. Sabelo will soon inform you formally." His eyes darted around to make sure no one was within earshot.

"S'khulu, you know me. I've always had confidence in you. I stood with Mzo to convince the late Pokela that you were the right man to be assistant chief representative in Botswana. Pokela didn't want to hear a thing, but with the help of Mzo I argued till he relented. You've now proved yourself. You must now do better and show the doubting Thomases that you're worthy of the new appointment."

My heart leapt. I enjoyed taking orders and implementing them, and had never dreamt of being in the High Command.

Three days after Toboti had tipped me, Sabelo informed me about my appointment to the High Command. I was placed in the Logistics Department.

I continued to operate in Harare, which soon buzzed with activity in preparation for the ninth summit of the Non-Alignment Movement. The streets were cleaned up and the city's prostitutes were locked up. Even women who were not selling their bodies were arrested if they were found walking in the streets at night. Women protested, but their protests were blown away by the wind as man asserted his domination in the streets. It was the usual story of man denying his sponsorship of prostitution, pretending to be spotless and shifting the blame to woman.

The summit took place at the newly built Sheraton Hotel; over a hundred non-aligned countries were represented. The summit went through the ritual of condemning South Africa's apartheid policies.

I watched the proceedings on television as they were broadcast live. It fascinated me to see the puppets of the Soviet Union and those of the USA assembled under one roof, asserting their imaginary independence and sovereignty and non-alignment. Even Lesotho, South Africa's hostage, was there, riding on the wave of this insanity.

I stayed in Harare for several months before I was sent to Bulawayo, and later crossed into Botswana with a bag full of arms.

We had arms and personnel but we didn't have the right network to infiltrate them into Azania. We had a network of professional people who were not familiar with guerrilla methods and ended up in the hands of the Boers. I discussed this dilemma with the old man Twenty Million.

He was known as Twenty Million because he always invoked the plight of twenty million people in South Africa, even after the population shot past that mark. He was born in 1913 and had left South

Africa in 1957, shortly after the independence of Ghana, in response to Kwame Nkrumah's offer to give military training to Africans who wanted to fight foreign rule on the continent. He travelled as far as Nyasaland (today's Malawi), where he was arrested and deported back to South Africa. He escaped from police custody in Mafikeng and returned to exile, this time to settle in Botswana. He gave up the dream of hitchhiking from South Africa to Ghana.

Twenty Million had been a member of the ANC Youth League. When the ANC and the PAC found him in exile, he decided to join the PAC. I got to know Twenty Million's real name, Jerry Zulu, only when I emerged from underground.

Twenty Million said he had a contact who could help us, named John Moatlhodi. I met John in Maduna's house in White City in Gaborone. He was a stocky man with a boozy face. The ANC and MK (Umkhonto we Sizwe, the ANC's military wing) had turned down his services, alleging that he was a drunkard. His mother was in the ANC in exile. He agreed to help us. After the meeting John asked me to drive with him to his home in Broadhurst as he wanted a word with me. He complained about Twenty Million and Maduna, saying they spoke a lot but never did anything. He said they should have been pensioned off from the revolution.

"Mchana – nephew, I tell you, a revolution is not an old-age home for crocks like Thirty."

"Twenty," I corrected him.

"I don't care whether he is Forty or Fifty Million. All I know is that he must be pensioned off from the struggle."

Mchana, as John was called, said he wasn't impressed by words – he wanted action and nothing less.

The following day Mchana took me to reconnoitre the border. He was fast but careful as he drove on the sandy road to Pitsane Molopo. We chatted as if we had known each other since childhood. He cracked jokes and laughed heartily, and mimicked Idi Amin speaking after the coup in Uganda. Mchana said he was studying at the University of Makerere at the time of the coup.

"Mchana, you were at a university?" I exclaimed in disbelief. "Stop joking." He was wearing a yellow helmet and had a face that had gone through many bottles of liquor. He could easily be mistaken for an illiterate railway worker. His English, however, confirmed his university background.

"You're bloody stupid," he said. "Do you think universities prescribe what their students are to wear after they complete their studies? Dress is an individual's choice, if you didn't know."

In the village of Pitsane Molopo, John drove to an old friend of his, who was extremely happy to see him. Mchana spoke deep Setswana and addressed the old men by their totemic names. He left me in the village and, using his Botswana passport, went to chat up the police and the immigration officials on both sides of the border. He crossed to Makgobistad, the village in the erstwhile Bophuthatswana on the other side of the border.

He came back and told me what he had found out – the lie of the village, the bus services, the places for crossing without having to go through the border post, and the village code of hanging white washing on the line when there was no police patrol and coloured washing to warn of one.

That evening Mchana drove to Johannesburg. The following day I hiked back to Lobatse and then was driven to the border with Zimbabwe.

When I reached Harare and gave my report, Romero was happy. He ordered me to get Rufus Zonyane and Themba Phikwane into Azania. I left for Botswana with the two but Mchana wasn't there. He surfaced after weeks, beaming with smiles.

"Mchana, the mission was successful," he said, puffing at a cigarette. "The route is clear and people are ready to receive the cadres."

Mchana didn't seem to care that there was a state of emergency in South Africa. Zonyane and Themba each stuffed a bag with two Scorpion machine pistols, six fully loaded magazines, two stick grenades, TNT slaps and extra ammunition. I wanted all the arms concealed, but Mchana said each fighter had to have a gun ready for action if the need arose. As we stood by the border fence shortly after nightfall, I gave the final instructions.

"Comrades," I said. "This moment has eluded many cadres. You have to regard yourselves as lucky because you're now about to cross. In that village across the border, you'll find a car with its park lights on. You'll travel to your destination by car. Any questions? If there's none – Izwe lethu, MaAfrika!"

"IAfrika!" the two voices, one baritone and the other tenor, chorused. I watched the two scale the fences and disappear into the dark, into history. With Themba Phikwane in command, within a week the Yugoslav-made Scorpion machine pistols set Alexandra Township ablaze. On December 16, 1986, the Scorpion fatally stung soldiers deployed in the township to enforce the state of emergency.

Themba and Zonyane had separated, with Zonyane moving to the Cape for his operations. Themba teamed up with local operatives.

One of these operatives, Fana Sabela, died during a shootout with the police in Bramley in Johannesburg. Four others eventually left the country for formal training in Apla camps abroad.

In Gaborone I used Maduna's house as one of my hideouts. Maduna and Twenty Million were bosom friends, and their friendship was forged in their shared suspicion of the leadership of the PAC and the ANC. I was told that they once visited the Chinese and Soviet embassies in Gaborone and asked that the two countries terminate support to the two organisations. The support should be resumed, they argued, only after the organisations had told the world what they had done with the money they had received in the past, and witnesses from Azania had been called.

Tata, as Maduna was affectionately called, had been expelled from the ANC for allegedly promoting factionalism and for saying the organisation was dominated by Communists. He and others formed an organisation they called ANC (Nationalists). He loved and admired Chris Hani, MK's Political Commissar, and distrusted ANC president Oliver Tambo. Tata liked saying Tambo was a Marxist atheist when he was in Moscow and a Christian when he was in London.

Tata's neighbours suspected that he was doing something illegal, but they could not put their fingers on it. He in turn suspected them of collaborating with a former lover of his to bewitch him. He consulted sangomas throughout Botswana; every time he heard of one he hadn't seen, he would promptly pay him or her a visit.

One morning a group of his neighbours came to complain about the cars that drove in and out of his yard at night and disturbed their sleep.

"Voetsek – go away, you dogs," Tata responded. "It's none of your business who visits me, or when or how. We are very close to the busiest road in Botswana – have you ever stopped the drivers and complained to them about what they do to your sleep? Voetsek, man. You think I'm not a human being just because I'm a refugee. You call me mtsakwa. That's shit. If you have complaints, go and report to the police. Mtsakwa! Mtsakwa! You Batswana are very rude – call an old man like me mtsakwa?"

He spat in disgust. By that time Tata was speaking to himself: his neighbours fled at the first outburst of his fury. He entered the house and filled and tamped his pipe, gloating after his victory.

"Mtsakwa! You know, Batswana are silly. They call us batsakwa. They are a silly nation, ndiyakuxelela – I tell you." He blew a cloud of smoke that filled his small kitchen and drifted into his even smaller bedroom.

He was still castigating Batswana when Lindela Madondo arrived, bringing the two live chickens I had asked him to buy. Chicken was Tata's favourite meat and he cooked it well. He liked the breast and gave me the drumsticks.

"Most people don't know the best portions of chicken and go for the drumsticks. The best tasting portion is breast." He said this each time we ate chicken.

Lindela laughed as Tata told him of his neighbours' visit.

Lindela was the first to react when the police stopped their car in front of the door. "The police!" he exclaimed, and headed for the door with Tata in tow. He got into his car and drove away, leaving Tata with the security police. I remained in the house and heard every word they said.

The police said they had come to investigate after complaints by Tata's neighbours.

"Who is in the house?" one policeman asked politely.

"No one, I'm just by myself," Tata replied. I looked around the two tiny rooms – there was no place to hide in the event of the police coming in.

"Who's the man who drove away when we arrived? And whose car was that?"

"He's Lindela Madondo and is a student at the Botswana Polytechnic. He is a friend of mine and the car is his."

Tata was cool, completely different from the demon that had just poured obscenities on his neighbours. He said he understood his neighbours' fears of raids by the Boer.

"But they mustn't concoct stories about me," he said.

The police said they understood and would explain to his neighbours. They left.

Bozzo arrived soon afterwards. He had been watching the whole drama from a discreet distance. I took one live chicken, bade Tata good-bye and asked Bozzo to drive me to another hideout in Mogoditsane, just outside Gaborone.

Bozzo was a big man. A former member of the South African Police, he was a citizen of Botswana and had his finger in all manner of illicit deals. He was useful and brave, but charged too much for his services. He once charged me a thousand pulas to transport weapons from Mochudi to Lobatse, a distance of about hundred km.

Bozzo mimicked Twenty Million trying to speak Setswana. "What's wrong with these old men?" he asked. "They've been in Botswana for decades but can't say a sentence in Setswana. Did you hear Tata say mtsakwa? What's that? Why can't he say motswakwa?" Bozzo laughed. (Motswakwa is the disparaging Setswana word for foreigner.)

I continued my work in Gaborone and Harare for a few more weeks into 1987; then it came to a sudden halt.

It all started when I infiltrated two members of our sister revolutionary organisation, Qibla, into Azania. Qibla is a Muslim organisation that worked closely with Apla and is largely based in Cape Town.

A few weeks later, Apla in Harare sent me a message that the two Qibla comrades were ready to receive four cadres who had been waiting to cross into Azania. These four had been with us in Gaborone for a few days.

We didn't know that the Qibla people had been arrested by the South African security police on their return to Azania and turned against Apla. When the four cadres crossed, the enemy was waiting for them.

Lindela Madondo, an Apla cadre who was studying at the Botswana Polytechnic, drove me and the four to Pitsane Molopo at dead of night. Lindela remained in the car while I helped carry weapons to the border.

There was no sign of the car that was to meet the cadres. We decided they should take the smaller guns, the Scorpions, and walk to a bus stop on the other side of the border. They left me with the rifles.

Just before dawn, as I was walking back to Lindela in the car, I heard rifle fire from Makgobistad across the border, rattling with demonic ferocity. I immediately conjured up a picture of my four comrades lying dead, with frozen hands still clutching the zips of the bags as they tried to reach for their Scorpions. The sound of the gunfire suggested that only one side was firing.

I cursed myself for not having called off the mission. It had been drummed into me and I in turn had taught others that if a courier failed to turn up, the entire mission had to be aborted.

The angry guns roused Makgobistad and Pitsane Molopo from their sleep. The sound of the guns settled into a staccato rhythm, and I imagined the gunmen finishing off the wounded.

I wished I could take the place of my comrades – either shot dead or about to be finished off, a just reward for my madness. I remembered Pokela's prophetic words during that marathon meeting years before: that I should not be made a commander.

Lindela had driven off when he first heard the gunfire. I walked to Lobatse, haunted by images of what I imagined had happened in Makgobistad. I had covered a long distance when I decided to hitch a lift. After all, I found no reason to avoid arrest after I had sent my comrades to their deaths.

A car stopped for me, but when we reached Lobatse, the driver drove straight to the police station. Here there was frenetic activity, and overhead an army helicopter droned towards Pitsane Molopo.

I bolted out of the car and unthinkingly tried to run away. The pistol tied to my waist with a rope fell off.

"O tshotse tlhobolo! – he's got a gun," the citizens of Lobatse shouted as they helped the police to apprehend me.

The police searched me and locked me up.

— Chapter Sixteen —

AFTER A SHORT WHILE Clifford Poni and Mpush Makambi were brought into the cell. They were surprised that I had been arrested, and I was pleasantly surprised that they were alive. Mpush was wounded and had a bullet lodged in his heel. He said two comrades had been captured by the enemy.

"Are they alive?" I asked incredulously.

"Yes they are, unless the Boers decided to kill them later. They surrendered when the Boers ordered us to surrender. I ran and jumped the fences on the border. It's a miracle they didn't kill me. They continued shooting at me even after I had reached Botswana soil."

An ambulance picked him up in the village of Pitsane Molopo and took him to the Lobatse Hospital. After he had been treated, the ambulance then drove him to the police station. Mpush was excited and I felt relieved that they had not been killed.

Cliff said when the shooting started he had dashed, jumped over the fence and bolted into the Botswana police station at the border post. The Boers were right behind him. They stormed into the police station and asked the commander if any terrorist had sought refuge there. Cliff was in the corner where the station commander had hidden him. The commander denied that any person had come into the police station. The Boers left.

Villagers found the rifles and ammunition we had abandoned in the bushes, and we were charged with possession of weapons of war.

Sabelo Phama visited us a few days after our arrest. I guess the prison warders told him he could see only one of us. He shook my hand firmly and hugged me. He promised to do everything in his power to get us released, and said there was a strong possibility we were not going to be prosecuted. He said Romero and Barney wished us well, and asked me to convey his regards to Cliff and Mpush. Sabelo's visit buoyed our spirits.

We were transferred to the Gaborone Central Prison, but we continued to appear in Lobatse.

One day out of the blue the prosecutor withdrew all the charges of possession of arms of war. One charge, of possession of an unlicensed firearm, remained against me. We returned to the prison in high spirits. Immigration officials came to the prison to serve deportation orders on Mpush and Cliff; I was already persona non grata in Botswana.

On the charge of carrying an unlicensed firearm, I pleaded guilty and was sentenced to six months imprisonment, suspended for three years.

We informed Phineas, who had replaced Mzo as the PAC's chief representative in Botswana, that the charges against us had been dropped. He told us he would ask headquarters in Dar es Salaam to send us air tickets – and then he stopped visiting us.

We waited in vain for him.

One day the heavily armed police Special Support Group stormed into the prison, handcuffed us, shackled our legs, threw us into a van and drove towards Lobatse. We thought they were going to hand us over to the Boers. They drove us to the magistrate's court, where we were told that the charges that had been dropped were being reinstated.

At the end of the trial, months later, I got five years in jail. Cliff initially got two, but on the automatic review of the case, it was raised to seven years. Mpush was released after I pleaded guilty in exchange for his release. I agreed to the deal because Mpush was ill with severe ulcers.

We returned to Gaborone Central Prison, also known as Maximum. It was built to house criminals in the common sense of the word. Botswana maintained it had no political prisoners, and that no one would desert his country, for whatever reason, to come and claim political status in the country's prisons. So to our captors we were all criminals and were treated as such. PAC, ANC and BCMA cadres in jail were all criminals.

The ANC cadres we found there welcomed us warmly. They had teamed up with other Azanians who were in jail for drug trafficking. Bongo Qina, a stocky, ever-smiling man, immediately nicknamed me Mzalwana – born again Christian – because he thought I looked too innocent to be a guerrilla. He was a member of the ANC and was serving seven years for possessing arms of war. All the Azanians called me Mzalwana.

We also lived with a man who had murdered a six-year-old girl, carried the corpse to the mountain and had sexual intercourse with it daily till it decomposed. Another, named Matopo, had had sex with a horse. A likeable young man, he was a fitness fanatic and ran gracefully around the courtyard to keep in shape. He wasn't offended when other prisoners reminded him of his crime. He flashed his white teeth, and said when he was released he would look for another beautiful horse: "Dipitsi di monate go gaisa batho" – horses are nicer than women.

There was also Mpshe, a Mosarwa from Serowe. I don't remember what crime he had committed, but most Basarwa in Botswana prisons were convicted of stock theft.

When Mpshe's brown prison clothes got thin and discoloured with age, he went to the stores for new ones. The storeman, a warder, refused to give him clothes, arguing that Mpshe's fellow Bushmen were roaming Kgalagadi (the Kalahari Desert) naked and he was lucky to have something on his back.

Mpshe's clothes started to tear apart when he washed them. I was one of those who offered him some clothes, but he refused to take them because he felt he was entitled to new clothes like the rest of us.

One morning he stripped naked and walked about the prison yard in full view of female visitors and warders. When he was asked why he was naked he answered: "Gatwe ke Mosarwa, diaparo di a nthona" – they say I'm a Bushman and clothing doesn't suit me.

On hearing this, the storeman retorted: "If you don't cover your tall and skinny body with your torn clothes, you'll remain naked until your release."

In the afternoon, just before lock-up, the officer in charge ordered the storeman to give Mpshe two sets of new clothing. When triumphant Mpshe came back to the cells, he was dressed in 'springbok' colours, clothing with red stripes across the belly and the back given to 'springboks', prisoners who had escaped and had been recaptured.

We greeted him with congratulatory chants: "Rragwe Dee, rragwe Dee!" (The father of Dee.) Dee was his daughter Dikeledi.

I used to spend days with Mpshe; he spoke longingly of his family and hunting. He was one of seven prisoners I taught how to read, write and count. He in turn tried to teach me his click-laden mother tongue, but I gave up when I realised how difficult it was.

Mpshe lamented that his people were treated as inferior both in prison and outside. He told me of a man who killed a Mosarwa in Serowe. At his trial he got off with a suspended sentence, after telling the court that he was brought up in a society that regarded Basarwa as animals.

Moarabi, a cobbler from Serowe, confirmed this story. Moarabi also didn't hide his belief that Basarwa were not fully-fledged humans. He was serving five years for cruelty to animals, because he had cut off a horse's tail and it had died. In his defence in court, he said the tail was going to be used as a charm by the opposition party to win the general elections.

We killed time playing ludo, table tennis, darts, chess, Scrabble and Monopoly. I was the worst table tennis player. Bongo jokingly called himself Professor Es'kia Mphahlele, and said no one could beat him in the game of English words. He was proud when he played Scrabble against the two British mercenaries locked up in the prison, and hammered them.

News of daring action by both Apla and MK combatants reached us. Our spirits soared when we heard of clashes between Azanian guerrillas and the South African forces. One afternoon Radio Botswana boomed from the giant prison speakers that MK cadres had fought fiercely with the South African forces at a roadblock in Lichtenburg in the Western Transvaal. We shook the hands of ANC comrades and congratulated them. The whole prison buzzed with the news of MK heroism.

The story was the main item in the news bulletins that night and was music to our ears. The next day we were itching to read the details of the battle of Lichtenburg in the newspapers from South Africa. We usually borrowed newspapers from ANC comrades. Bongo lent me his newspaper after reading it. He smiled, patted me on the shoulder and said: "It was Apla that fought the Boers in Lichtenburg. Well done, comrade." The other ANC comrades also congratulated us.

I must have read that story more than twenty times before I returned the newspaper.

That afternoon we listened to Radio Botswana with anticipation, but the newscaster said nothing about Apla. By ignoring the follow-up, the station promoted the lie that Apla was not fighting in Azania. A large section of the South African and international media, together with the South African government and the ANC, promoted this lie.

Every shade of offender, from assassin to askari (a former guerrilla who turned coat and joined the Boers), was imprisoned in Maximum. The most hated prisoner was an askari named M'german. When he was in the ANC, he had served a five-year sentence in the same jail. He was back again, this time for trying to murder his former comrades. He said he had quit the ANC because the organisation was dominated by Xhosas, and Zulus like himself were treated badly.

"M'german, you're talking shit, my brother. If you found the ANC tribalistic, why didn't you join the PAC? Why did you join the ene-my?" asked Mohammed Garamroudi, an Iranian national who was found in possession of PAC arms. He could tolerate anything but be-trayal, and hated M'german more than anyone else.

We were joined in the prison by leaders of the BCMA. They had been arrested after their military wing, the Azanian National Libera-tion Army, stepped up the infiltration of its cadres into Azania through Botswana. The BCMA leaders who joined us were Mpotseng Kgokong, Nkuts'oeu Motsau, Strike Thokoane and Vuyisile Qunta.

One morning the warders ordered us to strip naked, stretch our legs and stoop. They examined our anuses, searching for concealed dagga.

I felt sorry for the BCMA leaders who were humiliated along with us. They were not ordinary cadres like us and deserved better treat-ment. No dagga was found because some warders had tipped the cul-prits off.

After breakfast, I met Kgokong at the dispensary and told him I was sorry about what had happened to him and his colleagues. He said it was nothing compared to what he had suffered at the hands of the South African authorities when Jimmy Kruger was Minister of Police.

He then switched to the question millions of Azanians had been asking: "Why don't we BC and PAC unite?" He said the PAC leader-ship was making a serious mistake by treating his organisation as ju-nior partners in the revolution.

"Comrade, as general secretary of BCMA, I've written many letters to PAC headquarters in Dar es Salaam, suggesting that we meet and work out a strategy to liberate our country as a united force. Guess what? My comrades in Dar don't even acknowledge receipt of my let-ters. When I meet some of them in the streets of Gaborone, Harare or London, they bluntly say, 'You must dissolve your organisation and join the PAC as individuals'."

He and his colleagues did not stay long in the prison, but were de-clared prohibited immigrants and deported to Zimbabwe. His ques-tion rang in my mind long after they had left.

We PAC members rarely got visits and supplies from outside. We sponged off ANC cadres, who shared everything with us, including their s'mokolo – foodstuffs, especially meat, smuggled from the kit-chen for the prison currency of cigarettes. I hated it that we had be-come parasites, but I rationalised it by telling myself that everything the ANC possessed was raised on behalf of the victims of apartheid, including us.

One day Vulindlela Majija of the ANC called me aside and spoke in a subdued voice: "My colleagues have sent me to you. They complain we are many and the bread is no longer enough for all of us. They are asking if you can't pretend to have a stomach ailment to get the doctor to prescribe bread and milk for you."

I pitied Vulindlela. He didn't relish his mission, but had been forced to come and talk to me by ANC people who resented our sharing their supplies.

"You see, Mzalwana, some comrades simply don't understand we're one family in spite of our political differences. They are small-minded. These are the same people who boast of over ten years in exile. I wonder what they've been learning in all these years. At home we co-operated with PAC people when the need arose."

I said I'd have to discuss the matter with my comrades, Cliff and Thembinkosi Siyone. Thembinkosi had been arrested some time after us. We decided against faking illness because of pressure from the ANC. We could survive on our own. I told Vulindlela about our decision, and we stopped eating their bread and sharing their toiletries.

Other prisoners, particularly Jonathan Basil, Moarabi and George Arbie, gave us toiletries and s'mokolo.

Bread was at the centre of our discontent. We asked for the criteria used to give bread and milk to one prisoner and not to another. The locals said this diet seemed to be the prerogative of foreigners. All Indian and European prisoners got bread, because the prison authorities believed they were not used to the normal prison diet of porridge and samp. Indigenous Africans from countries such as Ghana and Nigeria, who were seeing samp for the first time in their lives, were forced to eat it like the rest of us. Sadly, this discrimination was enshrined in Prison Act of nineteen what-what, which the officer in charge once read to us when we really got angry.

We had hoped to further our studies in prison. We asked our chief representative in Botswana, Phineas, to facilitate registration and sponsorships, but all in vain. His successor, Xola Mketi, alias Raymond Mvelase, was also of no help. We appealed to the PAC's army commissariat, but all we got were promises and promises and nothing more. We asked for newspapers, but the supply was irregular at best.

One day Ray visited us. He was drunk and carrying a bundle of newspapers. We thanked him profusely. Since publications first had to be checked by the censor before we got them, we left the pile at the reception. When a warder eventually brought them to us, there was a scramble, as everyone wanted to lay his hand on his favourite newspaper. Alas, it turned out some of them were up to three years old – I had read them long before I was arrested. We were deflated.

And the struggle continued.

I joined Vulindlela's accountancy classes. The subject was fascinating and the teacher superb. Mohammed taught us chemistry and physics and Benjamin Lecheko taught us biology.

Siyolo Jafta, from Qumbu in the Transkei, came to teach us English poetry. He loved poetry and infected everyone. He recited Percy Shelley's 'The Skylark' from the first verse to the last from memory, moving his body gracefully to emphasise the beauty and magic of the poem. Religiously, he would then move on to John Keats's 'Ode on a Grecian Urn'. At the end of the two poems, he would be drenched in sweat. He would tell us about his deceased uncle, a teacher who had worshipped poetry. Jafta also wrote poetry, which was moving. His sonnets, however, were too difficult for me to grasp.

We drew books from the mobile Botswana National Library Services.

One day the PAC members met under the chairmanship of Cliff to discuss prison conditions. (We used to rotate the chairmanship among us every three months.) Thembi and I were sick and our requests to see a private doctor had been turned down. Thembi had sores all over his body. My heart was beating furiously and I couldn't sleep. My feet were so wobbly I felt like a drunk about to drop down.

We resolved that immediate release was the only remedy for the prison conditions. We decided to go on a hunger strike till we died or were released. We also refused prison medical treatment. Cliff went to present a letter, addressed to the Minister of Presidential Affairs, to the prison authorities demanding our release. The ANC comrades pledged their moral support, as did Mohammed and Jafta.

On the first day of the hunger strike the warders separated us. Cliff was taken into death row, where they kept prisoners awaiting execution; I was taken to another section of the prison; and Thembi was kept in the main section.

On the fourth day I felt no hunger at all, only the wild beating of the heart and shaky legs. A doctor, a Ghanaian, came to see me. He pleaded with me to rethink my decision as my condition was worsening. I refused and he left.

On the sixth day we reviewed the hunger strike through smuggled notes, and decided to intensify it by abstaining from water too.

A prisoner arrested for drug dealing, Desai, beckoned me to his corner and whispered: "Listen, Stone," – the English translation of

Letlapa – "you're sick and you can't sustain this hunger strike. I'll stand at the door and you get in the toilet and eat. It will be a secret between you and me. Here's bread and milk and a few chunks of meat." He dug his hands into his many cardboard boxes.

"Look, Stone, you won't be the first to do this. Banda – another prisoner – sustained a hunger strike for three months because he ate secretly. If you don't feel like eating now in daylight, I can arrange for a night meal when everybody is asleep. I'll leave food in the toilet and come to alert you. You must eat, Stone. Never allow these bastards to destroy you."

Desai was deeply sympathetic and persuasive. His sparkling eyes darted around the cell as he talked in conspiratorial tones. I flatly rejected his proposal. Nothing would torment me as much as the memory of such weakness: immediate gratification at the expense of well understood principles.

Desai's face fell in disappointment.

The next day the acting commissioner of prisons, Lenong, came to persuade us to eat. On this day the prison swarmed with warders of all ranks. Lenong promised that our diet would be vastly improved if we terminated the hunger strike. He said on that day, the seventh and severest, we could order any food and drinks we wished to have. He was calm and didn't show the anxiety his colleagues had displayed. Lenong was huge and didn't look like a cross-country marathoner, but he had just won a major Botswana race.

We told him we would not compromise on our demands.

On the eighth day I was grabbed from my bed and carried shoulder-high to the sick-bay, where I found Cliff and Thembi. I was forced down onto the hospital bed, handcuffed and chained. The toughest warders forced sorghum porridge into my mouth. Their nails tore at my cheeks and lips as they forced my mouth open. Cliff also bore ugly scratches on his cheeks.

We vowed we wouldn't eat voluntarily.

Once a day they would force the porridge and water into us. One day after such a meal, the officer in charge accused me of being irresponsible. He said Cliff and Thembi were younger than I was, but they had come to their senses ahead of me. He said they had written him a note suspending the hunger strike.

I told him we had democratically decided to go on the hunger strike, and if my comrades were to suspend the strike, they would consult with me rather than write to him.

He fished out a creased paper from his pocket and claimed Cliff had written it. I wasn't sure of Cliff's handwriting but I concluded that this wasn't his.

I told the officer that I would carry on with the strike till we collectively agreed to end or suspend it. I returned his scrap of paper and inwardly vowed never to fall into the traps of mischievous warders.

That afternoon I got a smuggled note from Cliff, apologising for himself and for Thembi for deciding to suspend the hunger strike without me, and communicating their decision to the authorities first. He said they were still committed to the strike, and had not started eating yet. I was digesting Cliff's note when I received one from Thembi, also apologising.

I was touched by the openness of my comrades. In the depth of my being, I knew I owed them an apology for my intransigence and inflexibility.

I accepted their apologies and we asked the authorities to allow us to meet and review the strike. They happily granted us permission. We decided to abandon the farce of being fed by force. We had aimed for a hunger strike, but if the authorities deprived us of that right enshrined in the Tokyo Convention, there was nothing we could do. We agreed to stop the strike, but to save face we claimed we were suspending it. Cliff communicated the decision to the officer in charge and the strike was over.

Cliff and Thembi were re-united, but I was placed in a different section of the prison. On weekends the warders on duty allowed me to visit my comrades in the main section; only one, a warder called Alosious Sesikwe, always refused.

It was again Sesikwe who once turned away books from our visitors, arguing that criminals were not allowed to read books. I cried when he did that.

I remained in this section for more than a year, until the prison authorities tightened security and moved all convicts into the main section.

We learnt that Zephania Mothopeng, the PAC president, would be visiting Botswana. But when Ray told us Mothopeng would be visiting us in prison, we thought that was one of those exhibitionist statements PAC leaders were notorious for. The same things that had stopped other leaders from visiting us would also stop Uncle Zeph, the Lion of Azania.

We accepted that the top leaders of liberation movements wouldn't visit their imprisoned cadres for diplomatic reasons. Johnson Mlambo and Gora Ibrahim of the PAC and Oliver Tambo and Thabo Mbeki of the ANC were often in Botswana, but never visited their soldiers in prison. We had resigned ourselves to this and appreciated messages of support and well wishes from them.

Even though we didn't expect the Lion to come to us, we prepared for a visit just in case. We rehearsed songs and poems and spiced them with revolutionary slogans. His visit was postponed a few times, but we continued rehearsing until the morning the warder shouted for the PAC group.

Was the Lion here? Who else could it be? We asked the warder who our visitor was.

"The old man who was in the Sunday newspapers," he replied tentatively. Mohammed jumped up and danced indlamu. King Shaka must have turned in his grave at this distortion of the warriors' dance.

Led by Thembi, we filed into the visitors' room. The prison grounds were swarming with prison warders, as they had done in the days of the hunger strike. This time there were also plain-clothes security police clutching walkie-talkies. Thembi started singing 'Give A Thought To Africa'. We lifted our open palms in the PAC salute and sang. The air was electric. The cooks deserted their pots and positioned themselves where they could peek; the warders were amazed.

Uncle Zeph was with other PAC leaders from Azania and Botswana. He leaned on his walking stick, got up after a struggle and joined in the singing. The warder sitting in the room didn't know whether to stop us or not. Hesitantly he rose, stopped halfway, half-raised his half-opened palm and moved his lips to a song he didn't know. I restrained the laughter welling inside me.

The song is long and we were in no hurry to shorten it. Instead we prolonged it by punctuating it with humming and the recitation of poems. Mohammed was first with his poem. I still remember a few verses, recited in his emphatic Arabic accent:

De Klerk!
Where is my cock?
You tell me you didn't steal it
But I see its tail protruding from your jacket
De Klerk!
Must I believe what you say?
Or what I see with my own eyes?
De Klerk!
Where is our land Azania?
Bring it now
Or we'll take it by force!

Uncle Zeph seemed entranced. The song rose to a crescendo; then we switched to another song to back Thembi's indlamu.

Only after this dramatic prelude did we exchange greetings. Ray made the introductions and then the Lion roared: a hoarse, prolonged "Izwe lethu!"

He said he had come to tell us our sacrifices were not in vain, and also to ask the Botswana authorities to release us so that we could rejoin the fighting masses in the trenches. He blamed his deteriorating state of health on the "Dutch boys" who tortured him with the hope of breaking his spirit. He said recent research had revealed that the PAC was the only political organisation in South Africa that was growing.

We ended up singing five songs, although we had only planned to sing three.

Then we shook hands once more, and Mothopeng and his entourage left. We were joyous and overflowing with admiration.

"Stone!" Abe Sishuba, an ANC cadre, called me. "Bamba nas-'isandla – let me shake your hand. You have a real leader. I respect that old man."

The unprecedented visit, the ceremony and the electricity in the prison air touched Sishuba deeply. PAC and ANC soldiers understood the language of war and Uncle Zeph was with us in the trenches.

Steve Burnett, a British mercenary who had been arrested for attempting to kill an ANC activist, was writing a book. We were on good terms and he often asked for my views. He told me that he had been warned by the ANC cadres in the prison to avoid PAC members – that we were violently anti-white and that he would not be safe from us even in prison.

Initially he kept a discreet distance from us and we felt no obligation to befriend him. However the narrow confines of prison locked us in conversation. He disagreed with us on some issues but said he admired our consistency and strength of character. He was not the first to pay us this tribute: other prisoners and the warders alike kept saying we were different, even after bruising battles with them.

We established that ANC cadres warned the whites who entered the prison against PAC racism. And most of them, who did not stay as long as Steve, left with hostile attitudes towards us.

Truth is that white people are allowed into the PAC. There is no clause in the organisation's constitution that excludes them from membership. In recent years Dr Costa Gazi, for example, left the ANC to join the PAC. Even after Pedro, a white man and an Apla operative, visited us in prison before we were convicted, the ANC cadres continued to spread the lie that we excluded whites from our ranks. Pedro was sent by Apla High Command in Harare to look at the prison security, with a view to mounting a rescue operation. The plan was later called off.

However, the PAC hasn't done enough to recruit white members.

Our repeated challenges to the ANC to have joint political discussions were ignored. Somehow we rubbed shoulders, two political organisations living cheek by jowl and talking about everything except politics. The irony was that we found it easier to exchange ideas with a mercenary from abroad, who had come to our shores on a mission to destroy our cause.

Ray visited us one Monday morning. He had a huge smile as he announced: "MaAfrika, you've been released. Yesterday President Masire signed a release order for all freedom fighters."

We were overjoyed, but quickly sobered up and reduced our expectations. Hadn't S'fiso and Themba completed their sentences five months back? They had then been declared prohibited immigrants and were still with us in jail, because the PAC didn't have money to buy them air tickets out of Botswana.

We were happy but we left room for disappointment. We even resigned ourselves to the possibility of serving our full jail terms.

We shared the news with our ANC comrades and they were jubilant. Later that day an ANC representative came to inform them about the release order and confirm our story.

Ray had promised to fly us out of Botswana before the weekend, but we had our doubts. To our surprise, he kept his promise. On the Thursday we flew out of Botswana, bound for Harare in Zimbabwe.

— Chapter Seventeen —

WHEN WE ARRIVED in Harare, the immigration officers wouldn't allow us into Zimbabwe because we didn't have visas. They also held back the plane, saying it had to take us back to Gaborone.

The stern officials meant business – why else would they have delayed the plane's departure? The PAC officials who had come to meet us just couldn't move them.

The Air Botswana airliner finally took to the sky, leaving us behind. The battle was half won. However, the Zimbabweans insisted they were not going to let us out of the airport: we had to fly out of their country.

We were satisfied just to see the sun rising in the horizon free of any walls and bars – magic I had last witnessed more than three years before.

We stayed at the airport for about a week, and were released after negotiations between the PAC and the Zimbabwean government.

I stayed with Romero and other cadres in a house in Strathaven, a suburb in Harare. Romero was the army's political commissar and I was his deputy, having been appointed to that position while I was in prison. I asked Romero why they had appointed me as his deputy at a time when I couldn't perform my duties: much as I felt honoured, I didn't feel indispensable in the organisation.

"Rraetsho – sir," Romero said in his cool, unruffled voice, "it wasn't because you're indispensable – you know that in the PAC nobody is indispensable. We in the military commission looked around. Fihla was qualified, but he had just been appointed to the High Command and wasn't well versed in the dynamics of the body. That's why we appointed you."

Harare was dull, with very little military action. I thus left for Bulawayo, where I stayed for a short while before crossing back into Botswana.

The Botswana front was manned by Boyboy Mbethe, alias Ntsiki, Castro Phillips and Andile Ntabeni, alias Junior. Ntsiki and Junior worked with demonic zeal, infiltrating an unprecedented number of people and weapons. They were highly resourceful and had established a wide range of contacts inside Azania.

The technique of infiltrating people had changed. Instead of infiltrating a unit comprising a commander, a political commissar and a person responsible for logistics, each department deployed its own personnel and weapons. Operations, the Political Commissariat and Logistics operated almost independently of one another. As a result, three distinct armies were taking shape within the small Apla army.

The first thing I did when I reached Gaborone was to hand over to Logistics the weapons that we had stashed away before my arrest.

I then watched in disgust as the three departments gnawed away at each other. The people who were splitting Apla apart said the practice ensured secrecy and security. I continually reported my disquiet to the military commission, but it was a while before Apla was restructured.

One day at sunset I left my hideout, a two-roomed house in Mogoditsane, about five km from Gaborone. I hadn't eaten all day and strange thoughts buzzed in my heavy head. It was chilly and I kept my hands in the jacket pockets. An army jeep whizzed by, missing me by centimetres. I was jolted from my reverie and swiftly moved away from the road. The jeep stopped and the soldiers swore at me. When I went to them and apologised, they were surprised to see I was sober.

"Be careful next time or we'll run you over." Accusing fingers wagged at me and they drove off.

I walked to Gaborone, to Ray's flat, where I was sure there'd be something to eat and provisions for the following day. The flat was lit and that was a promise of food. I heard excited voices inside: the group seemed to be playing Scrabble. There were women in the group. I knocked and the voices fell silent. I knocked again and heard soft footfalls approaching the door. The lights went out. I knocked harder and identified myself. There were giggles inside the flat, and that infuriated me.

"Ray! Ray! Vula – open, man. Open!"

The giggles grew louder and ended in mocking laughter. I hit the door with my palms and shouted. The evil laughter stopped abruptly, but the door remained locked. I kicked the door and threw my weight against it. It didn't budge. I got tired and left with tears welling in my eyes.

I thought of Joe Mkhwanazi, who was in Botswana at the time and had a safe house near mine in Mogoditsane. He would be my salvation.

He was home.

"Comrade Khwani, I must apologise for waking you up . . ."

"No, no, no, my friend," he cut in with his gravelly voice, "don't you know that the revolution is executed at night? Revolutionaries are witches. They work at night. In fact, I would have fought you if you had come here in daylight."

I felt immensely relieved. "Comrade Khwani, I used to ask you for money for our work. Now I must ask you for something else – food. I'm hungry."

Khwani foraged in his cupboards and brought out a half loaf of white bread and an orange. He offered me coffee. Since I don't drink coffee or tea, I took only the bread and orange, thanked him and left.

I then walked to Jabulani Tshabalala's house in Phiring in Gaborone. The last time I had been there Jabu's wife, Nthabiseng, had served my favourite meal of porridge and meat. The couple had also offered me a room, but I'd decided against staying there because the house was frequented by Azanian exiles.

On this night I could either remain underground and starve, or expose myself and eat. I chose food.

Jabu – also known as Maria after the Kaiser Chiefs player Maria-

Maria Lamola – and Nthabiseng were happy to see me. They were happier when I asked them if I could stay for an indefinite period. Nthabiseng served us a memorable breakfast, and I ate heartily.

Afterwards I sent for Ray. I was angry: "Why didn't you open for me last night? I knocked till my knuckles bled." He said he didn't open "for security reasons". He said he also thought I was Ntsiki and he wanted to teach him a lesson.

"If I had a gun I would have opened the door with it and your security argument would be valid," I said, and meant it. I demanded duplicate keys to the flat.

Ray was a charming man, who bore no grudges. His battles were fought and settled on the same day. He had a sharp sense of humour that helped resolve the quarrel in Jabu's house.

A few weeks later I was on my way to Zimbabwe. It was in the early hours and Ntsiki was driving. After filling up with petrol in Francistown, we cruised towards the Zimbabwean border.

"Tell me, S'khulu, what's your position on 'repossession' in Botswana?" Ntsiki asked.

"You know the High Command doesn't approve of armed robberies in countries that are hosting us, like Botswana."

"Mfondini – man, are you the High Command? I'm asking you as S'khulu. Tell me *your* opinion on the matter," he chuckled.

"Kwedini – boy, my position is clear: I'm opposed to our forces carrying out armed robberies in friendly territories like Botswana. Amen," I said emphatically.

"Oh, are Batswana your friends? Was it your friends who sentenced you to five years in prison? My friend, you've got funny friends. Tell your friends they'll never take me alive if they find me with guns. Even their army will never come near me. I'll sweep them." Ntsiki was agitated, like a bull goring an anthill before a fight.

"Tell me, S'khulu," he continued, "as a member of the High Command, what do you discuss in your meetings? I'd like to know. In fact, every cadre is eager to know."

"In the last HC meeting we discussed the size of your head. It's too big and needs to be chopped to size."

He laughed, rocking his big head – a loaf of bread, we'd call it back home in Manaleng.

"Do you know what I'm laughing at?" he asked when the laughter subsided. "A person who doesn't know our High Command would think you're joking, when in fact you're telling the truth. Instead of discussing strategy and analysing the enemy, you discuss the size of people's heads. We still have a long way to go. The HC member I respected was the late Madoda Myoli. He treated the revolution as roughly as it should be treated. He wasn't like you and the High Command, a bunch of Christians."

"Perhaps you want to say he treated the revolution like a Christian. Personally I don't equate Christianity with peace and harmony. Christians have executed the worst and most savage violence. The only two nuclear triggers ever pulled were pulled by Christian fingers. And it was a Christian Pope who decreed that Africans be uprooted from their land and taken across the Atlantic Ocean to serve as slaves," I said, as our conversation took a new turn, less heated and confrontational.

Ntsiki dropped me just before the border. I crossed on foot and walked to Plumtree. When I arrived in Bulawayo, I learnt the Botswana police had arrested our cadres in Mogoditsane.

Modiegi Mohapi later told me in detail how the unit had been arrested. It was after sunset when three cadres went to a shop for cigarettes. They deviated into the Blue Note disco. In the crowd, one strayed from the others. Not finding his friends back at the base, he took a Scorpion sub-machine gun and returned to the disco. He still couldn't find them, so he went back to the hideout and exchanged an AK47 assault rifle for the Scorpion, and returned to the disco.

When I heard this, I burst out: "The damned fool could as well have taken a tank if we had one, and gone to look for his friends at the disco!"

"Or a Mirage fighter plane, if he had his way," Modiegi quipped.

The rifle is big: it protruded clumsily from his clothes and a suspicious person alerted the soldiers. They beat him thoroughly, suspecting he was an askari looking for Azanian freedom fighters. The man could have led them to the PAC chief representative's house and claimed his credentials there. No, he led them to the base, where they arrested his two comrades. A day later the arms were dug up in the yard and the cadres got five years' imprisonment each.

After inspecting the haul, a sympathetic Botswana soldier is said to have commented: "Guys, with this quantity of ammunition, a platoon of guerrillas could have operated effectively for four months without asking for fresh supplies."

In my operations I continued to shuttle between Bulawayo and Gaborone.

On one occasion, I went to visit Maduna, who I hadn't seen since my arrest by the Botswana police in 1987. Tata chuckled: "Now you're a prison graduate, my boy. You'll appreciate the importance of time."

It was 1990 and exciting things were happening on the home front. De Klerk had lifted the ban on the PAC and other liberation movements. He was talking about negotiations with the ANC and the PAC.

Tata spoke excitedly about changes in South Africa, and was looking forward to returning home after thirty years in exile. His friend Twenty Million didn't share the excitement.

For Tata, the return of all exiles was "a golden opportunity for the masses to put Oliver Tambo and his corrupt colleagues on trial". Tata was preparing himself to give "damning evidence that would shock Nelson Mandela and his co-accused in the Rivonia Trial". He had prepared "evidence" to present to Winnie Mandela, who was due to visit Botswana for consultations with the refugee community.

"What do you think you'll benefit out of going home to the same oppressive system?" Twenty asked Tata with a frown.

"What do you think we benefit from rotting here," Tata asked, "being called batsakwa by disrespectful Batswana? We must go home and warn the masses about people like Tambo and Mlambo. Otherwise they'll overtake us and by the time we get there, they'll have swung the masses in their favour. Mandela and Mothopeng need to be informed about these crooks." He lit his pipe triumphantly.

It was during those heady days that Romero instructed me to stop everything I was doing and get to Harare as soon as practicable. I had phoned him as usual from my hideout in Mochudi.

Junior drove me; we played reggae all the way from Gaborone to the border.

When I arrived in Bulawayo I learnt that Willie 'Siyaya' Nkonyeni, deputy chief of operations, and Sello 'Mjomba' Kungoane, deputy chief of logistics, had received the same urgent call from Sabelo.

"Sabs says he wants me in Harare but he knows I haven't got a cent," Mjomba said. "He says I must borrow money. I've got so many debts I can't walk freely around Bulawayo. Just last week I was served with a summons to appear in court for unpaid debts. If Sabs wants me in Harare he must first send money."

I proceeded to Harare by train. I converted the pulas I brought from Botswana into Zimbabwean dollars on the black market, and they doubled. The money was enough to take the three of us to Harare, but I didn't even broach the subject with the others. Theirs was much more than just a quibble over fare to Harare.

"Siyaya and Mjomba are defying us," Barney said when I arrived in Harare. "Look, S'khulu is here all the way from Botswana. Those two are defiantly stuck in Bulawayo." Barney went on to read a catalogue of sins the two had committed, as voluminous as the ones Siyaya and Mjomba had compiled against him and the military commission. I listened and kept quiet, as I had when my colleagues in Bulawayo had attacked the top military leadership.

No one among us was a saint.

Meanwhile, Sabelo mounted pressure to get Siyaya and Mjomba to Harare. He said the High Command wouldn't meet without the two.

They finally arrived and the High Command met. As usual, speakers moaned about the lack of resources, particularly money, and the military commission was accused of not knowing its tasks.

Fihla said his visit to West Germany had been fruitful, as some support groups had donated sophisticated intelligence equipment and were willing to give more support.

The meeting ended with Sabelo Phama announcing a new structure for the High Command: the Secretary of Defence became the Army Commander; the Logistics Department was phased out and became a directorate under the Chief of Staff; and the Political Commissariat was sub-divided into a number of directorates.

Sabelo, the Secretary of Defence, became the Army Commander. Barney became the Chief of Staff and Romero, the Chief Political Commissar. My heart raced when it was announced that I was to be the Director of Operations. I had made the Political Commissariat my home and thought Ops were the territory of others.

Sabelo's final words were a call for more HC members to go into Azania and direct the armed struggle there.

Shortly after the meeting I consulted with Barney and Siyaya about our strength inside Azania and about how the country was zoned. There were areas without any PAC structures and others with large concentrations of cadres. As Chief of Staff, Barney would still have a hand in operations. Siyaya, on the other hand, was moving out of Operations but pledged his co-operation for a smooth transfer of functions.

Barney gave me five thousand rand and I returned to Botswana. On my way I stopped in Bulawayo, called a meeting and informed the comrades there about the decisions of the HC meeting. The meeting was a mere formality, since the comrades already knew everything about the meeting – some even congratulated me on my appointment when they came to fetch me from the railway station. As I enumerated the directorates and their heads, the cadres I was supposed to be briefing constantly corrected me. They laughed at me and said I needed to be briefed by them.

In a few days I was in Botswana. I asked Modiegi to arrange for my entry into Azania as soon as possible.

"Do you mean even now, if our contact is ready?" Modiegi asked and looked at me mischievously.

"Yes, I'm ready." I meant it.

I told my girlfriend Mosalagae in Lobatse about my imminent journey across the border and what that entailed. She wept profusely.

"You mean we'll never see each other again?" she asked.

"If that is what the revolution prescribes, yes," I said, and comforted her. We parted and I haven't seen her since.

Modiegi accompanied me as I drove to the border. I instructed him to tell no one about my departure until I sanctioned it. As we neared the border, I told him I admired his efficiency and that of our other operatives based in Botswana, and the way they worked with contacts in Azania. In the past it took one month to get a person from home to come and fetch literature or weapons. This time it took Modiegi less than a week to alert his internal contact to fetch me from the border.

We arrived at the pre-arranged spot and the engine stalled. I tried to restart it but failed. Our contact Thabo responded to Modiegi's whistle and emerged from the bush to join us. The two pushed the car as I tried to jump-start it. In Harare comrades had tried to teach me how to jump-start a car; I grasped the theory but couldn't do in a practice. All I needed was a bit of adrenaline to jump-start me. To our joy the engine growled to life.

We said goodbye to Modiegi and he drove back. I had been teaching him to drive, and now wondered if he would reach Lobatse. But as I saw the red tail-lights receding, I knew that he would make it. I had advised him to stay overnight in Lobatse and get the car fixed the following morning before proceeding to Gaborone.

It was January 1991 when I jumped the fences near the Ramatlabama Border Post, the same place where I had crossed into exile on a train twelve years before. We crossed several fences, erected to keep freedom fighters out of our land.

"This is the last fence," Thabo said, and leapt over. I handed him my bag and followed. Joy, fear and hope electrified my whole being. I unzipped the bag and took out the Scorpion machine pistol.

"You look nervous," Thabo said. "Is this your first time in the country since you left?"

"No, this is not my first time," I lied to cover my nervousness.

He didn't pursue this further. "Okay, you remain here. I'll be back with the transport."

He disappeared into the dark night. I leaned against a tree trunk with the gun in my hand. Distrust is an essential part of vigilance. A long time passed and Thabo hadn't come back. I then noticed I had no watch: it must have slipped from my wrist while I was crossing the hurdles of the border. Truth is that it was probably only half an hour before Thabo came back. He was with a man and a woman who gave me the PAC salute of "Izwe lethu!"

We drove to Mmabatho in Mafikeng.

A fortnight in the township was too much for me. I was indoors most of the time, avoiding exposure to the askaris who frequented it in search of people like me.

I asked Thabo to take me to the countryside where I could have more freedom. I went with him to PAC members in Mmabatho, asking them if they had a place for one person in a rural area. Thabo always introduced me as a relative of his. I was struck by one common feature among PAC members, who were just a handful – they lived in big houses. Their plump children, judging from their mannerisms, no doubt had joined the stampede to 'multiracial schools', where the African child's mind is disfigured and distorted to hold everything that is white as right and the symbol of might.

We finally found a place, not from among the PAC members but from one of Thabo's non-PAC friends. There were four of us in the car as we drove to my new hideout in Madibogo: myself, Thabo and his two contacts. The one drove like a lunatic, slacking only at points where he knew police liked mounting roadblocks. We drove over a snake and he stopped and declared confidently: "This is a good omen: there is no roadblock ahead."

He tossed the dead snake into the boot. His friend protested bitterly, saying the snake was a harbinger of trouble. The driver didn't give him a chance – he started the car and sped off. The argument between the two raged on.

When Thabo, who was seated in front, was asked for his opinion, he said he didn't know.

"Of course, Thabo is a township boy who knows nothing about snakes," the driver commented, and asked what I thought. It was now my turn to break the deadlock. Although I've outgrown all superstitions, I felt this wasn't the time to contradict the beliefs of my helpers.

"Good luck awaits us," I said, to the driver's delight. Reluctantly his friend conceded defeat and promised to check with the old men when he visited his home village.

I stayed with old man Plaatjie in the village. We had sold him the story that I had run away from Johannesburg because of the fratricide that was sweeping the city. We said I had been harassed by the police. He in turn told his friends and neighbours that I was his nephew. When the friends came visiting, they were interested in life in Johannesburg.

"Dipola'no – the killings, the senseless violence, brother against brother . . ." I would start. They would end up expressing deep hope that the release of Nelson Mandela and the unbanning of the ANC would bring peace and liberation. No one in the village, not even my host Plaatjie, seemed to have ever heard of an animal called PAC.

"We don't know what the old man holds for us – Buthelezi and Mangope are disappointing," Plaatjie commented after the evening news that we normally listened to on his portable radio.

"Which old man is that?" I asked, though I knew he was referring to Mandela. He and FW de Klerk had dominated the entire bulletin.

"I mean Mandela. What's your opinion of him?"

"Politics is a tricky game," I said. "Just yesterday de Klerk and his Boer brothers were telling us Mandela was a terrorist who had to be kept away from us. Mandela and his ANC on the other side were telling us that de Klerk was a snake that had to be destroyed. Honestly, I'm as confused as you are now that the two men are singing each other's praises."

"Let's hope and pray Mandela will free us. He's God's gift to us," Plaatjie said and stood up.

"Let's hope so," I said as the old man disappeared into his outhouse.

Both in the news and in the village, the PAC was conspicuous by its absence. I wondered what had happened to this "fastest growing organisation in the country". I consoled myself by believing that the polls didn't say the fastest growing organisation in the countryside. That night I slept with a sore heart.

Plaatjie and the other villagers knew me as Thabo. During the day I helped Plaatjie glaze windows in the village crèche, where I met two of the teachers.

"Abuti – brother Thabo, did you know that my colleague is married?" one asked me one day. She must have sensed I found it difficult to choose between them.

"I didn't know. What about you?"

"Oh, me? Marriage can wait. I'm still too young to think about it."

"But you look the same age as your colleague."

"Yes, which means she was young when she married," she said.

The direction of our conversation was crystal clear. She spoke of a music festival and asked me to take her to it to break the monotony of village life. I agreed, but hoped that by the time the festival happened, I would be out of the village.

That evening she came to the Plaatjies' house for a casual chat and left after a short while. As she exited through the front door, I slipped out the back one and we met outside and walked towards her home.

"I live with my uncle and my younger sister," she told me. "Next week he'll be away for a few days and my sister is no problem."

We held hands as we walked under the cover of the night. We stopped occasionally and kissed and exchanged promises. I ran back to the house hoping nobody had noticed my absence.

I was late. Plaatjie's wife had already dispatched children to look for me around the neighbourhood.

"Thabo, where have you been?" she asked agitatedly.

"I'd just gone out to get fresh air," I said, and wondered why such a short absence should have unsettled her. It was so short I could well have said I had gone out to pass water.

"You know, Thabo my son, here in the villages a person can lure you out of the house with muti, and kill you to make medicine for wealth with your body parts. It would bring us a bad name if our visitor disappeared. We'd be the first suspects. So take care, my son." She went out to call back the search party.

The next day Thabo came to see me.

"I'm going back with you," I said as I packed my luggage. I thanked Plaatjie and his wife profusely and promised to come and see them one day. That promise is still hanging.

As for my girlfriend, I kept her address for some time and then tore it up with other addresses of contacts. I hope she too tore up my fictitious name and address.

— Chapter Eighteen —

A FEW DAYS LATER Thabo and I boarded a taxi to Mabopane, a township just outside Pretoria. PAC member Isaac Lekubu and his sister Gloria welcomed me. Gloria had just had a baby boy, Tiro, named after Azanian hero Onkgopotse Abram Tiro who was killed by a parcel bomb in exile in Gaborone.

Mabopane became my base as I visited Apla underground units in the Pretoria, Witwatersrand and Vaal areas. Modiegi co-ordinated my movements from Gaborone, and I spoke to him every day using code. He told me he had succeeded in deceiving Apla members, including the High Command, that I was still in Botswana, but had retreated to a remote area.

On the political plane, the PAC had finally settled on supporting negotiations with the Boers, with the aim of pushing for a one-person-one-vote election of a constituent assembly to write a new constitution for our country. A faction opposed to talks and the constituent assembly, calling itself the Watchdogs of the Revolution, emerged. It was strong in the PWV (Pretoria-Witwatersrand-Vereeniging) area.

Apla cadres found themselves caught between the two warring factions. A rumour spread in Watchdogs circles that somebody had been despatched from Harare to eliminate their key leaders. The rumour coincided with my arrival in Azania.

"Comrade, I suggest you meet the Watchdogs and allay their fears," a unit commander, Thapelo Maseko, said when I visited his unit in Soweto. He added that his unit depended entirely on the Watchdogs for survival. They even paid the rent for the backroom he shared with me, from which I'd peep out and see a police uniform flapping on the washing line. Under our bed there would be AK47 rifles and plenty of ammunition. Nothing could have been better than that – being housed by a member of the police force, who didn't know what we were doing.

I agreed to see the Watchdogs. Later, Thapelo brought one of their leaders to meet me. S'thembele Khala, who had served ten years on Robben Island, was driving a car and was well dressed. After the introductions we went straight to the matter: I told him I hadn't come into Azania to eliminate PAC members. I also told him that as far as I knew, the High Command, of which I was a member, would never send an assassin to kill PAC members.

S'thembele criticised the PAC's decision on the constituent assembly, saying it was inconsistent with the organisation's struggle for the land. He said the organisation's second congress, where Clarence Makwetu was elected president, had been a farce; that Gora Ibrahim was the circus master, and that delegates had applauded deliriously without critical analysis. He planned to remain with the original Sobukwe-Mothopeng PAC. I reminded him that Mothopeng had called for the establishment of a constituent assembly.

From this meeting, I got to know some Watchdogs like Themba Hlatshwayo and Vincent Mama, who was to drive me as and when I needed help.

Mama was also then organiser of the Media Workers Association of South Africa (Mwasa). The two of us went to Mmabatho, and with the help of Thabo we loaded arms at the Bophuthatswana government offices where Thabo was employed. We hid them in the body of the car.

It was drizzling and the night was solid dark as Mama and I drove to Soweto to deliver the weapons. Vincent couldn't see beyond fifteen metres, and the car was crawling slowly. He suspected its lights were faulty. After a while the lights brightened again, and it was only then that we realised we'd been driving through thick fog. Vincent was a fast and exceptionally careful driver. He picked up speed and cut through the sheet of drizzle.

As we passed the small town of Ventersdorp, Vincent said he hoped it would also be raining in Soweto when we arrived. He was worried about Operation Thunderbolt mounted by the police and the army, searching homes and vehicles in the PWV area. I drew courage from the fact that the weapons were concealed.

"Malume – uncle," he called me by my newly acquired name, "the police are thorough. They use a long iron bar to detect weapons in cars. If there are weapons, a red light goes on and there's a bleep. Concealed or not, the weapons can be detected."

I feigned fright.

We arrived safely at our destination in Pimville, parked the car in the yard and began the arduous work of retrieving the weapons from the secret compartments. We had offloaded them and were busy putting the car panels back when a police van came crawling around the corner.

"Police!" Vincent and I exclaimed together.

The van passed by at a snail's pace before disappearing around the corner.

"They nearly caught us," Vincent said, and we continued with the work. The two policemen in the van must have had their doubts about us, because just as we thought the van had disappeared, it came back in reverse. This time it was moving fast.

"There they are again," Vincent announced unnecessarily. He deftly removed hand grenades from the back seat and pushed them under our car.

"Shoot! Shoot them," I whispered to him. Then police van was behind me and I didn't want to alarm the police by turning abruptly. He was on the other side of the car, facing the van. Besides, my right hand was shaking and too cold to operate the trigger.

"No, Malume, that would alert them. Bring the gun here: I'll hide it under the car." He stretched out his arm to receive it.

"I'll give you the gun only if you're going to shoot."

The van stopped a few metres from us. I held my breath waiting for their doors to open, when I would be forced to shoot them. Inexplicably, the van slowly pulled away.

"I respect your judgement," I said as I shook Vincent's hand. "Thank you."

He laughed and replied: "No, Malume, it's I who should praise you. Other cadres would have shot at the police or run. You at least have time to debate with us civilians."

I continued my visits to various units.

"Oh, Saddam Hussein – you're our Saddam Hussein," one commander commented at the end of my visit to his unit. This was at the height of the US-UN-Iraqi war. The Iraqi leader had captured the imagination of the world's poor by visiting the battlefield, chatting with his forces and dishing out food. Whether that was an authentic gesture or public relations for television cameras, it earned Saddam the admiration of many around the world. The unit commander's words humbled me.

But unlike Hussein, there was no food for me to dish out. Cadres were literally starving. They complained that most PAC members were not taking care of them – a fact I was later to establish myself. Members urged the cadres to commit robberies to survive. When they refused to do that, they were called cowards who were beaten by mere criminals who had not been given military training abroad.

It's a sad record that during the nineties Apla suffered more casualties on 'repossession missions' than on combat with the enemy.

My argument was, and still is, that it's better to turn criminals into revolutionaries, than to turn the revolution into crime. If every Apla cadre had used his or her gun and skills to rob banks and shops, the results would have been an army of criminals.

If some cadres infiltrated the world of criminals, educating and sensitising them to the needs of the revolution, teaching them not to 'repossess' from the dispossessed African communities but from the affluent oppressors, we would have achieved the goal of turning criminals to work for the revolution.

Revolutionaries should strive to lead a life free of crime. If a revolutionary steals or buys stolen property, he opens himself to unnecessary arrest. Usually the State plays down the crime, and bargains with him to spy on his comrades in exchange for the dropping of charges or acquittal. A person who is wont to commit crime is dangerous to the revolution. It is silly for a revolutionary to ignore the rules of the road or to board a train without a valid ticket, for example. A serious revolutionary should know that one needs to obey most of the rules of a state one wants to overthrow, in the same way that a chess master will sacrifice pawns to get to the opponent's king. More so, a revolutionary should be the embodiment of healthy social behaviour that anticipates life after the triumph of the revolution.

A disturbing phenomenon I discovered was that our cadres were concentrated in urban centres and went into rural areas only when they were hunted by the police. We were not stretching the enemy across the country as we should have been. Some cadres stayed with PAC members, and the majority built shacks in the mushrooming shantytowns.

I visited a cadre in his shack in Pretoria. He sat in the car with me, and introduced himself as Selby.

"I'm S'khulu," I said and firmly shook his trembling and sweaty hand. "You might have heard about me outside."

He looked nervous.

"MoAfrika, I want to see inside your mokhukhu," I said, and headed towards the cluster of shacks.

"No, comrade, not today. I haven't swept."

He also whispered something to Isaac, who had driven me to the place. I stopped and waited for him. Reluctantly he caught up with me and led me into his home.

"By the way, comrade, what did you say your name was?" Selby asked, and looked into my eyes.

"S'khulu."

"S'khulu? Is that your real name?"

"It depends on what you mean by real name. To me a name is just a label, especially in our case. If I'm in a group of people and you call out 'S'khulu!' I'll respond. Really. That way S'khulu is my real name."

He nodded but obviously had doubts about what I said.

A paraffin stove stood in the middle of the shack, and a clumsily made bed that sagged in the middle hugged the corrugated iron wall. The smell of dagga hung thickly in the air. I picked up the stove and shook it. There was no paraffin in it.

"How do you cook, comrade?" I asked, with the stove still in my hand.

"There's no food to cook," Selby said, lifting a cardboard box and turning it upside down to demonstrate that his pantry was empty.

"How do you survive without food?" I asked as I put down the stove.

"Bakhona abafowethu – my brothers are there. Like the one who stays next door. He works and he and others share their food with me."

I dilated my nose and sucked in the air. "You share everything, eh? Including dagga?" I asked after breathing out heavily.

"No, comrade," he said looking down.

"Oh, you don't share it with them. You simply smoke alone?"

"No, I don't smoke dagga, comrade."

"If you don't smoke it, it certainly smokes you. Very soon it will finish you off. And you'll be an unlamented martyr to dagga." I spoke at length about the evils of smoking dagga.

Revolutionaries are builders of communities and nations, and must neither take nor traffic in drugs. Some people in the liberation movement used to argue that they could traffic in drugs in order to inebriate the enemy forces and render them ineffective. They forgot that drugs are like landmines – once laid, they mutilate both foe and friend. Once drugs hit the streets, you can't control them; they turn around to haunt the society long after the warring parties have agreed to lay down arms. Moreover, how can we liberate people when we turn them into violent beasts and unthinking zombies? Revolution is sacrosanct and should be executed by sober men and women.

I gave Selby thirty rand from the hundred rand that remained in my fast-drying coffers.

"Izwe lethu!" he said in appreciation, and we parted.

Three days later I was at Isaac's place when he burst into the room: "Selby is here to see you. Should I let him in?"

Before I could answer, Selby appeared. After greeting me, he said he wanted to see me outside. It was already dark.

"Comrade, forgive me – what's your name?" he asked when we were out of earshot.

"Go and ask your unit commander what my name is," I said and went back inside. I told Isaac to drive him back to his shack, and to tell him never to come to the house again.

Isaac got into the car and motioned Selby to get in. Selby dragged his feet, but he got into the car and they drove off.

When Isaac returned, I asked him to drive me to Selby's unit commander. The commander was back after having been away for a few weeks. He laughed when I told him Selby's story.

"Selby is right to suspect you, comrade," he explained. "We had a cadre called S'khulu who turned coat and became an askari after the Boers had arrested him. That S'khulu is short, but Selby doesn't know both of you. That's why he was suspicious and nervous."

The commander said he would talk to Selby the next morning.

Only a few of the cadres were well-off – those who had been embraced by generous members of the PAC who were outside Apla. Some of these dressed well and called their suits 'city camouflage'.

Starvation drove numerous cadres to their old family homes, where they were warmly welcomed and well looked after. Some of these continued to operate from their homes, while others simply disengaged and applied for indemnity.

I guess it was a combination of homesickness, poverty and the lack of direction in the PAC that drove them home. This led to tension and suspicion in the units. I was warned by some cadres to avoid others. As a result, I sometimes met only two members of a unit of seven and avoided those who were not trusted.

Because of operating in an environment of suspicion, I made a serious error: I sent a number of cadres back to exile to be interrogated by our military intelligence. A few of them had to be flown right up to Tanzania. They were all cleared after that costly exercise and had to be brought back into Azania.

I continued my visits and inspection of the units. At one time I had to visit cadres in the Transkei; S'thembele and Vincent got me a forged South African passport in which my name was Zweledinga Ngombane.

I arrived in Umtata by taxi on a misty Monday morning. The trip from Johannesburg had taken us well over twelve hours, because we had two punctures and no spare wheel. Another taxi that wasn't full came by, and passengers who had to be at work the following day were transferred to the second vehicle. I said I was rushing to work in Umtata even though I had never set foot in the town.

I phoned Vuma Ntikinca from the Umtata Hotel and he came to fetch me. We drove to Ikhwezi location, where he stayed with Nomvakaliso, an amiable woman with a long history of helping Apla cadres. The two opened their arms and hearts to me.

Vuma was operating openly, and in media interviews was introduced as an Apla field commissar, a title he probably gave himself. He had good relations with members of the Transkei Military Council, including its head Bantu Holomisa.

The meeting with the Umtata unit took place at night in Vuma's house. I expected a handful of cadres, but an early trickle into the sitting room swelled into a flood. I was overawed. As the numbers rose, Vuma asked me to go into another room. Later he fetched me and led me back into the sitting room.

"Up!" he shouted and the mass of humanity rose to attention.

I sat down, and then Vuma instructed the crowd to sit. Many remained standing since there was no place on the floor. Vuma introduced me in glowing terms, which heightened my nervousness. When I spoke, my voice was shaky, as it usually is when the audience is large and expectant. I grappled with Xhosa and English to find suitable words to express my feelings.

I thanked them and their commanders, particularly Vuma and Bulelani Polite Xuma, for their work in both the PAC and Apla. The numbers present that night showed how much work they had put in. I went on to point out that the Transkei honeymoon would soon come to an end, and we had to plan for that day. It was a brief talk, and I gave the cadres a chance to ask questions.

One cadre asked if Apla would continue the armed struggle if the PAC lost in the elections for a constituent assembly.

"The victory or defeat of the PAC, or of any liberation movement for that matter, will be measured by whether land is returned to the Africans or not, and not by the ballot box. We are in the armed struggle because European aggressors stole our land. Sekhukhune, Moshoeshoe, Makana and Dingane did not mobilise their glorious armies and fight for the right to vote. They fought for their land. We their descendants are fighting for our land and the right of self-determination.

"The sacrifices of generations of Azanians will have borne fruits the day every square centimetre of the land is taken back from the alien conquerors, not the day the PAC flag is hoisted on the Union Buildings in Pretoria."

Another cadre asked if the PAC was a socialist party.

"The PAC is neither a party nor socialist," I answered. "The PAC is a movement embracing all social classes. The colonised African people, irrespective of their class origins, rally around the movement's call for the liberation of our country from settler colonial domination. We should be aware that the PAC has great potential to become a bourgeois party. Liberation movements across Africa are known for their vociferous socialist rhetoric before they occupy seats in parliament, and in some countries the rhetoric continues into parliament."

Vuma differed with me; he said the PAC was a socialist party, and cited the Moshi Conference in Tanzania where the organisation adopted Marxist-Leninist-Mao Tse-tung thought as the organisation's guiding ideology.

I maintained that the PAC was not a socialist party.

Asked whether Apla should attack the Transkei security forces, I said that would run counter to the PAC policy that bars our army from engaging Bantustan – including Transkei, Ciskei, Bophuthatswana and Venda – forces unless it was in self-defence.

"But these are puppets of the Pretoria regime," a cadre I later got to know as Thembelani 'Mshishi' Xundu protested.

"Let's destroy Pretoria and the puppets will fall on their own," I said, and also pointed out that the Transkei was unique in that it recognised the liberation movements and their respective armies.

The meeting ended with a song and the comrades dispersed.

While in the Transkei, I also visited Cala, Cuwa (Butterworth) and Centane (Kentani). When I went back to Umtata, the PAC leaders organised a barbecue for me in the house of Gilbert 'Jojo' Sineke, a top Transkeian civil servant, in the suburb of Norwood in Umtata.

Men in dark suits, some driven by chauffeurs, arrived in flashy cars. These were businessmen like Mavume, who owned a construction company, 'Fidel Castro' Komsana, the ombudsman of the Transkei, Ndoni, a lawyer, and other professionals. Majama, a slightly built man dressed in flowing West African robes, was in charge of the team that roasted the meat. Never before had I seen men eat meat with such passion. "Ndili Mpondo mna – I'm a Pondo, and we Pondos are famous for eating meat," Sineke said between mouthfuls. It was meat all the way – no porridge or anything else to accompany it down the throat.

When I left Umtata, Vuma got me a forged Transkeian passport and I assumed the name of Thabo Lethola. I took a taxi from Umtata to Sterkspruit near Herschel. Herschel was Transkeian territory, but there was a stretch of about 200 km of South African land between it and the rest of the Transkei. Several Apla cadres had been arrested by South African police on this stretch.

The taxi got a puncture as it snaked along the treacherous road leading to Satansnek, but otherwise the journey was uneventful. Vuma had told me to contact Swartbooi, the manager of the only bank in Sterkspruit.

The bank was closed when I hesitantly knocked on the glass door. My heart warmed when I heard footsteps rising in volume as they approached the door. Then a man spinning keys on his forefinger appeared. He opened the door and waved me in, saying: "I'm Swartbooi."

"I'm Happy," I said.

He locked the door and led me into his inner office. "Izwe lethu," he saluted and hugged me. He was expecting me, and had asked his staff to leave him behind because he had a lot of work to do. He took me to his house, a short way from the bank, and introduced me to his relatives.

Swartbooi said his wife was a nurse in his hometown of Queenstown, and that he would phone her to come over on the weekend. He begged me not to leave before I saw her. He told me he had been in and out of prison, including Robben Island.

"I hosted Enoch Zulu in this very house, and that is why Matanzima's police arrested me. Only death can stop me from working for the liberation of Africa," Swartbooi said – prophetically, as he was gunned down with an AK47 early in 1995, in the same house that used to be an Apla base. To this day, no one has been prosecuted for his death.

The PAC in Herschel was fairly strong, boasting former Robben Islanders and others.

"Right away," Buyafuthi Tsembeyi, a former mayor of Sterkspruit, said after meeting me. "Kuzasetshenzwa, tata – we shall work, man. We have guns but the boys don't want to fight. I'm happy you're here to tell them to fight."

Buyafuthi, also known as Jomo because of his undying love for Orlando Pirates Football Club, was right. Our cadres in Herschel were drowning in social pleasures and must have thought they were on holiday. I learnt that one cadre had emptied a rifle magazine in a tavern, shooting into the air to scare away members of a rival gang. He belonged to the Spartans. Solly, another cadre, did not turn up for an appointment with me, for no reason. As punishment I made him run 30 km in the rain.

I soon dismantled the unit and asked Vuma and Polite to send other cadres to Sterkspruit. The new unit, under Vusi Dolo, did well. Vusi was later arrested by the Boers in Barkley East and sentenced to fourteen years for terrorism for the attack on the Lady Grey police station.

From Sterkspruit I went to Maseru for a meeting with Thapelo Maseko. He was nursing wounds he had sustained during a shootout with police in Johannesburg. His family were originally from Lesotho and had a house in Butha-Buthe, north of Maseru; but most of them lived in Bekkersdal near Johannesburg.

He took me to Moipone Mpondwana's house in the Maseru suburb of Lower Thamae. During our stay in Lesotho, Moipone helped Thapelo and me acquire Lesotho passports. In mine I was Sello Happy Mabitle from Mokhotlong in the Lesotho highlands.

Months later, Thapelo told me how his Lesotho passport had saved his life. He had gone back to Azania to visit some of the cadres under his command. He went to a shack used by his comrades in Diepkloof.

It was locked, and the cobwebs around the door told him it had long been abandoned. As he left the shack, he saw men armed with spears, sticks, knobkieries and firearms approaching him. He looked around and realised that he was encircled.

Thapelo said he dashed into another shack, where he found a huge man slicing and munching cold meat. He asked the man to defend him from the Inkatha army. The man laughed mirthlessly: "Welcome to an Inkatha home. I'm the leader of Inkatha in this area. Who are you?"

"I'm Mopenyakatse Nkhabu. I am from Lesotho."

"Any troublemaker can claim to be a foreigner when he's in trouble. What proof have you got?"

Thapelo said he fished the Lesotho passport from his pocket. At that moment the armed men were all around him, their eyes already burning him to death. They were just waiting for the order to charge. After examining the passport, the leader nodded. "Oyisilwane esimsulwa lo – this is just an innocent animal."

The giant returned Thapelo's passport and invited him to share the meat with him. Thapelo said the meat tasted like rubber – his taste buds had shrivelled in those short minutes. The leader then ordered his impi to escort Thapelo out of the shantytown. As they walked along, he realised he would not have escaped if he had tried to run. Armed men had swiftly mobilised against a lone intruder in their political dominion and were at every street corner.

This encounter happened at the height of the violence sponsored by the white minority government, the so-called 'black-on-black' violence. Instead of turning their guns on members of Inkatha, the Apla cadres followed long-standing PAC orders, which were to promote peace among the African people and wage war against the white minority state. They chose to ship out their guns and leave the area instead of spilling the blood of fellow Africans. If a war had to be waged in the residential areas, it should not be in the African shantytowns or in our dry and dusty villages. Whether we loved or hated it, Inkatha was a predominantly African organisation, and a military attack on Inkatha would be an attack on the African masses. It would not further the objectives of the revolution.

From Lesotho I went back to Johannesburg. However, I travelled to Lesotho frequently, because I wanted many immigration stamps in my Transkeian passport to make it appear authentic. But I was careful not to enter at South African-controlled border posts.

I reported and sent any requests I had to chief of staff Barney

Hlatshwayo through couriers. Eventually the two of us agreed to meet in Manzini in Swaziland. Buyafuthi gave me the airfare and Tikiso, the chief of Thabalesoba, drove me from Sterkspruit to Maseru, where I boarded a plane to Swaziland.

Ambrose Simelane fetched me from Matsapa International Airport. Barney had already arrived and was staying at a hotel. I stayed with the Simelane family in Fairview.

Our meeting took place in town, at the beauty saloon run by Simelane's wife.

I briefed Barney about the political and military situation in Azania. I also asked him to send more cadres and weapons into Azania as quickly as possible. He told me lack of funds had halted the movement of cadres from the rear to the front. He also said that most African states, including our main backers, Tanzania and Zimbabwe, were irritated by PAC's continuation of the armed struggle. They had reduced their support.

At the time the Apla camps were overflowing with militant youth, and this had resulted in starvation and disease. Barney said several cadres had recently died of malaria and that HIV-Aids had begun to take its toll in the camps.

"So, comrade, do your best in Azania and don't expect much from outside," he said bleakly.

"We have known this from the day this organisation first came into existence," I said. "We knew that the revolution wouldn't survive on handouts from foreigners. We are now reaping the harvest of dependence. Self-reliance is the cornerstone, the very foundation of the revolution."

"You're preaching to the converted, comrade. In the PAC we have great ideas. The problem is, we don't practise what we preach."

When we parted, Barney gave me one thousand five hundred US dollars. Simelane then took me to a village on the outskirts of Manzini, where I stayed in a room for two days before I flew out of Swaziland.

— Chapter Nineteen —

THE TINY Lesotho Airways plane shook violently above the mountains. At last it landed, luckily, at the Moshoeshoe I International Airport. About a dozen of us disembarked. It was mid-winter.

After the immigration formalities, I headed for the exit. A man came running after me. "Tshwarelo, Ntate – excuse me, sir – you're wanted upstairs," he said and took my bag. I followed him.

Unspoken questions assailed me: what law, besides using a forged passport, could I have broken? The man in plain clothes, who was no doubt a security policeman, ushered me into an office, where a woman in her late forties or early fifties waited.

"Where are you from?" she asked, her voice vibrating with authority.

"I'm from Swaziland," I said.

She demanded to see my passport, and passed it over to the man to photocopy. She wanted to know why I'd been to Swaziland.

I told her I was a social worker and I had gone to Swaziland to organise scholarships for needy children. The man returned with so many copies of my passport photo that I wondered how many departments would be supplied with them.

"Please spare me a few of the photos for my album?" I said to relieve the tension in the room, but my captors were devoid of humour. Copies of the photos were used extensively in the South African press when the police announced they were looking for me.

The woman ordered the man to search my bag thoroughly. I was relaxed because there was nothing incriminating in my luggage. He ran his hands over my body and again found nothing.

After extensive questioning – about my address in Maseru and how long would I be in Lesotho, among other things – I was released. The bus was still waiting – apparently for me, because it pulled off as soon as I boarded. I knew the woman had placed a tail behind me but I wanted to confirm it. When the bus stopped at the traffic light I grabbed my bag and made for the door. A man followed me. I stopped and sat near the driver. The tail hesitated and then returned to the back seat.

When the lights flashed amber at the next robots, the driver stopped the bus. As soon as they turned green, I bolted out and mingled with the scores of people coming in and out of the Pitso Grounds. My tail was left confused in the bus.

The following week I converted some dollars and got about two thousand eight hundred rands. After changing the money I started my journey back to Azania. I reached Tele Bridge border post at dusk. The immigration officials were packing their books and preparing to leave because of the biting cold. They let me through without even looking at my passport.

I walked towards Sterkspruit. There was no car in either direction. I went into a shop by the roadside and bought half a loaf of bread, tinned beef and a can of cold drink.

As I was starting to eat, a drunken man staggered towards me from the direction of Sterkspruit. After greeting me, he asked for some of my food. We shared it. He advised me not to try hitchhiking to Sterkspruit at that time of night, and said I should rather go with him.

We walked towards the river Tele, where he led me into a ramshackle shanty crowded with men. He half asked and half instructed them to accommodate me for the night. They murmured disapprovingly, but agreed on condition that I did not share their blankets. I squeezed myself between two of them. My drunken friend staggered out into the darkness, mumbling to himself till the night swallowed the sound of his voice.

It was cruelly cold, the cold piercing through the gaping holes between the roof and the walls. I wore every piece of clothing in my bag. One man gave me a threadbare blanket that he had been using as a pillow. I thanked him, and held the blanket tightly around my shivering body and was comforted. Another man gave me a blanket, and so did a third. Though my body was shivering, my heart was warmed by the generosity of these men.

I slept fitfully that long night.

In the morning I realised the men were brick-makers, and the shanty was in a brickyard. They were the casualties of widespread retrenchments, especially in the mining industry. I gained the impression they were all from Lesotho, from where the people of Herschel recruited the cheapest labour imaginable.

I thanked them and gave them ten rand to buy meat. They were grateful and invited me to come back anytime I had a problem with accommodation.

In Sterkspruit I arranged transport to get to Johannesburg:

"MoAfrika, did I hear you properly the other day, saying you're ready to execute any PAC mission?" I asked Cetshwayo Mbelebele, a tough man whose age was hard to estimate because of his agility. He was old enough to have been at the founding of the PAC in 1959.

"Yes. I will leave my wife and answer the call," he said. "I belong to the old and hardened PAC, where we translated the slogan 'serve, suffer and sacrifice' into action. I'm not one of the present crop of slogan shouters."

"Okay, let's prove that. Organise a car – you and I are going to Jo'burg. Bring your driver's licence."

We took a taxi from Sterkspruit to Thabalesoba, where Mbelebele had been promised a car by Tikiso. A taxi owner, Tikiso was expecting one of his cars to come back.

The sun set and rose as we waited in Tikiso's house, and still there was no car.

"MaAfrika, the car hasn't come," Tikiso said. "What do we do now?"

Mbelebele looked at me enquiringly.

"We are going to Jo'burg," I said. "We are already 15 km into our journey and we won't take a single step backwards. All our moves must be towards our destination."

Tikiso grasped my meaning and organised a car to drive us to Rouxville. Arriving in the small town, we headed to the shop of Mangesi in the township of Rweleleathunya. Mangesi was a PAC member.

The shop was partly burnt and sparsely stocked. ANC supporters were boycotting the shop after having torched it. 'Comrades', thugs battling for control of the dispossessed African communities, constantly threatened to kill Mangesi. He and his family were harassed and ostracised by the equally intimidated Rouxville community.

Mangesi was accused of being a police informer, but the root cause of his misfortune was his association with the PAC. He was a victim of the 'One township – one organisation' slogan. In areas like Rouxville, the ANC was implementing it with demonic resolve. The 'comrades' had soiled and debased the fond connotations that the word carried for its Greek inventors.

Nonetheless, Mangesi's relationship with the police disturbed me. As he led us from one section of the shop to another, he told us that it would have been completely gutted had it not been for the quick response of the police. He said he was grateful for the regular patrols of the police around the homes of PAC members like him, and that he had friends among the police.

Mangesi knew me quite well. In one of my previous encounters with him, I had asked him to monitor the movements and strength of the police and the army in and around the town. He didn't refuse to do this but slipped out of it, arguing that his first priority was to hit his enemies in the township hard.

In turn I argued that the thugs who burnt his shop and intimidated other residents were as oppressed and dispossessed as he was. I said when slaves fight among themselves, they sink deeper into their slavery and make liberation that much more remote. He didn't like my argument.

I still felt uneasy as he drove us to Botshabelo, about 50 km east of Bloemfontein. If it were true that he was an informer, I would be a sitting duck for the security police. As Mangesi drove over tar and gravel roads, taking the short cut from Rouxville to Botshabelo, he talked about nothing else but ANC intimidation.

We arrived in Botshabelo at noon.

After telling Likotsi about us, Mangesi returned to Rouxville. Likotsi said he would take us to the nearby location of Thaba Nchu, to Molefi Litheko, an attorney and PAC chairman in the then Orange Free State. Likotsi thought Litheko would help us.

As Likotsi got ready to drive us to Thaba Nchu, Mbelebele looked at me and grinned: "We're a football, being passed from one player to another."

"I don't care how many players kick us, so long as we're being kicked towards the goal mouth," I said and Mbelebele laughed.

Litheko couldn't help us: his credit card had reached its limit, and he could thus not get us a hired car. We had to turn to public transport – the dreaded taxis. We boarded one from Botshabelo to Bloemfontein, where we could connect with one to Johannesburg.

It was early afternoon when we arrived at the taxi rank in Bloemfontein. There were only two passengers in the waiting taxi, and we increased the number to four. By eight o'clock in the evening we still hadn't filled the taxi. Some of the passengers abandoned their journeys because they didn't want to arrive late in Johannesburg and fall prey to thugs, who now wore the cloaks of political activists.

A few paces from us, the taxi drivers debated their next step. Some said the taxi had to leave with the passengers already in it, and others said the passengers should be told to go home and come back the next day. The measured low voices of the drivers became loud and angry. The debate was finally settled when we were told to get out of the taxi and board another. The second driver joined us and in no time we pulled off.

"I haven't slept for two nights," he said, addressing no one in particular. He fumbled in his pockets and fished out a folded paper. He unwrapped it, took out a tablet and chewed it – I suspected he was drugging himself against sleep.

I loathe taxis because they are always involved in horrific accidents, and because of the fratricide among the operators. Most taxi drivers don't respect their passengers and don't care for other motorists sharing the road. The taxi industry is the only business where businessmen harass and sometimes kill their customers to promote their 'product'. Unfortunately, it remains the major mode of transport for the wretched of the earth.

Somehow we arrived in Johannesburg safely.

I gave the bulk of the money to the units operating in the PWV area, leaving some for Mbelebele's trip back to Sterkspruit and my trip to Umtata.

In Umtata I asked Vuma to take me to Enoch Zulu's home village in Cofimvaba.

"I must see comrade Zulu," I said.

Vuma told me the village could not be reached by small cars like his.

"Never mind, I'll go by public transport," I said.

However, Vuma wouldn't allow this. Using the same small car, we reached Hoita, Zulu's village.

Scores of people were gathered at a homestead in the village. We asked somebody to find Zulu and tell him we had come to see him. He walked out of the multitudes with his confident, stately strides. We shook hands, reunited after many years.

Vuma left for Umtata, and I was to stay overnight. After introducing me to his relatives, Zulu excused himself and went into a hut to join other family elders in some ritual there.

The family had slaughtered a beast and brewed beer for the ancestors. Men cut pieces of the roasted meat, and I regretted that I had put off buying a knife. Each time I went into a shop with the intention of buying one, I saw other items that I needed more urgently. Zulu's friends, however, were generous with their knives and the meat. And the roasted meat was just the first course: it was followed by cooked meat at noon.

Men with blankets wrapped around their waists emerged from the hut, singing and shuffling their feet gracefully. Zulu was among them. His fleshy, dark-skinned body contrasted with the other, light-complexioned bodies. Three decades of exile and imprisonment had not cut him from his roots, his belief in his ancestors.

As I watched the poetry unfolding in the drought-ravaged village of Hoita, the cynical atheist in me questioned the validity of African rituals in this age. Yet another part of me affirmed them. As long as we worship the god of our conquerors, so long will the contradictions between them and us be blurred.

The debate inside me raged as the song and dance filled the afternoon.

After the ceremony, Zulu called me. He was back in Western dress, and was as I had known him for over a decade. The only difference was that he wasn't smoking his pipe: he said he had given up smoking on Robben Island. As for liquor, he said he'd stopped drinking long before he was arrested. As a guerrilla, he didn't want to be caught drunk by the enemy.

I stayed in Hoita for three days. I could have stayed longer but Zulu was leaving for Johannesburg. When we parted in the town of Cofimvaba, he gave me a full chicken and home-baked bread.

"These peasants don't know that food and drinks are served in the plane," he chuckled.

I thanked him for the food, and recalled the day he had shared his porridge and meat with me when I went to join the PAC in Botswana.

My nomadic life continued.

I was in Lesotho when I heard of the coup in the Transkei and the flight of the homeland's military leader, Bantubonke Holomisa. The news shocked me, and the following day I rushed to Herschel, worried about the effects of the coup on Apla cadres. I found Holomisa had not been overthrown. The media had exaggerated a minor mutiny. I went back to Lesotho, from where I rang Umtata to find out how the instability in the Transkeian army had affected our cadres. Vuma said Apla had teamed up with the officers who were fighting the mutiny, and that they were mounting an operation to recapture the Ncise Military Base.

"Don't worry, son," Vuma reassured me. "Sabs knows about this operation. Fihla (the head of the Apla Military Intelligence) knows too. So do Romero, Mlambo, Zulu and Makwetu. I should have informed you, but you know how you sometimes disappear from everybody. I can assure you the preparations are advanced. Zero hour will be anytime from now. That's why I advised Makwetu and Mlambo to leave the Transkei."

Makwetu's home was in the Transkei, while Mlambo had been visiting in the homeland.

"You say Sabs knows about the operation?" I asked.

"Yes, he knows and actually gave his blessings to it," Vuma said. He went on to elaborate on how the operation would elevate Apla above the status that MK enjoyed among the homeland's officials.

"What is MK's stance on this?" I asked.

"You know MK – they are dilly-dallying as usual."

"What about Holomisa?"

"He's undecided. It's known that the man is a coward."

"I see. Where will Apla get the arms to fight the mutineers?"

"We'll have to bring all the available weapons to Umtata. I've already started the process. You'll have to send us all the weapons you have that side – and the personnel."

"You'll have to come and fetch them," I said emphatically.

Just before he replaced the receiver, I heard a voice asking to speak to me. It was Thapelo Maseko, a regional commander. He asked me if it was true that I'd given an order to recapture Ncise from the mutineers.

"I've only now heard about the operation. I couldn't have issued the order."

"You'd better come down here," he said. "We shall send a car to fetch you. Otherwise things will get bad."

"Okay, I'm ready. Send the car. Tomorrow I'll be in Sterkspruit and whoever you send will find me there."

Before Thapelo dropped the phone, another regional commander asked to talk to me. I ended up speaking to several of them and they all had one appeal, that I come to Umtata. Then I phoned Sabelo Phama in Harare. He said he knew about the operation in the Transkei, and had approved it because Vuma had told him that I knew about it.

I was furious. "Comrade Sabs, I must be frank with you. I'm angry with you. I can excuse Vuma but not you. Do you think an operation of this magnitude could be planned over the phone?"

"No, ngwaneso – my brother," Sabelo said sagely. "Cool down. That's exactly what surprised me. Vuma was phoning us every hour, and I concluded he was just exaggerating. I didn't think he was serious when he said they were going to recapture the camp. That's why I gave him the go-ahead."

"Without contacting me?"

"Vuma said you were nowhere to be found."

"Well, if you share Vuma's fantasy to fight well-armed, professional soldiers with petrol bombs and revolvers, you'll excuse me. I'm not going to be part of that circus. I see no political justification for the operation. It's going to be a tragi-comedy that will dent our image."

"Ngwaneso, let's do this," Sabelo said. "Please exercise your powers and restrain Vuma from plunging us into this mess."

When we ended our conversation, I wished I had wings to fly to Umtata to stop the farce before it started.

The following day Zingisa Mkabile came to fetch me in Sterkspruit, and we travelled through Lesotho via Qachasnek. When we arrived in Umtata I convened a meeting of regional commanders. All of them were opposed to Vuma's plans.

"You all say you're opposed to the Mother of All Battles," I said to the eruption of laughter, "but you were preparing for it and didn't tell Vuma how you felt. Why?"

"A soldier is a soldier," Thapelo said. "Ours is to take orders and never ask why."

Taking orders seemed to have taken precedence over their consciences. It was this subservience that annoyed me more than Vuma's unilateral decision.

"Comrades, do you want to tell me you are robots? You do only what the operator instructs you to do?"

"No," Sabata protested. "We were told the order came from you."

I said: "Even if it was from me, that wouldn't make you any less robots. I for one wouldn't have obeyed an order like that, even if it was from Sabs."

I called off the operation and later informed Vuma, who was not at the meeting. The following day he handed me a letter resigning from the High Command, and I praised him for his courage in reaching his decision.

After I stopped the 're-capture' of Ncise, I decided to use the Transkei as my base. I had several hideouts in Umtata, organised by people like Charge-in Mabaso and Tyhilana. One of the hideouts was the stately house of 'Fidel Castro' Komsana, which was once the home of former Bantustan leader George Matanzima.

Komsana's domestic helper Mambhele cooked a lot of mgqusho – samp – because she believed an army must march on full stomachs. She called me Overall because I used to wear blue overalls.

Because Apla operations were increasing, I thought the Boers would raid the Transkei. I called a meeting of commanders based in Umtata to discuss this possibility. We agreed that Apla members shouldn't stay in large groups in their hideouts, and should find accommodation in the rural areas. We also closed the Apla office in Sigqibo Mpendulo's house. We advised him to avoid sleeping in the house for fear of an attack.

I asked Gilbert Sineke to find me another hideout outside Umtata, and that's how I became a member of the Mjali family in Misty Mount in Libode.

Mama Nothembile Mjali named me Vuyani Mzazi, and I was introduced to neighbours as her nephew from Gauteng. She said that originally I was from her home in Mqanduli. Her five daughters – Lulama, Tozama, Tandeka, Zanele and Andiswa – and her son Kadephi called me Mzala, cousin. The whole family, even Lulama's son Kutu, ended up calling me Mzala. On month-ends the family showered me with gifts.

Tata Tyelinzima Mjali was an avid reader and had a good library. A teacher by profession, he was fond of telling us he was Nelson Mandela's former schoolmate.

"We were together at Clarkebury College in Ngcobo, when education was still a serious thing," he would say. "It was unheard of those days for teachers to leave their students and go out to toyi-toyi and demand one thing or another. Teachers were in the profession because they loved teaching, not for money."

We nicknamed him Nonkala ka Dzedze, and teased him to tell us the story of his tough upbringing and his epic fight with the legendary stick-fighter Nonkala ka Dzedze. Tata would chuckle.

"Nonkala ka Dzedze!" he would start, his eyes flickering with a longing for halcyon days. "I'll never forget the day uncle brought him home and told me to fight him. Uncle turned to Nonkala ka Dzedze and said, 'You're good, kwedini – boy – but you won't beat my nephew.'

"I wondered if there was something wrong in Uncle's head. By that time Nonkala ka Dzedze was raging like a veld fire, jumping up and down and beating his sticks together and coming down to squat with one knee on the ground. The onlookers cheered and ululated. Nonkala ka Dzedze lunged forward, slashed the air with his whistling stick and danced on his left leg.

"I took my sticks and faced him. He charged and struck me on the ribs, and the crowd cheered loudly. I struck a blow and he parried it. He hit out again, aiming at my head, but I ducked. He unleashed several blows but I was careful to protect my head. The fight became fast and furious, but as it raged on longer than he had expected, his confidence waned.

"Uncle's voice in the crowd soared, urging me to kill the man. I struck Nonkala ka Dzedze with a series of powerful blows and he staggered and fell. Uncle jumped up and turned to the incredulous crowd: 'I told you no boy could beat mchana – my nephew'."

By that time Tata would be in his own world, several decades in the past: "In those days men and boys settled their differences with sticks. Your generation believes in guns. What possesses a man to shoot a woman?"

Years later we lost Tata. He was in his eighties when he fell while crossing a stream in the village and died.

The early nineties saw Apla imposing itself on the Azanian military landscape. This was not the beginning but a continuation of Poqo's military culture, which emphasised killing the enemy. Apla combatants are heirs to the history of resistance spearheaded by Makhanda, Cetshwayo and Bambata. Apla owed its mid-eighties revival to the decades of hard work by PAC members inside and outside the country. Their selfless services pushed it to the heights it reached. The list of women and men who hoisted the flag of Apla is long, but some individuals stand out.

They are people like Sabelo Victor Phama Gqwetha, the man under whose command Apla became a household name and was celebrated in the streets, villages and valleys of Azania. While he was captain of the ship, his crew included people like Barney Hlatshwayo, Daniel Mofokeng and Vuma Ntikinca.

The name Karl Zimbiri was once synonymous with Apla. I first heard it after an Apla unit consisting of, among others, Patrick Muchindu and Godfrey Mathebula had attacked and killed five SADF soldiers in Soweto. A man calling himself Karl Zimbiri telephoned newspapers saying he was an Apla commander and that Apla was responsible for the attack. Inquisitive cadres asked me who the man was. I didn't know, and I tried in vain to find out.

Apla combatants continued to gun down security forces, and would assume the name of Karl Zimbiri when they telephoned the media to claim responsibility. There were, however, other operations that we did not know about, which the media attributed to Zimbiri. Songs were composed in Zimbiri's honour and poems were recited in his praise. Baby boys were named after him.

It soon became clear to us that the operations we didn't know about were operations where African policemen were killed.

The Apla High Command, which included me, was worried about Zimbiri's growing popularity, but we could have grudgingly continued using his name if he hadn't denounced us when we sent a delegation to meet Hernus Kriel, the South African Minister of Law and Order, in Botswana. The mystery warrior also condemned the PAC participation in the Codesa negotiations.

Given the stance he was taking in the media, the High Command decided to stop using his name in our operations. The cadres were told, but the decision was not and could not be relayed to the person central to it, Zimbiri himself. He continued to claim both his and our operations.

His popularity with the media and the people grew. The names that we wanted to promote just fizzled away in the dry sand. We fell short of denouncing him publicly, because when Apla was going through a drought in military activities, he would come up with operations that would capture the newspapers' front pages. We kept our ignorance of his identity to ourselves.

When the cracks started to show in PAC ranks following the suspension of the armed struggle, some senior PAC members declared that Zimbiri had died in combat in Durban. Others said he died in a road accident. Still others claimed he was alive. One group denounced him and another defended him.

Some Apla cadres died in combat. High Command member Mpinzimpinzi Zaba died in Durban; regional commander Sabata Mabinyane died in Pretoria; Moses Mothapo died in Roedan in the Northern Transvaal; Zukile Tolibadi died in Botshabelo outside Bloemfontein; Phanuel Mudau died in Tzaneen. Other cadres just disappeared without trace, among them Hasp Namba, last seen in police custody in Richards Bay. The police say Hasp escaped from their custody.

The dead inspired the living to pick up the fallen spear and charge at the colonial monster. The fighters struggled to get arms, but that didn't dampen their spirits. Instead they made petrol bombs, and spiked PVC pipes with nails – to throw across roads when retreating after an attack. At the time the armed struggle was abandoned, Apla cadres were developing a petrol bomb launcher. We realised late in the day that in guerrilla warfare, every fighter had to be a weapon manufacturer. Nozuko Ramokhele, Refiloe and Shadrack Ndzaba spent whole nights making petrol bombs.

Umkhonto we Sizwe (MK) gave us limpet mines, a bazooka and an assortment of arms and ammunition. Apla regional commander Polite Xuma was the link between Apla and MK and he received the consignment. He also arranged for MK comrades to train Apla cadres in the handling, transportation and setting of limpet mines. One of the people that were trained was Hasp's brother Vuyani Namba. He successfully used a limpet mine in Queenstown, but was killed by one in Durban. The bazooka was used by a unit of five Apla cadres against a petrol depot in East London.

The PAC external mission continued to send us arms, but the lion's share always ended up in the hands of the Task Force, the PAC's version of a people's militia, whose role was to defend the organisation's members from political thugs. The PAC armed the Task Force better than it did Apla. There were even times when Apla had to borrow money from the Task Force.

This imbalance in the sharing of resources existed because Enoch Zulu, a member of the National Executive Committee and a close associate of PAC president Clarence Makwetu, was leader of the Task Force. Apla inside the country was headed by me, Director of Operations, a junior position compared to that held by Zulu.

Transkeian soldiers and police were the main source of weapons for Apla. Polite Xuma and Sandile Njikelane brought us a lot of arms and ammunition from members of the Transkei Defence Force based in Umtata. Misile Stemela and Sichumiso Nonxuba regularly fetched grenades and ammunition from members of TDF Special Forces stationed in Port St Johns.

I was once approached by the Transkeian police in Sterkspruit, offering to lend Apla their service arms. They said we could use the weapons for a mission and return them after the operation. They were disappointed when I told them the arrangement would compromise them – anything could happen to those arms, and if they landed in the hands of the Boers they would be traced back to their origin. However, Apla operatives in Sterkspruit enjoyed the support of the Transkei police and army.

Earlier, when I was arrested at a police roadblock in Thabalesoba in Herschel with rifles, grenades and ammunition, I was taken to the Sterkspruit police station. On learning that I was an Apla cadre, the station commander, Phenduka, invited me to join him and other senior police officers for a barbecue. I had lied to the police, telling them that I knew no PAC members in Herschel and that I was on my way from Johannesburg to Umtata. They believed me because they had arrested me in a taxi from Zastron.

After the feast of meat, the commander of the local riot squad, Captain Skwatsha, took me to his home, where I spent three days. He then drove me to Umtata through hostile South African territory. He assured me that no South African Boer would dare arrest me, because I was under Transkeian protection. To quell my fears, he gave me a fully loaded gun with spare magazines, and said in the event of South African Boers attempting to arrest me, we would both fight them.

We arrived in Umtata safely, and government officials returned the weapons to Apla. When Thapelo Maseko and I were arrested with a large quantity of weapons at a roadblock in Umtata, we identified ourselves as Apla and were immediately released. The weapons were returned to Apla the following day.

As the white-controlled media in South Africa condemned Apla as a racist army thirsty for the blood of whites, the people of Azania sang and danced in praise of Apla. The prolonged negotiations and the rise in state-sponsored violence caused resentment and Apla's popularity rose. A soccer player in the elite professional league was nicknamed Apla by soccer fans. During the festive season, thousands of revellers on Eastern Cape beaches sang and shouted slogans in praise of Apla. Sadly, Apla was fighting a losing battle, because in the end this fervour did not translate into votes for the PAC.

The battle that Apla was fighting was already lost in 1960 when, without thorough preparations, the PAC resolved to use armed struggle as a principal form of struggle. War is a serious venture that should be well planned. Our initial attempts at war were not planned but were an emotional reaction to the brutality of the enemy in, for example, Sharpeville. Anger is like a mist: it blurs the vision. We needed sober and visionary minds to plan for a protracted war. In the haste to action, we scorned theory and risked our destiny on the fortunes of the gun.

In the mid-1960s, we had the chance to train and to understand the theory of guerrilla warfare, but we were let down by poor leadership. Even when Apla was belatedly shooting at the enemy, the PAC leadership did very little to support military strikes with political campaigns. Instead, the ANC captured the people's imagination when it organised campaigns like the marches against the South African blockade of the Transkei. Ironically, the blockade was mounted to uproot Apla from the Transkei: Apla was fighting and the ANC was scoring political points. It was only in Herschel that the PAC branch joined hands with the ANC to march against the blockade of the Transkei. We were cocooned in the shell of the 'bullet and war' slogans.

As Apla mounted attacks on fertile and rich farmlands occupied by European settlers, farms lost their value and some farmers hastily sold to wealthy Africans. A farm that was once owned by a white man with an Afrikaans or English name now displayed a freshly painted African name. This development complicated the planning of operations by Apla cadres, because their orders were to attack white farms and spare those owned by Africans.

Another irony: it was painfully clear that the land of our ancestors was on auction to the highest bidder. While some fighters had shed blood for the land, the stern auctioneer didn't care. Our moneyed African brothers took advantage, and are now sitting on a dormant volcano – because it is an abomination in Africa to auction, sell or buy the property of the dead, the living and the yet to be born.

— Chapter Twenty —

WE ARRIVED in Mqanduli on the morning of October 7, 1993. The likeable and plump John Gumede, whom we called Sangoma, was at the wheel. He boasted an accident-free record, despite the fact that he was always driving. Thapelo Maseko was also with us.

The Mpendulo family welcomed us warmly. "Is there water in the house?" Sangoma asked. "As usual, we are thirsty."

'Amanzi' – water – was Apla code for food. It also meant women. Everybody knew he meant we were hungry.

The Mpendulo twin boys Samora and Sadat swung into action to prepare food. The twins were born in 1976 while their father was in prison in the Transkei. A former Robben Island prisoner, Mpendulo named his sons after the two political giants. Samora was the bigger and taller of the two teenagers, but the smaller Sadat always reminded him that he was not the bigger brother. They were together most of the time.

We ate sumptuously with them and their friends, amid jokes. An addict of communal eating, I greatly enjoyed the porridge and sausages. After we had slaked our 'thirst', Sadat and Samora cleared the dishes and disappeared into the kitchen.

I remained in Mqanduli while Sangoma, Thapelo, Samora, Sadat and their friend Thando Mthembu drove back to Umtata. I spent the night in Thando's home.

When I switched the radio on in the morning, I was stunned.

"Five schoolchildren were killed in a house in Umtata in a pre-dawn SADF raid," the newscaster said. I was alone in the house because Thando's mother and father had left early for work.

I immediately went to the house where cadres were waiting for our meeting to start.

The meeting had been called because they had grievances they wanted to discuss with me. They had just heard the news too, and the mood was sombre.

We had expected an attack on Mpendulo's house, and that was the reason we had closed our office there and advised him not to sleep in it. We couldn't take it in that it was his twins who had fallen to the Boers. The house had been locked up for a while, and on the one night when the children go back there, they are ruthlessly killed. I remembered the breakfast with them the day before . . .

The greatest tribute we could pay them was to continue to fight for the return of every grain of our soil.

We finally turned to the reason we had gathered there. I urged the cadres to be open, even if their problems were about me.

We were still talking when somebody knocked at the door. It was bespectacled Mpendulo, clad in denim jeans and jacket. Instinctively I rose to my feet, and the rest of the cadres followed – more as an expression of our condolences to a bereaved father than as military decorum.

With his hand Mpendulo motioned us to sit down.

"Abantwana bam' babulewe – my children have been killed," he said. "Whose children must die? Somebody's children had to be killed because the Boers are still fighting us. It's my children. So be it. But how I wish it was me they had found. Not the children . . ." His voice trailed off.

He told us how he had found the bodies of the five children soaked in blood that morning – his twins, Thando, Sandiso Yose and Mzwandile Mfeya. He had come to Mqanduli to tell his wife and Thando's parents.

I was quiet. In my mind I had been rehearsing the words I would use to comfort Mpendulo when I met him – but here he was, actually comforting me with his stoicism.

"I don't know what to say," I said as he stood up to go.

After the meeting I boarded a taxi to Umtata. When I arrived I convened a meeting of commanders. We met in the rented room of Mfanelo Skwatsha, an official in the Department of Education and an underground Apla operative. Only three commanders – Bongani Dlamini, Mandla Yende and Sandile Njikelane – turned up. We didn't make a quorum but we went ahead with the meeting.

There was a standing order in Apla that in the event of an enemy raid like the one in Northcrest, we were to go on the rampage and kill whites and destroy their property. It had been hammered into us in meetings and outside, like religious indoctrination. Every cadre knew it, even those who had defected to the enemy.

"Are we ready to retaliate?" I asked.

Bongani Dlamini, alias Mongezi, answered: "Everything is ready. We are waiting for nightfall to strike. The other commanders are busy with final preparations."

It seemed all the commanders were raring to go. All but me.

"Comrades," I said, and cleared my throat like someone about to renounce his religion. "Retaliating in the Transkei won't work. The enemy knows our plan, and surely they have devised their counter. They will come into the Transkei under the pretext of protecting their citizens, in the same way the US bulldozes its way into any country under the pretext of protecting US citizens. Nothing will stop arrogant South Africa from coming here to crush Apla and demoralise the PAC."

We discussed it intensely, and finally agreed we would not retaliate in the way the Boers expected. We then started the task of contacting all units to tell them about our decision. Njikelane, a brilliant administrator and a workaholic, was given the duty of informing the Transkei authorities of our decision to remain calm. They applauded it.

I believe that by refusing to give Pretoria an excuse, we succeeded in frustrating its plans to wreak havoc in the Transkei.

A few days after the mammoth funeral, I asked Mpendulo to take me to the graves, since I hadn't been at the funeral. Five graves in a row. Silently I renewed my pledges to liberate my country from the evil men who had killed these children.

The Umtata massacre showed one front on which we faced the enemy. The other was where ANC supporters were slaying PAC members. Some amakhosi – African royalty – fled their homes with the ANC in pursuit. One of them was Tshekedi Pitso, a PAC member and inkosi of Jozana's Hoek in Herschel. At Fort Hare University, members of the Pan Africanist Students' Organisation (PASO) fled the campus and sought refuge in the neighbouring villages.

In Port St Johns, PAC members intercepted a hit list drawn up by ANC hooligans and took it to the police. The names on it were Magabuko, a school principal; Mapipa, a businessman; and Mposelwa, a prosecutor. The police dismissed the list as fake, but within weeks the three were gunned down. Magabuko was shot on his school grounds, Mposelwa in his house; and Mapipa was ambushed while driving his car a day or two after I had visited him.

Mapipa always told fascinating stories, such as how in the early 1960s he used to tie a concertina around his neck and pretend to be a professional musician. He would take PAC recruits masquerading as musicians to Botswana en route to Tanzania. On the way they would entertain fellow passengers in the train with their music. His travels took him as far as Rhodesia (now Zimbabwe). The South African police caught him on one of his trips and he was sentenced to imprisonment on Robben Island.

Instead of arresting the known authors of the hit list, the Port St Johns police arrested PAC members, and concocted the lie that there was a power struggle in the organisation. The real culprits were subsequently caught when Umtata investigators took over the case. These killers have been granted amnesty by the Truth and Reconciliation Commission.

Mapipa was not the first former Robben Island prisoner to be killed by thugs wearing political robes. Maliwa, another PAC stalwart, died a gruesome death in Paarl when members of the United Democratic Front, the ANC's front organisation before it was unbanned, doused him with petrol and set him alight. A police van rushed to the scene, but when the police found out that the burning man was Maliwa, they drove away without helping him or attempting to arrest the dancing and singing culprits.

Mposelwa's death drove the South African media into a frenzy. A national weekly said he was a prosecutor by day and an executioner by night because his farm was an Apla base. The media tried and condemned the dead man.

In Port St Johns four PAC youths were killed and their bodies burnt beyond recognition. Their charred remains had to be sent to Cape Town for DNA tests.

In its bloody trail the ANC left gutted huts, helpless orphans and widows and frightened African people. Miraculously, the organisation was not condemned by the local and international media. Instead it was hailed as a torchbearer of democracy and peace. Was this because its senseless violence was directed at Africans and not European settlers? Who cares when Africa bleeds? The blood of Africa was flowing thick and fast when Nelson Mandela and FW de Klerk jointly received the Nobel Peace Prize. As champagne was flowing in Oslo, so was the blood of the African people at the hands of the followers of the two men.

Local and international businessmen, foreign governments and organisations continued to pour millions of dollars into ANC coffers and starve other liberation movements.

One of the places I frequented at this time was Nozi's in Umtata. I first met her in 1992, when Thapelo Maseko and I went to fetch some Apla parcels that had been mailed to Joe Renene, an advocate who was also a member of the PAC. She was working for Renene's legal firm. Before she gave us the parcels she insisted that I sign for the goods. I told her that I attended night classes and therefore couldn't write in daytime, and she laughed. When we said goodbye, I told her to expect a call from me. Later that day I phoned her proposing love. She laughed me off and told me how her life was nearly ruined by the man she had divorced. She said men hadn't been fair to her, and at any rate she was in love with somebody else. We settled for friendship.

As our friendship blossomed, Nozi introduced me to her boyfriend, a taxi man. I also got to know her parents and brothers, her son Lusapo and daughter Tando.

I asked her to type my manuscript, *Mantlalela*, a collection of poems I started writing in prison in Gaborone. After reading the manuscript, she encouraged me to publish it and to write a book about my life.

One morning Nozi phoned me. Her voice was hoarse as she gave me an address in Southernwood in Umtata, and said I should come to her urgently. I went to the house and found she had been beaten: her left eye was closed tight with swelling and she peered through her right eye. She was bruised all over her body and walked painfully.

Nozi said it was her boyfriend who had beaten her up, and she had

had to flee her house. She had reported it to the police, but from their negative remarks she knew they were not going to help her. She asked me to drive her to her father in Qumbu, about 50 km east of Umtata.

On the way to Qumbu, Nozi asked me if I still loved her and, fearing to hurt her more, I said yes.

She left the man, but he still stood between us. Once she had healed, I told her I would not have an affair with her because I knew her former boyfriend, and he would conclude that our relationship had started before their break-up. We spent evenings in her office, and she tried to convince me the break-up was not caused by our friendship. She said her boyfriend had started beating her up long before she knew me. I was torn between my love for her and the fear of betraying a man I knew, and I would cry.

This was the beginning of our tearful and loving relationship.

One Sunday I was resting in the bedroom in Nozi's double-storey flat. She was preparing lunch downstairs and her two children, Lusapo and Tando, were playing outside. Nozi brought me the Sunday newspapers and tried to chat.

"Shh, it's time for the one o'clock news," I said, increasing the volume on the radio. The voice of a newsreader droned: "The PAC has suspended its armed struggle, the organisation's leader, Mr Clarence Makwetu, told a press conference in Johannesburg today."

Nozi looked at me.

"Since when does the PAC use the media to communicate with its fighters?" I said. I was angry and Nozi walked away.

I didn't believe the radio report, and reminded myself that the media have always been mischievous, stuffing words into the mouths of our leaders to sow confusion and distrust among us. But the evening TV news bulletin vindicated the radio reporter. There were Makwetu and his lieutenants, dressed in suits and ties, posing in front of cameras and a host of journalists and calling off the armed struggle.

I had known some PAC leaders to be clowns, but I had never thought they would stoop to such depths of absurdity on life and death matters. How could they suspend the armed struggle without first talking to the fighters?

Early Monday morning I kissed Nozi goodbye and went around Umtata and the surrounding areas, informing the cadres to ignore the media reports. I told them that Makwetu knew the channels of communicating with his forces. I also appealed to them not to insult Makwetu or any PAC leader in song or slogan, because Makwetu and the leadership of the PAC were not the oppressors.

The High Command hastily met that morning. Morgan Gxekwa, a member of the Military Commission and a Poqo veteran, chaired the meeting.

"I couldn't sleep last night, MaAfrika," he said. "The leadership has sold us out. So what do we do? What do we tell the cadres?"

I raised my hand because I had an answer to Gxekwa's weighty questions. He hesitated for a moment, confused by the many hands that shot up, and then motioned me to speak.

"I defy the order," I said, and saw his eyes dilating with astonishment.

"What did you say, S'khulu?" he asked.

"Comrade Gxekwa, I say as an individual I am defying the order."

Magagula, a bearded, pipe-smoking man and an eloquent speaker, was next. He said he also defied the order. Magagula is said to have wept after he heard the news. Sandile Njikelane spoke after Magagula. In a meeting we had with Mlambo weeks before, he had said if the PAC was suspending the armed struggle, Apla would defy it. He stood by his word and said he defied the PAC leadership.

Everyone agreed to defy the PAC leadership. It was a short meeting, and we agreed to formally inform the cadres throughout Azania to ignore the order and continue with their operations.

On their side, the leadership of the PAC didn't condemn the attacks that occurred after they suspended the armed struggle, like the Vryheid, northern Natal, disco attack in which a white woman was killed and several people were injured. The PAC merely attributed these to Apla cadres who had not yet heard of the suspension because they were operating in remote areas.

I believed we should not suspend the armed struggle until we had wrung out some concessions from the other side, like amnesty for all Apla cadres and the release of all those who were in prison. Our leaders had been too hasty to call off the struggle.

The controversial Karl Zimbiri was again in the media, condemning the PAC leadership for suspending the armed struggle. This time he was not alone: Ropa Hondo and Mahmadou Bello, who claimed to be Apla commanders, joined him in his ritual of condemnation. We later established that Ropa was Polite Xuma and Mahmadou was Thapelo Maseko.

Njikelane phoned Sabelo in Harare to ask about the suspension. Sabelo said he hadn't been informed about the decision and, like everyone else, had first heard about it in the media.

Sabelo said he wanted to speak to me and asked that I phone him that night. I rang the house in Harare but he wasn't there, and had not left a message. I tried the PAC office but he wasn't there either. I replaced the receiver and vowed the next time I spoke to him would be in a face-to-face encounter. That wasn't to be – he died in a road accident in Tanzania before we could meet.

His death came at the worst of times. I heard about it on the radio when I was in Misty Mount and had started writing this book. I stopped in mid-sentence.

I immediately went to the PAC office in Umtata, and the story was confirmed.

"Why do you look so sad?" one cadre asked me.

"I wished Sabs a long life," I said.

"Do you weep for someone who suspended the armed struggle?" he asked.

I dismissed him, and told him I wasn't going to celebrate the death of a comrade.

Sineke, Rev. Mutwa and I went to Baziya, to Sabelo's family, to express our condolences. As we were preparing for Sabelo's funeral, the same cadre who had spoken to me earlier asked me to sanction the killing of Romero Mofokeng and Barney Hlatshwayo. He said he was ready to carry out the mission to protect the revolution.

I told him one couldn't protect the revolution by killing the oppressed – and I counted Barney and Romero among them.

A few days after Sabelo's funeral I went to Baziya to pay my last respects. Sabelo's younger brother Bandile took me to the grave. I gave the PAC open palm salute and was silent for a moment.

I broke the silence with the PAC salute: "Izwe lethu!" Bandile responded: "IAfrika!"

We returned to the house, washing our hands at the entrance as tradition demands.

A day or two later I went to see Sabelo's widow Dudu at Vuyisile Dlova's place and expressed my condolences to her.

"How are things going these days?" Dudu asked.

"Okay," I said, even though I didn't believe it.

"But they don't seem so," she said. "When you have time, please call again and update me on what's going on. Things are not well at all."

I agreed to come back when I had time. But events moved like hundred-metre sprinters: one surprise followed another in quick succession. I couldn't find time, and Dudu's questions were left unanswered.

I had last seen Sabelo early in 1994 in Umtata. He was optimistic that the PAC would win the election or, at least, be second after the ANC. I saw it differently. I thought the organisation would be very lucky to win one percent of the votes. The reason was not because the organisation had no following, but because it had antagonised its constituency. Even the decision to go to the polls was not well canvassed among its followers: it was simply pushed down the throats of the membership by a panicking leadership, who had secretly prayed for the failure of negotiations at the 'World Traitors' Centre' (World Trade Centre).

The PAC was not united as it went into the April 1994 elections. The organisation's Western Cape region, under chairperson Theo Mabusela, voted overwhelmingly against going in. This was by far the PAC's strongest region. The fast-growing southern Free State region under Mofihli Likotsi also rejected the April elections, as did the Transkei. These regions accounted for a large portion of PAC membership.

But that was not the end of the story. All the PAC's component structures – PASO, the Azanian National Youth Unity (AZANYU) and the African Women's Organisation (AWO) – also rejected the elections.

I argued with Sabelo, using all these facts, hoping to influence him to restrain his optimism and wake up the dozing PAC leadership. Sabelo, however, was confident that miracles were in the offing: "The PAC victory will surprise most people, as ZANU's in Zimbabwe surprised the world."

I wished I had such boundless hope.

— Chapter Twenty-one —

April 11, 1994.
THE TRANSKEI, which had been a safe haven for Apla cadres, was about to disband and rejoin South Africa.

Some comrades wanted to help me avoid arrest: Vuyisile Dlova, a professor at the University of Transkei, had said that he and Joe Mkhwanazi had secured a safe place for me in the countryside in Zululand. S'thembele Khala, Isaac Lekubu and Frank Vaaltyn had also approached me separately, and assured me they had prepared hideouts for me in Gauteng.

But I had my own secret plan. I had asked Philemon Sicwebu and

Phambili Mei of Herschel to get me a safe house in Lesotho. The house had to be far from Maseru, and have electricity and a phone. The owner of the house had to be an ordinary citizen who wouldn't draw the attention of the police or the media.

Sicwebu and Phambili had come back to me after two weeks: they had secured a house in Leribe, about hundred km north of Maseru. They gave me day and night marks to identify the house.

As Freakout drove through mountainous Lesotho landscape, I knew where we were going.

We arrived at night in the suburb of Lisemeng II, nicknamed America, in Leribe. We went straight to the house and I introduced myself as Sello to Fabia Makau and her brother Mabusetsa, who were looking after the house.

Freakout drove back to Umtata the following morning, leaving me in the house of Gifford and Gladys Faku. The Makaus were their relatives from the neighbouring village of Sebothoane.

Mabusetsa told me that Gifford Faku was a lecturer at the Lesotho Agricultural College in Maseru. He also lectured at the Leribe Agricultural College on Tuesdays and Thursdays. Gladys was the principal of the Bishop Allard Vocational School in St Michael in Roma.

We arrived on a Sunday, so I had to wait till the Tuesday to meet Gifford, a reserved and soft-spoken man. He said his wife usually came to Leribe at month-end, but that she would come that weekend to see me. She did come.

"Sello, my child, this is your home," she said after we were introduced. "You're a big brother to my two daughters, Pondi and Fundiswa, and my sons, Liphapang and Nyawuza."

The following morning I was woken up by a scraping spade – it was Gladys cleaning the fowl run, her stout body bulging in the blue overalls. She mended fences and watered the garden before preparing a sumptuous breakfast. Her pantry was full of homemade jam, tomato sauce and canned fruit.

She cursed people who always bought vegetables and fruit. She would say: "Poor people – some of them are unemployed but they spend the little money they have on wilting vegetables. Lesotho is poor but we have land and plenty of water. We must work hard to feed ourselves or we'll be the slaves of those who feed us."

I had been in Lesotho for less than ten days when it was shaken to its foundation by the assassination of Deputy Prime Minister Selometsi Baholo. He was killed by members of the Lesotho Defence Force in broad daylight. The soldiers were reported to be unhappy with their low pay. Thousands of angry mourners packed the sleepy town of Leribe to bury Baholo.

Across the border, South Africa held its first non-racial elections. The ANC won by a big margin, and ANC president Nelson Mandela became president of the Republic.

Mandela didn't declare a general amnesty, thus ignoring many freedom fighters who were still in prison, in exile or operating underground.

A few months after I arrived in Lesotho, Nozi told me during a telephone conversation that the rose I had planted when I left Umtata had died. I don't know if it had lived its full life or if it had died prematurely.

She later visited me in Lesotho. She drove from Umtata to Maseru via the Ficksburg border post, as other posts were closed by 10 p.m. The Ficksburg gate was then the only one open twenty-four hours a day. She booked in at a hotel, and we were together from Saturday morning to Sunday noon. She drove back to Umtata and I took a bus to Leribe.

About five hours later, Nozi phoned from a hospital bed in Barkley East. She said the car had rolled several times and was now a heap of metal. A farm boy who had hitched a lift with her had died in the accident. Nozi had fractured a leg.

The leg took several months to heal, but thereafter Nozi visited me often, hitch-hiking from Umtata to Maseru.

Sichumiso Nonxuba, who had been one of my three deputies in the directorate of operations, also visited me. He was now a major in the South African National Defence Force (SANDF), the new army comprising Apla, MK, the armies of Transkei, Venda, Bophuthatswana and Ciskei, and the old South African Defence Force.

Sichumiso came with his girlfriend in a hired car.

He told me he wanted to leave the army because he felt unsafe. He believed intelligence agents were monitoring his movements and he feared he could be killed. Sichumiso, an exemplary warrior, had taken part in many Apla operations, including raids on police stations when we desperately needed weapons.

I advised him to stay in the army. It took a long time to convince him but he finally agreed. He was one of many cadres I persuaded not leave the army in spite of their problems, mainly white racism. I argued and still argue that the National Defence Force belongs to the African people. It would be national suicide if we let this asset slip into the sole control of whites. Although whites may resist change and cling to the positions they obtained by virtue of their skin colour, the liberation forces should not give them a blank cheque by excluding themselves from the defence force.

We talked till late that night, and the following day Sichumiso left Leribe for Umtata. He died mysteriously in a 'road accident' near Kokstad in 1996. His family has not been able to trace the Good Samaritan who took him to hospital, nor the driver of the other car in the head-on collision.

Likotsi and Freakout visited me regularly in Lesotho.

In December, Nozi, her son Lusapo and daughter Tando visited me. They flew from Umtata to Maseru via Johannesburg. Likotsi had lent me a car for the festive season and I drove from Leribe to Maseru. Nozi and her children brought me gifts wrapped in glossy, colourful paper. It was hot but the swimming pool was there, noisy with children and adults who cavorted in the shallow end because they couldn't swim.

One man at the poolside was absorbed in a book, *Swimming For Beginners*. I laughed at him and told him the only way to learn to swim was in the water. He told me he had learned golf from a book before he went out on the golf course, and he was now one of the best golfers in Lesotho.

Indeed, once the man finished the book and dived into action, he progressed faster than all the other learners.

Everything seemed to be going well till the end of our stay at the hotel. When Nozi tried to settle the bill with her credit card as she had done before, the hotel management demanded cash. We sensed there was something fishy, and I slipped out of the hotel after midnight.

The same day, two or three days into the New Year, the Lesotho Police arrested me at the Fakus' house in Leribe. They took me to the police station and asked me who I was. I told them my real name and place of origin. They asked for my passport and I told them I didn't have one. I didn't want to show them my false passport, because they would have accused me of overstaying and would simply have driven me to the South African border post.

"Are you in Lesotho illegally?"

"Yes," I said.

"How long have you been in Lesotho?"

"Since April last year."

I told the police that I had fled from South Africa because the police were looking for me for my role in the liberation struggle. I said I had crossed the border illegally and was on my way to report my presence in the country when I heard the news of the assassination of Deputy Prime Minister Selometsi Baholo. When I heard the news, I decided against going to report and went to stay with Uncle Gifford.

The police said that since I was seeking political asylum, they would take the matter to the administrator of the Leribe District. Meanwhile, they would not lock me up in a cell but would keep me in the charge office.

That evening Gladys Faku and a family friend, David Tsebo, brought me a large mattress, clean sheets, a pillow, blankets and plenty of food.

"Take these things back," a policewoman joked. "You are spoiling this bandit."

I shared the food with the police.

Just in front of the charge-office, there were bags of dagga piled two metres high. They had holes in them as if they had been nibbled by rats. The police poked their hands into the holes to get the dagga, which they smoked till the summer night air was choking with the acrid smell.

When Likotsi heard from Gladys Faku that I had been arrested, he came to Leribe to help stop my deportation to South Africa. After a meeting with Likotsi, the District Administrator ordered that I be released and travel with Likotsi to Maseru to sort out my papers with the Ministry of the Interior.

When we arrived in Maseru we picked up two staunch Basotho Congress Party (BCP) members, Moipone Mpondwana and Anna Chicha, and PAC member Mtimkulu. The five of us drove to the headquarters of the BCP. Anna and Moipone presented my case to the party leaders, who promised they would do their best to prevent my deportation.

Anna and Moipone lead us as we moved from office to office, canvassing support. Old man Mtimkulu commented: "Women now lead the struggle. We men have taken the back seat."

Satisfied with their efforts, the two women took us to the office of Deputy Prime Minister Molapo Qhobela. Unfortunately, he was not in Maseru that day.

As Likotsi eased the car out of the parking area, police in plain clothes stopped us. They said I was under arrest and ordered me out of the car.

"Don't argue with them, my child," Anna said as I surrendered to the police. "They'll never take you back to South Africa. The party and the government support you. And of course we, your mothers –

Moipone, Sophie, Mmapolo, Mmafako, Mmasello and I – we all support you."

The National State Security (NSS) officers drove me to what looked like a private house in the Maseru suburb of Katlehong. They questioned me about the relationship between the PAC and the BCP, and between Apla and the Lesotho Liberation Army. My interrogators were not satisfied with my answers and said I would be detained till I was deported to South Africa.

"This is Lesotho," a young officer said. "'Not even the office of the Prime Minister will help you. After all, the Prime Minister is a terrorist like you."

After the stormy questioning, the NSS officers drove me to the police headquarters and handed me over to the International Criminal Police Organisation.

I protested: "You can't do this to me. I'm not a criminal and have nothing to do with Interpol."

One policeman by the name of Nkeane said dismissively: "You know you're a murderer. We are processing your papers and very soon you'll be in South Africa to answer for the massacres you committed. Is that clear?"

In the afternoon the police led me to the cells, where I was locked up without water or food. I peeped through a window and saw holidaymakers diving into a swimming pool, and thought that not long before I had been one of them.

The cell had a stale smell and the blankets smelled of urine, sweat and dust. Political slogans and sexual obscenities were scribbled on the grime-coated walls. Among the slogans were: 'Release Nelson Mandela'; 'Viva ANC'; 'Viva PAC'; and 'Viva Azapo'. I slept on a mat, rolling one blanket for a pillow and using another to cover myself only in the early hours when it became chilly. Mosquitoes buzzed around and bit me.

The following day Anna, Moipone and PAC member ZB Molete visited me with plenty of food, newspapers and novels. They told me Prime Minister Ntsu Mokhehle and his deputy Qhobela had assured them that they would prevent my deportation. Advocate Zwelakhe Mda, attorney Sooknanan and ZB Molete spearheaded the legal battle, while Mafumahali a Ts'oenyehileng, a women's pressure group in the BCP, mounted the political pressure. When I ultimately appeared before the Supreme Court, the judge released me.

A white South African policeman called Muller was in the courtroom. I asked questions about his presence, and the Lesotho police said he was their security advisor. Muller could not conceal his anger at the verdict. We rode in the same car to the police headquarters, where I was to fetch my odd possessions from the cell. In a strong Afrikaans accent he said: "Happy? I know you – you are Happy."

"Yes, I'm very happy indeed," I said.

"I told you," Muller said to his Lesotho police cronies, "his name is Happy. Happy," he turned to address me, "you've won this round with the help of your BCP friends. But the battle isn't over yet. We'll get you."

Looking at the silent, brooding faces of the Lesotho police, I could feel Muller and his band were going to regroup; next time they would hit with a telling blow.

My Lesotho mothers escorted me to the Ministry of Interior, where I was given a document signed by Lesao Lehohla, the Minister of Interior, stating that I could freely live and travel in Lesotho till the Minister determined my status in the country.

We had a busy day thanking the people who had helped in the case. Likotsi and other PAC members joined us when we went to the BCP headquarters.

Likotsi, who led the delegation, praised the BCP, the government and the people of Lesotho for taking a revolutionary stand in the intimidating shadow of a black-ruled but white-controlled South Africa. Ramolahloane, a Member of Parliament for Lower Thamae, said it was Lesotho's duty to protect Africans running away from injustice in their countries.

As we were leaving he called me aside, gazed at me in a fatherly manner, firmly shook my hand and said: "Aluta continua, comrade."

In the following days, the Lesotho press jumped into the fray. *Moeletsi oa Basotho*, a local weekly, condemned the Lesotho government for harbouring a terrorist whose hands were dripping with the blood of innocent people. The paper quoted unidentified police as its source of information. In *MoAfrika*, Candy Ramainoane wrote about the ordeal I had gone through while in police custody.

I phoned Nozi to ask her what had happened. She said the hotel management had called the police. The police asked who I was and where I had gone. She told them I was Thabo Lethola, and they apparently traced me to Leribe through a phone number. To settle the hotel bill, she had to go under police escort to the South African border town of Ladybrand to withdraw money from a bank.

Now that I was free, I settled in Maseru. I stayed in Upper Thamae and in St Michael. I also met regularly with other PAC cadres living in Lesotho – Nkopane Diahomonaheng, Thabiso Makoala and Thapelo

Maseko. Nkopane and Thabiso were sent to Lesotho by Likotsi, after the BCP had appealed for PAC cadres to train BCP youths to defend their leaders. Maseko was originally a citizen of Lesotho and his family had a house in Butha Buthe, where he had a job in the Lesotho Highlands Water Project. Nkopane and Thabiso ran a poultry farm in St Monica in the Leribe district.

There was also Oupa Khotle, who had ignored my advice not to leave the SANDF. He had a South African passport and shuttled between Lesotho and South Africa. Each time he came from South Africa he would bring us clothes from PAC members.

Oupa would also tell me about the position and strength of South African soldiers deployed along the border with Lesotho. He urged me to give the order to attack, and I always told him the war was over. Yet he persisted, gathering weapons and ammunition and selecting targets. When I realised that this was going too far, I called a meeting of the five of us. I made it clear that the era of armed struggle was over, and that history would judge us harshly if we started an era of armed banditry. Other comrades understood, but Oupa insisted that we should teach the SANDF a lesson. Reluctantly he eventually accepted the opinion of the majority. I also suggested that we inform our host country of our intention to go to the South African embassy to negotiate the terms of our return. We agreed to focus on making money. I was selling food at the National University of Lesotho and the surrounding schools in Roma and Nazareth. Thapelo pledged a portion of his monthly pay. We were now turning ourselves into economic activists, and agreed to open a bank account.

A day or two after the meeting, I was playing cards with Semakaleng Mokhae and Mokotjo in St Michael when I heard distressing news on the radio. Lesotho police had uncovered a large quantity of arms and ammunition in Ha Lesiamo in Leribe, and two men linked to the arms had been arrested in St Monica. The reporter said the police believed the arms had been intended for terrorist attacks against neighbouring South Africa.

The cards shook in my hands, and after a few games I said goodnight to my friends. The following day, I drove a red mini-bus into Maseru and went to Sidzamba's house in the yard of the Lesotho High School where he was principal.

"MoAfrika," Sidzamba said when he saw me. "You'd better disappear. All your colleagues have been arrested. A large quantity of weapons was dug up in Dipu's house in Motimposo."

"It's a set-up," I said.

"This is no time for arguments. The police are looking for you. You'd better leave now." Sidzamba turned and left me rooted.

I boarded a taxi to Motimposo. Saddam Hussein, as we used to call Dipu's wife, told me what had happened. She said Oupa Khotle came with Lesotho and white South African policemen and pointed out spots in her yard, where the police dug out weapons.

"I mean Boers, my child. They swarmed this yard like ants."

She said Oupa was handcuffed but looked unruffled. Before the police left with him, he whispered to her that she should tell me there were more weapons at the corner of the yard, and I must recover them before the police found them. I told her to mark the spot and never again use it for ploughing because the bomb would kill her. She placed thorny branches on the spot. A few days later the police went back and dug up a landmine in the yard.

I said goodbye, but before I disappeared around the corner, she called me: "Ntate Thuso Motaung!" This was my name in the house of Saddam. I went back.

"Tell me the truth, my son. Did you know there were weapons hidden in my yard?"

I hadn't known of the weapons.

"Motho, never trust a person," she said. "I have housed and fed freedom fighters since 1960. I house and feed Oupa but he brings weapons into my house without telling me."

I hastened to Moipone's house in Lower Thamae. Moipone told me that Oupa had brought the police and led them straight to a maize-meal basket in her kitchen. The police emptied it and found a neatly wrapped parcel containing my three passports and firearm licence.

Oupa then led the police to her father's house in Upper Thamae. They found weapons, and old man Lethola, in his eighties, was dragged to the police station.

Moipone said I must be vigilant, because the police had told her I was behind all this and they would catch me.

A day after I had visited them, Saddam and Moipone were arrested and tortured, suffocated with plastic bags. The police wanted them to say where I was hiding.

Disguised, I moved around Maseru, getting bits of information about the fate of my arrested comrades. I wore a cooper hat and a blanket and carried a stick in the fashion of Basotho men.

More distressing news was pouring in. Oupa had led the police to

Butha Buthe to arrest Thapelo Maseko. He also led them to Al-wynskop to raid the house of Phenduka, a local BCP leader and a staunch supporter of the PAC since the early sixties. Oupa pointed out other BCP leaders and Members of Parliament, and the police arrested and tortured them.

Having thoroughly combed Lesotho, Oupa crossed the Caledon River with the South African police and took them to Qwaqwa, where more weapons were uncovered. He also led them to Herschel to raid Tikiso. Besides Tikiso's licensed firearm, the police found nothing.

Back in Lesotho, a BCP women's delegation met Prime Minister Ntsu Mokhehle to complain about the harassment of its members by the police. It also pleaded with him to stop the deportation of three PAC cadres who had been arrested. The Prime Minister told them his office had contacted the PAC headquarters in Johannesburg and the organisation had disowned the three. The PAC claimed that all its cadres had been integrated into the SANDF, and there were none in exile. This did not help Lesotho to fight their case.

Mokhehle told the delegation that his government and party were weak because of power struggles and internal wrangling, and the Lesotho police and the South African government had taken advantage of that.

Mmapolo, who was part of the delegation, said the Prime Minister told them that although Lesotho could not protect me against a powerful South Africa, his government would not revoke my permit to live in Lesotho. His deputy Qhobela advised me to stay underground until the storm had blown over.

Three weeks after their arrest, Thabiso, Thapelo and Nkopane and two trunks full of Apla archives were deported to South Africa.

David Tsebo drove me to Mafeteng to see Advocate Mda, who said the State had no case against me. He advised me to stay underground because the Lesotho police were uncouth.

From Mafeteng David took me to his relatives in a village called Sekhutloaneng in Thaba Bosiu.

Mmalekhooa, her husband Khotso Malefane and their children welcomed me. It was winter, and the towering Mount Thaba Bosiu spread its cold shadow over Sekhutloaneng long after other places got sunlight in the morning. The chilling act was repeated in the afternoon, long before the sun disappeared from other places. I slept in a hut a short way from the main house, joining the rest of the family around the hearth for meals.

"Don't forget to fill your hot-water bottle," Mmalekhooa would say as she stirred the ashes; the embers glowed and a wave of warmth swept across the room. "This fire is about to die."

When a full bladder awakened me at night, I would go out into the cold air and face Thaba Bosiu, imagining stampedes of African women and children scuttling for cover as European cannons rained death. In my imagination, steadfast African warriors rolled down boulders to crush the invaders. The warriors defended the mountain, but the fertile valley below was stolen. The alien land thieves celebrated with champagne.

"Ons vaderland! Our fatherland!" they said in drunkenness.

To this day the descendants of these thieves chant "Law and order" as they try to erase the pain from our collective memory. Where were law and order when Moshoeshoe's vast kingdom was reduced to the size of a man's palm?

I didn't linger for long in one place. David took me to HaMohalenyana, where I stayed in the house of Mmaphehello Ts'ehloane. I didn't stay long because of widespread stock theft in the village, and Mmaphehello told me the villagers were suspicious of strangers. Rustlers were not reported to the police: they were killed.

Thabo Ts'ehloane, not related to Mmaphehello, organised a hideout for me at the National University of Lesotho, where he was a student. He took me to Mmanthako Makhetha, a librarian in the university. I spent long hours with Thabo discussing his favourite subject, African literature.

He also introduced me to Khutlisi, a security guard at the campus. Khutlisi showed me footpaths I could use if I wanted to avoid the main entrance into the campus. He took his time, teaching me to fasten a blanket around the neck without using a safety pin, the way Basotho men do. I had to look and behave like a Mosotho man.

One night I was with David and Semakaleng Mokhae in Mmafaku's house on the grounds of the Bishop Allard Vocational School in St Michael. Suddenly, somebody knocked on the window and shouted: "Mmafaku, bring the keys of the minibus."

David and Semakaleng strained their ears, trying to identify the voice. A gun exploded with a deafening crash and the kitchen door was flung open. I jumped up and switched off the lights. We were all tensely silent. We heard soft tiptoeing in the kitchen, and I had a picture of a man carrying a big gun with his forefinger on the trigger. We heard boots stamping on the roof, and iron sheets and telephone wires being torn off.

David had a revolver with four bullets – he had started carrying the weapon after his brother was gunned down and he was left for dead in a fight over cattle. His father and another brother had also recently been shot dead in the war in the village.

"Give me your revolver, David," I whispered, surprising myself with my calmness. He gave me the gun. We were now in the passage, squeezed against the wall, waiting for the man from the kitchen with a big gun. I thought that with a revolver, we had the advantage over him. His long barrel would stick out first, and I would go for the head. But the man didn't come through.

Overhead the noise was getting louder and our attention was divided. Would some attackers descend from the roof? It seemed we were lost even before we could fire the first shot.

"David, give me the key of the front door," I whispered again. David fumbled in his pockets and found the key.

If these attackers could deploy men on the roof, surely they would have others at the door? They'd know we would expect armed men at the door, unless we were morons. I wanted to act like a moron and do the unexpected. Noiselessly I inserted the key into the keyhole, turned it and the handle simultaneously and flung the door open. The gunmen outside the door were caught by surprise.

"Shoot the dog!" one shouted. I intended to dive for cover but I was too late. A breezeblock tripped me and I fell. There was ferocious gunfire. Still on the ground, I turned and shot twice in the direction of the attackers. There was a brief respite and I ran, jumped a fence and headed for David's house, a kilometre away.

Vicious dogs charged at me and I shot into the air. They scuttled away. I shouted, "Koko!" (knock-knock!) and identified myself. David's younger brothers, about five of them, came out and restrained the dogs. Inside, the women were crying.

"Where is my son David?" David's mother, Mmamoeketsi, asked. She was still dressed in black, mourning the death of her husband, who had been married to three women and thus left three widows.

I told her David was alive, and I had come to ask for the hunting rifles that David's father had left behind, and donkey carts to block the road.

David's brothers got excited and were raring to go. They whistled and made shooting sounds as they fired imaginary guns. But Mmamoeketsi refused: she said too much blood had been spilled in her house.

"We are widows because of these mad killings. Where is my son David?"

"He's alive," I said, and dashed out of the house.

"Ntate Sello, Ntate Sello!" an agitated voice called from the dark. It was David.

"Where is Mme Maki?" I asked. "How did you get out of the house?"

David said he had followed me out of the house but didn't jump the fence. He used the rear gate. He'd left Semakaleng in the house.

I felt guilty. Two men, one armed, had run away, leaving a woman to the mercy of the vultures on the rooftop. Beastly men have been known to do ugly things to women before they killed them. We were cowards.

David and I ran to his sister's house to phone. We phoned the Roma police station five km away, but the phone rang with no one picking it up. We tried the Maseru police station and again had no luck. We spent over thirty minutes on the phone. We even telephoned some people in Maseru, asking them to phone the police, but they all phoned back to say the phone was ringing but nobody was answering.

Why did the armed men take so long to drive away? I feared for Mme Maki. Just as I was getting agitated, we saw lights of a car crawling out of Bishop Allard. It reached the main road and the lights of another beamed. The two cars drove slowly towards Maseru.

"Ntate Sello, give me the revolver," David said. I gave him the revolver and we walked towards a point on the road where the vehicles would pass. Our minibus that they had stolen was in front. We sheltered behind some trees, and David readied himself to shoot the last bullet. I hoped that he would hit the driver. The single shot rang out and triggered a massive bark of gunfire. The thieves sprayed our position with bullets before slowly driving away.

David drove his late father's battered van to the Roma police station and I resumed the ritual of phoning the police. David later told me the phone was ringing when he entered the charge office. The police were there, chatting and warming themselves around a heater. He said they should pick up the phone before they attended to him, but the commanding officer asked him who he thought he was to teach them their job.

"Tell us your problem and forget about the phone."

David reported the crime.

When he came back, without the police, we returned to Bishop Allard. Semakaleng was there, unhurt and happy to see us alive. She had hidden under the bed, and the gunmen hadn't ransacked the house. They had spent a long time tinkering with the car as it had an immobiliser.

David drove me to Maseru the same night. The police went to the scene of the crime the following day, interested more in my where-abouts than in the stolen car.

In Maseru, Sophie Kau, a retired nurse, attended to my painful and bruised knee. She ran a health centre, Ntlo ea Kuena, named after her hundred-and-something-year-old mother.

"Cadres of the Lesotho Liberation Army were also treated here," she said as she cleaned and dressed the wound.

After a few days, I left Upper Thamae for Lower Thamae, to stay with Sophie's younger sister Mmasello Rakometsi. Mmasello lived with her son, Sello, a mechanic. I ventured out of the house only at night. Sello's cousin Fako Mothebesoane, also a mechanic, took me to his workshop in Butha Buthe for a few weeks.

I was back in Maseru when Dina, from Thabong in Welkom, visited her friend Mmasello. The two women spoke about my plight, and one day they called me. Dina said she was on her way to her home village in Semonkong and would take me along. She would introduce me as the son of Mokete, a member of her family who had disappeared forty years before. I would tell her relatives and friends that Mother had told me I was Mokete's son. Mokete was a farm labourer who left Mother on the white man's farm when I was a few months old, and never came back. When I grew up I made it my mission to look for him or his relatives. One day somebody led me to Dina, and I agreed to go to Semonkong.

When we left Maseru, I wore a blanket and a cooper hat. Sello drove us to the Mmanthabiseng bus terminus. The most celebrated buses in Lesotho those days were 'Saddam Hussein' and 'Ntsho Ma-ketola', operating between Maseru and Maputsoe. Whatever its name, the Semonkong bus was not famous. It left Maseru at about 11 a.m., lumbering uphill and groaning under a huge load on its roof carrier. Door and window frames, mattresses, wardrobes, washing basins, a car seat, a flat tyre and other odds and ends were tied down with ropes.

The music of Apollo Ntabanyane and Tau ea Mats'ekha was blar-ing inside the bus. Men heaved their shoulders and nodded to the beat of the music. A woman in the back seat yelled to a woman seated in the middle, complaining about soaring prices and men who forgot about their families once they were seduced by city girls.

The tarred road ran out and the bus kicked up brown dust. We closed the windows but the dust found its way through the cracks in the body of the creaking bus. We were forced to re-open the windows. The smell of dust, sweat, stale perfume and soiled nappies filled the bus.

As we drove up the Maluti Mountains the mountaintops were white with snow, and the bus windows misted over. It was night when the bus finally slowed down, stuttered and stopped. The driver victoriously announced: "The joy of riding the bus ends here."

The conductors got out first and the rest of us scrambled to disembark. We followed the conductors to the back of the bus and noisily identified our luggage.

A man barked at his son, telling him to bring their horse nearer. People clustered around their bags. The first to leave were men on horseback, riding into the cold Maluti night. Some walked home, but we boarded a van to our destination.

That night Dina told her Makholokoe clan my story: the homecoming of the son of a lost son. Neighbours came to see me. They sat around the fireplace in the smoky hut and furtively studied my face. I overheard somebody whispering that I looked like Mokete. "What is your work, Lekholokoe?" somebody asked, addressing me by my new clan name.

"I'm a farm labourer," I said.

"Do you have donkeys?" he asked.

"No, I don't. But a friend of mine has plenty of them and would like to get rid of some."

"Talk to your friend and bring those donkeys here. With donkeys you'll be a great man in this village."

After a delicious supper of homemade bread and pork, I faked a headache and said I wanted to sleep – I was running away from more questions. It was cold outside as Dina and her ageing mother led me to the hut where I was to sleep.

Dina's mother raised her eyes to the dark sky and said: "It looks like it's going to snow tonight. We need snow for our wheat fields."

I fell asleep while thinking about Mokete.

The following morning I woke up to a cloudy and freezing day. Instead of snow, there was tsheole – fine ice – raining down.

The village was perched on a ridge on the slopes of the towering Maluti Mountains. Women and girls filed to and from the spring, carrying containers filled with water. People shouted, asking which house would be slaughtering a pig that day: it was cold and they needed fat for their bodies.

At noon the sun tore the flimsy blanket of cloud and shone brightly over Semonkong. In the afternoon Dina took me to Maletsunyane, the Labihan Falls, and we watched the beautiful workings of nature from the high banks of the river: water flowing languidly over the riverbed before falling noisily and wildly, breaking into droplets to form a cover of mist. The water crashed down to the pool below, forcing it to ripple and splash against the walls of stubborn ice and snow. A short way from where we stood, herdboys wearing blankets pushed rocks over the high stony banks. The falling rocks sounded like thunder and their echo continued after they had dropped dead on the riverbed. It was a magic sound. The Victoria Falls on the Zambezi might be broader, but the Labihan Falls is deeper.

I spent a week in Semonkong. I didn't like a sanctuary that cut me off from the world – there were no newspapers and I couldn't even get a single channel on my portable radio. The morning I left with Dina, the old lady was concerned that I hadn't met the village chief. He was to allocate me land for farming and for building a house.

"Will you come back?" Dina's mother asked me with love glowing in her eyes.

"I shall come back. Tell the chief I'm sorry I couldn't meet him. I have to go back to fetch my belongings from the farm in South Africa," I lied to her.

Dina left me in Maseru and proceeded to Welkom. As a parting shot, she said: "Collect whatever you'll need in Semonkong, go back there, find yourself a makoti – bride – and lead a normal life like your peers."

I didn't return to Semonkong. I kept asking myself how long I was going to run. Did I run to advance a cause or had the running become my cause?

Back to Maseru – back to the edge of a dagger. I secretly met people from Azania and sent Lesotho people to different parts of Azania. I relied on Pakela, an old man with a limp who continually spoke about Robert Sobukwe, Kimberley – the Northern Cape town to which Sobukwe was exiled after his release from Robben Island – and its diamonds. He said Sobukwe was the best lawyer he had ever seen, and that Prof had once defended him and got him acquitted.

Nzondelelo Mpondwana, Moipone's son, helped arrange my meetings with different people. One was PAC Deputy President Motsoko Pheko, whom I met in the house of ZB Molete. He had come to Lesotho to meet with BCP leaders. I hadn't met Pheko in person before but I had read his militant books, including *The Story of a Dispossessed People*. We discussed the false liberation that South Africa had attained, the plight of freedom fighters still languishing in South African prisons, and the besieged government of Ntsu Mokhehle in Lesotho.

Winter came and passed, and so did spring. And we were in summer when, on a hot afternoon, a large contingent of Lesotho police in many vehicles pounced on me in Mmasello's house. After they had interrogated me briefly at their headquarters, the police put me in a dark, windowless and stuffy cell. I could tell time only by listening to the chirping of birds: when they stopped I knew it was nightfall and when they started again it was dawn. Amazing how we get back to nature when our crutches are removed.

On the day I was arrested, I went on a hunger strike, demanding that I be released immediately.

From the second day Anna and Moipone visited me regularly, but each time I saw them I'd weep. They really cared for me.

The police wanted to cut a deal with me. They said they would release me if I confessed that I had secretly met the Prime Minister and his deputy to establish ties between Apla and the Lesotho Liberation Army (LLA). I refused to confess to something I did not do.

When I was taken to court I saw Anna and Moipone in the yard of the building and I waved to them. I was taken to an outbuilding that looked like an office. A casually dressed young woman was sitting at the desk. A policeman whispered something to her, and another led me into an adjacent office, apparently to allow the two government officials to talk in private.

After a while I was taken back to the woman's office and told to sit on a chair. I was then told to stand up as the policeman who had whispered to the woman read a charge sheet. He started by calling me Zweledinga Ngombane, a South African male aged thirty-five years.

I interrupted him: "I'm Letlapa Mphahlele, not Zweledinga Ngombane. What's happening here? Am I in a kangaroo court or what?"

"Order," the woman barked at me. "I'm the presiding magistrate in this case. You are the accused. This policeman is the prosecutor. Behave yourself, Mr Ngombane. Go on, officer."

The officer told the court that I had three passports in three different names from three different states. I'm not certain if the charges were fraud or something else, but the magistrate ruled I was to be tried for the Lesotho passport only because it was the property of Lesotho. She asked if I pleaded guilty or not guilty. I pleaded guilty, but reminded her that I was not Zweledinga Ngombane. She cut me short and fined me five hundred rand. When we emerged from the office block, Moipone and Anna asked when the court was going to sit. I told them I had already been fined.

"Thanks God," Moipone said with relief. "This is the last money I have and it's exactly five hundred rand."

She gave me the money and I went back into the office to pay.

"Now that my son has paid the fine, I beg you to release him," Anna said to the police.

They refused, saying they were continuing with their investigations.

The police drove me back to the dark cell. The following day, December 22, a band of noisy police burst into my cell.

One shouted: "Get out of here, you dog. We have found arms in Lower Thamae, in the same house where we arrested you. Come now and see for yourself."

They pushed me onto the back of a bakkie, handcuffed me and chained me to the bars just behind the cockpit. Instead of going to Lower Thamae, the vehicle raced to the border with South Africa. As we crossed the river Mohokare – the Caledon – my whole being became charged with defiance.

— Chapter Twenty-two —

THE SOUTH AFRICAN police were waiting for me. There was a tall, bulky one who introduced himself as Brigadier du Plessis.

"Mr du Plessis, we've brought Letlapa Mphahlele. Here he is, sir," a Lesotho policewoman said, waving towards me.

"Oh, I thought I was Zweledinga Ngombane," I snapped. "You arselickers. You address white men as 'mister, sir'. Ask your boss du Plessis – he couldn't arrest me, but he set his dogs and bitches like you on me."

"Don't speak like that to me. Yes, I call white men 'mister' because I'm speaking their language."

"Okay, since you've known me, have you ever addressed me in your language as monghali – mister? Anyway, you're wasting my time because I want your master himself.

"Du Plessis." I faced the towering figure in front of me: "Phone your bosses in Pretoria and tell them you've got me. They may promote you."

After the handover, the Lesotho police drove back to their country – or should I say their shadow of a country?

I was taken to Ladybrand, from where a Captain Steyn and two African policemen took me to Bethlehem. Steyn said he was the investigating officer in my case. He persuaded me to eat and promised to buy me whatever food I desired, even from a hotel. I thanked him, but told him I was on a hunger strike to demand my release. He told me things had changed in the country and that people were happy with the new South Africa. We were driving through the vast expanse of treeless, flat land that is the Free State.

"You see this land," I gestured with the head as my hands were handcuffed behind me. "This land is still in the hands of the descendants of Jan van Riebeeck and the 1820 settlers. They took it from my forefathers by force of arms. Until this land is returned to the Africans, all the changes you speak about are just decorative."

The captain retorted: "Land, land, land, don't you people in the PAC know anything except land?"

"Yes, we also know economics because land is the basis of the economy. We know a lot about civilisation because civilisation began with land cultivation. We know history because it is a lie that the African soil belongs to all who live on it. We know agriculture because . . ."

"Enough. I am not a politician," Captain Steyn said.

We arrived in Bethlehem at night and the interrogation began. Captain Steyn, with whom I had spoken in English all the way, interrogated me in Afrikaans and an African policeman interpreted in Sesotho. I was asked to write a statement but I refused. Then Captain Steyn wrote a statement, read it to me through the interpreter and asked me to sign it. Again I refused.

"So you are not prepared to co-operate with us," he said lamentingly.

"How can I co-operate with my kidnappers?"

"You see, things have changed. In the old days, you couldn't speak to me like this. Say thanks things have changed."

"Do you think that in the old days I could have been delivered to you so easily? One of you would be lying in a mortuary. Say thanks things have changed."

Steyn looked at me with hatred. He barked angrily in Afrikaans, but whatever he said wasn't interpreted to me. The interrogation ended and the police led me into a cell.

Anna, Moipone and Sooknanan came to see me. After their visit, I decided to end my ten days' hunger strike. When Mofihli Likotsi and his entourage from Botshabelo visited me, he inspected my cell, and insisted that I be given a foam mattress instead of sleeping on a mat. The police complied.

On New Year's Day, a policeman brought me rice, plenty of meat and delicacies. He said his wife had prepared the meal especially for me and that she did the same on Christmas Day – but unfortunately I was then still on a hunger strike.

On January 3, 1996, a large convoy of cars drove me to Bloemfontein for a court appearance. As I walked up the stairs and through the corridors from the holding cells to the courtroom, I jostled through an excited crowd, shaking hands and shouting "Izwe Lethu!"

In that buzzing crowd, I spotted Mother, Father and my brother Seputule, who had shed his childhood name of Mohlolatlala after his initiation. My heart pounded and I trembled. All my brothers and sisters were there except Mafokeng, who was a new mother after her son Lethabo was born a day after I was kidnapped from Lesotho. He was named Lethabo – Joy – because the family was happy to hear I was still alive.

Father wept. I restrained the tears building up in my eyes; I wanted to cry but I feared the people and the media particularly. A warrior was not supposed to cry in public. I imagined what the headlines would read like the next day: Tearful Terrorist Meets Mum. Weeping is an expression of emotion, but unfortunately most people associate it with weakness. That day I betrayed my emotions.

Among the press people I recognised Benison Makele, a former Apla underground operative and the journalist who had covered my trial in Botswana. It was a strange twist indeed – covering my case first as a freedom fighter operating in a foreign land, and now back in my own land, in a country I had helped 'liberate'.

Supporters had descended upon Bloemfontein from Lesotho and different places in Azania. I learnt Johnny Maseko had brought majorettes from Paul Roux to spice up the event. Jomo Makara had organised the residents of Bloemfontein to attend the court hearing. Sombu Majola, an activist from Gauteng, told me that members of the High Command of Apla said they were going to issue a public statement in my support. I was elated, but the statement was never issued.

In that excitement, I was introduced to my lawyer, Jake Moloi, the president of the Black Lawyers Association. Sooknanan had come from Lesotho, and briefed Moloi about my abduction. The case was adjourned to January 6.

Captain Steyn asked me if I would prefer to be kept in the Bayswater police cells or in the Grootvlei Prison. I told him anywhere – after all I wasn't consulted when I was kidnapped from Lesotho.

A massive convoy escorted me to Grootvlei Prison, 15 km south of the city. I found many Apla cadres there, some already convicted and others still awaiting trial.

With the help of Lenaila, a warder who was a PAC member and originally from Lesotho, I visited the comrades in the sick bay.

Malusi Nkabinde had a broken leg in plaster of Paris from thigh to foot. He had been in a car accident shortly before being arrested. Malusi was three months overdue for a doctor's check-up in town, but the white warders refused to take him, arguing that a terrorist was dangerous even on one leg. He threatened to sue the State for negligence, and a stern-faced white warder asked him: "Do you think you could sue the State if you were in Cuba?"

When I again appeared in court, PAC deputy president Motsoko Pheko was there as he usually was when PAC cadres appeared.

My lawyer Moloi phoned from his Welkom office to have the case postponed. This infuriated a lot of people who had travelled from as far as Cape Town to attend the hearing. Angry Sithembele Khala phoned Moloi and asked him to withdraw from the case and I appointed Sooknanan, who had come to court to support me.

Sooknanan succeeded in getting bail of thirty thousand rand after three days of intense arguing. The bail conditions were that I would be restricted to the Bloemfontein magisterial district, be under dusk-to-dawn house arrest, and report every day at Park Road police station in town.

Nobody had thirty thousand rand, so I returned to prison. I got visits throughout the day, every day. I learned other visitors were turned away because they had come on non-visit days without prior arrangements.

Pontsho Makhetha, a reporter on Sesotho Stereo radio, also visited me and brought me delicacies and good wishes from her colleagues. Nozi, still recovering from an operation, dragged herself to Grootvlei, and Karabo Motsapi was a regular visitor. Prisoners with radios in their cells told me some callers greeted and wished me well. A regular caller was Makhongoana from Hennenman, who would greet me even in the middle of the night.

One afternoon a month after I was granted bail, Likotsi came to pay it and drove me to the Bloemfontein suburb of Phahameng. I was to stay with the Motsapi family. Karabo, her mother and brothers welcomed me. Every time my family and friends from GaMphahlele and other supporters came to Bloemfontein, they were accommodated by the Motsapi family, using even the backrooms, which would otherwise be rented out.

During the first evening, Mmamotsapi put muti into my bath water and told me to wash away the bad luck. I washed because I didn't want to upset her, but afterwards I politely told her I didn't believe in the power of muti to assist in legal matters. She laughed and said I was too young to know these things.

Every morning Steve Motopi drove me to the police station to report. At the weekend, Likotsi and his quiet wife visited me. He said his wife was the one who had insisted that the family sacrifice some money for my freedom, limited though it was. I thanked them, but I don't think I can ever express the depth of my gratitude adequately.

Jabulani Khumalo sent me money from time to time till he later decided to deposit money into my account every month. Khunoana Ponoane visited me frequently. Originally from Hoita in Herschel, he was studying at the Bloemfontein Technikon. After qualifying as an electrician, he always gave me pocket money. Later he died in an electrical accident and left a void in my life.

When Nozi visited me, I had to apply for permission to be with her at a hotel for the weekend. The police gave permission, and she came with PAC Eastern Cape leaders Zingisa Mkabile and Victor Zamela.

I was back in my homeland yet far from home, Manaleng. It took a long while before the authorities allowed me to visit my home village, on condition that I report regularly at Pietersburg Police Station, 70 km from Manaleng. I set out on the journey home, boarding a taxi from Bloemfontein to Johannesburg and then another to GaMphahlele.

The taxi driver dumped me in Potgietersrus, now renamed Mokopane, about 80 km from my destination. He said he had changed his mind, and that he could do that because the taxi was his. It was about 9 p.m. when I started hitchhiking.

The first ride took me halfway home and I hired a taxi for the rest of the journey. It was nearly 11 p.m. when I arrived home. A dog barked viciously as I shouted, "Koko!" at the gate. My family didn't know I was coming, but the lights were still on and they were still awake. They have always gone to bed late.

Father came out to enquire: "O mang – who are you?"

"Ke nna Ngoato – it's me, Ngoato," I shouted, and the house burst into celebration.

Father opened the gate amid shouts of "Hallelujah" and "Amen" from Mother. We hugged and kissed and neighbours woke up to join in the jubilation. Aunt Ramaesela pinched herself to see if she was not dreaming. Each person woke his or her neighbour up and Manaleng became lively in the middle of the night. Women, some with children strapped on their backs, sang and danced and ululated. Malose went to Maralaleng and other villages to tell other relatives that I had returned home.

"On days like these we remember your late grandmother, Ntate," Aunt Ramaesela said. "She would blow a phalafala – a horn – and dance to welcome the hero returning from the spears, as was done in the old days."

As more people came, the gathering turned into a religious service. The congregation detonated into a powerful hymn:

> *"Tsohle di entswe ke wena*
> *Modimo re boka wena."*

> *(All was created by Thee,*
> *Oh Lord we praise Thee.)*

We sang other hymns and finally people prayed, each using his or her own words. I think Mother prayed loudest and Father longest. Mother prayed to the God of Israel and Father to a mixture of badimo – ancestors – and the God of Israel. The congregation dispersed after four and I struggled to sleep.

Barely two hours later, a new wave of visitors rolled in. There were some who came in cars and others wearing school uniforms. They brought me gifts of live chickens, fruit, vegetables, beans and money. Pebetse, our neighbour, brought a basket of fresh figs. Jacob Phala and Mperekeng Chiloane offered to drive me in their cars wherever I needed to go. Eventually they took turns driving me to the police station to report.

In the afternoon I excused myself, and asked Madimetja Molapo to go with me to Manaleng Mountain. As we climbed, memories of childhood flashed through my mind. From the summit I had a bird's-eye view of Manaleng and the other villages; I noticed that people were crowding the land. Several villages had sprung into life in the eighteen years of my absence. On the other side of the mountain, Maupaneng village lay dead and buried in thick mohloko bush – a casualty of time.

I finally knew what I was missing in Manaleng: the pigs. Madimetja told me that some years before, after an outbreak of cholera in the village of Mashite, the government ordered that pigs be kept in sties or be slaughtered. The villagers frantically slaughtered their pigs but Mogale, the village chief, defied the order and kept his flock of free-range pigs till he died. His pigs were slaughtered only after his death.

Manaleng looked strange without pigs.

We descended the mountain and went to Matane, the sangoma. We found him seated on a stool in a hut, stretching his legs on a goatskin and sniffing snuff. He had gone blind. Wild animal skins, the biggest that of a python, hung from the rafters. The scent of skin and snuff hung in the air.

"Phaahla," Madimetja and I addressed Matane at the same time – Phaahla was his salutation name.

"Who's that?" he asked as he sneezed.

"It's Ngoato and Mahlako," I said, using our salutation names.

"Ngoato'a – the son of . . . ?"

"Ngoato'a Mazwi – the son of Mazwi."

On hearing this, Matane stood up and fumbled his way towards me with an outstretched arm. I met him halfway and we shook hands, and then he groped his way back to his stool. He said he had gone to greet me, but was told I had gone to the mountain. He said I had done the right thing by climbing the mountain, and now should go to Molapo wa Mashoaneng Cave.

His voice rose emotionally as he said: "Molapong – that's where our forefathers camped when they fought the wars to preserve this tribe. Their spirits will be very pleased by your visit."

He said he was disturbed by the rumour that the government wanted to turn the cave into a tourist attraction.

"The ancestors will curse this tribe if it turns its shrine into a playing ground for tourists."

When we left Matane's hut, night had fallen over Manaleng. Once sprinkled with fireflies, the village now shone with brighter lights, in keeping with the ANC government's policy of electrifying rural areas. In my days in the underground I had remembered the Manaleng of fireflies and paraffin lamps; but I welcomed the Manaleng of electric power.

Most of the other villages in GaMphahlele were, however, still groping in darkness without electricity. Men from Bolopa still sold firewood, loading dry logs on donkey carts and moved from village to village. Even people who lived in electrified villages bought the firewood because they couldn't afford electricity. Women still gathered firewood from the bush, carrying bundles on their heads.

GaMphahlele was still dry and dusty. Several dams had been built in the mountains but the taps in the village remained dry. Rumour was that there was no water from the dams because the private company that built them and fitted pipes in the village intended to sell the water. The people vowed they would never buy water – a gift from God. The thirsty villages and the company deadlocked, and the people resorted to sinking boreholes for underground water.

Hlabirwa of Maralaleng was fond of saying: "Those dams are meant to provide water for the baboons, not us?"

Fields were shrinking as people built houses on the land. In fact, ploughing was left to the ultimate optimists: they scratched the dry soil and then assembled on the banks of the Hlakaro River, where once upon a time a formidable mokgapa tree towered, to kneel and pray for rain. But rain in this part of Africa is moody and indifferent to prayers. It comes rarely and when it does, it becomes matlakadibe – the carrier of destruction. It leaves a trail of fire and death: people struck by lightning, roofs flying off like dead leaves from a tree, and hailstorms pounding and flooding the crops.

Whereas the storms always blow over and the floodwater is soon sucked up by the thirsty earth and the vengeful sun, the curse of lightning remains to haunt and divide the villages into 'witches' and 'victims'. I learnt that Thema, a man who had been in my initiation regiment, had been shot dead by the police in Mashoene village after a crowd of angry people went on the rampage, burning huts and killing people, including old women, accused of striking others with lightning.

First lightning killed people. Then villagers killed the 'witches' who had sent the lightning. The police and the courts then completed this tragedy by killing those who had burnt the 'witches'.

Wonderful lightning, a natural electrical emission from a charged cloud, continues to cause more deaths than unassisted nature would achieve. The message that precautions can be taken against lightning has not reached our people. They don't understand that the 'victims of witchcraft' could have avoided death by not walking through open spaces during the thunderstorm, or by fitting their homes with easy-to-make lightning conductors. Africa continues to sacrifice her beloved children to the gluttonous goddess of ignorance.

There were other problems eating away at the people. Hunger had descended. Men complained they had lost their jobs in the cities, and asked if this was part of the new democracy.

"I used to work in Newcastle where I have a child with a Zulu woman," muttered Lehumo as he drank sorghum beer with other men. "Now I'm back here and our only rain is wind and dust. People blame me when I drink tototo, but that's the only liquor I can afford."

He lapsed into sleep on the stoep, a fly buzzing around the saliva trickling from his open mouth.

The liquor trade, both standard and illicit brews, was booming. Men, including Father, trooped into lounges to drink their senses away. Father continued to resist Christianity.

Religious fanaticism grew in tandem with the drunkenness: different denominations sang into the small hours. Loud sermons and confessions from the booming microphones punctuated the music, which was sometimes backed by instruments. Weekend nights were noisier than weekday ones.

I visited Mother's village of Rosenkrantz. The clusters of houses, once surrounded by open spaces, were now separated by thick bushes. Grandfather and Grandmother were about to celebrate their sixtieth wedding anniversary. Grandmother told me that Rampubudi, my maternal great-grandmother, died asking if anyone had heard about my whereabouts.

I wrapped up my home visit and returned to Bloemfontein.

Sooknanan withdrew from my case, and Ishmael Mthembu took over. Sooknanan said the State had told him bluntly that they were not happy with lawyers from outside Bloemfontein coming to defend cases there. It was worse in his case because he was from Lesotho, a foreign country. It still pains me that I couldn't pay Sooknanan for all his efforts for me. He told me he was happy that he got me bail and wished me well.

Attorney Ishmael Mthembu wrestled with the court to change the conditions of my bail. He succeeded, and the dusk-to-dawn house arrest was lifted. I was still restricted to the Bloemfontein magisterial district, but I could report to the investigating officer if I wanted to leave. I had to give him my itinerary and the address where I'd be staying. Instead of reporting daily at the Park Road police station, I was to report every Monday at any police station in South Africa and fax my reporting papers to the investigating officer in Bloemfontein.

This relative freedom gave me a chance to catch up with Nozi. She had told me while I was underground in Lesotho that she had another man in her life. I couldn't visit her then because I was in exile, and she couldn't visit me because she would probably be followed by the police to wherever I was hiding. She had already been questioned by the Lesotho police about me.

I persuaded myself to understand her situation. Exile, imprisonment and an underground life have always cramped my personal relationships.

I wanted to visit Nozi in Umtata, but she said there were complications and insisted on us meeting in Alice in the Eastern Cape. She drove from Umtata and I hitchhiked from Cradock, where I got off the train from Bloemfontein.

We met at the Alice police station, where I was to report my presence in town as instructed by the investigating officer in Bloemfontein. The Alice police were in turn to notify their Fort Beaufort counterparts about my presence in the area.

Nozi was looking serious as she drove to the local restaurant, which was empty. We sat in a corner with me facing the entrance, a habit that has become second nature since the days of the underground. She ordered spare ribs and chips.

Nozi told me about the new man in her life and how kind he had been to her. She said she had told the man about me and our inevitable reunion. But since my future was still uncertain, she felt she should continue with the affair until I was completely free.

A waitress interrupted us with two plates of chips and large, charred ribs. On seeing the size of the ribs, Nozi burst out: "These are not the spare ribs I ordered," and returned her plate to the waitress.

The manager came over. The Indian man said less about the spare ribs than about the Koran and the Bible. Quoting from both books, he explained that God had assigned pigs to clear all the mess in Noah's Ark during the Flood, and that was why he didn't have spare ribs on his menu.

Nozi was staring at the man. The zealot continued relentlessly, predicting the triumph of Islam. I burst out laughing. Even in the tensest of moments I look for the funny side – laughter sweetens some bitter realities that we are sometimes called upon to swallow.

Nozi settled for a cold drink, and we returned to our discussion. I told her to do whatever would make her happy.

"Is that all you have to say?" she asked accusingly.

"Yes."

Then she withdrew into a long, gloomy silence – punctuated by her deep sighs.

"You don't understand," she broke the silence. "It's difficult for a single woman to raise two children. I did tell him about you, but if I dump him today and tomorrow you go to prison, it would complicate matters for me and my children. Think of my family."

"I understand."

"You don't," she said.

We parted in the afternoon and I spent the night in a hotel. The following day I boarded a taxi to Cape Town. While I was there, Nozi phoned me daily. I understood the presence of another man in her life. What I didn't understand was my relegation to the role of a junior lover, nor why Nozi's house, full of fond memories for me while I was in exile, was now out of reach.

One lunchtime a few months later I met Nozi in Umtata and she invited me to her house. We greeted her domestic worker downstairs and proceeded to her bedroom, a floor above. I stood in the middle of the room and gazed at the bare wall just above the headboard. I wanted to ask her where the cards had gone, but I didn't want to hurt her. I simply told myself that our affair was over.

We didn't hug. We didn't kiss. We didn't cry.

Months later, I told Nozi over the phone that our relationship was over. For a long time we tried to mend it telephonically and almost believed we had reconciled. But whenever we met face-to-face, unpleasant thoughts aroused the unforgiving beast in me.

My relationship with Nozi was a casualty of our liberation struggle. I still respect her. Among her many accomplishments, she established a private school in Umtata and is involved in community projects aimed at improving the welfare of women. I have encouraged her, and wish her well.

During the storms in my relationship with Nozi, police led by Des Segal ransacked her house looking for evidence that would link me to the attack on the St James Church in Cape Town. Segal was then the head of the Cape Town Murder and Robbery Unit. They took away an electric typewriter for forensic tests and promised to bring it back. Six years later, they still haven't returned it.

In May 1997, I learnt that Des Segal and another detective had died in a car crash between Ceres and Touwsrivier in the Western Cape. A Russian-made RPG 7 rocket launcher, an R4 rifle and ammunition were found in the boot of the private car they were driving. The weapons were linked to Eugene de Kok, commander of the notorious Vlakplaas anti-terrorist unit that specialised in killing opponents of the state. This incident confirmed my long-held fear that the ANC government had unleashed the right-wingers in the police force, the courts and the prison services against freedom fighters.

Now that I could move around, I visited my comrades still languishing in prisons around the country. I went to Haeldestroom Prison, in the freezing shadows of the snowbound Boland mountains; Goedemoed Prison on the banks of Qili (Orange) River; sun-baked Barberton Prison, which once captured world headlines when scores of African inmates died during a heat wave; the seemingly forgotten Rooigrond Prison in the North-West Province, and the massive and overpopulated Durban-Westville Prison.

When I visited comrades at Johannesburg Prison to brief them about planned marches, picketing, night vigils and a million-signature campaign to release all freedom fighters, Thapelo Maseko was moved.

He said: "I'm sorry about your abduction from Lesotho, but I'm very happy it happened."

Nqaba Xulu echoed these words when he was released from Leeuwkop Prison.

Nqaba Gubanca and his wife Nohlangule hosted me in their home in Khayelitsha when I visited Cape Town. He also drove me to Pollsmoor Prison to visit freedom fighters there.

Thobela and other former Apla cadres in the SANDF such as Major Thembelani Xundu were arrested shortly after my abduction, and rumours were rife in the PAC that I had broken down under interrogation and sold them out. This, of course, was rubbish.

From Pollsmoor I went to Victor Verster in Paarl, then to Haeldestroom in Caledon and Brandvlei in Worcester. There was no public transport to any of these prisons except Pollsmoor. I relied on Gubanca and other PAC members for transport to visit these prisons regularly. The PASO students at the University of the Western Cape sometimes helped to transport me.

Twelve Fudumele, a trade unionist, gave me a few hundred rand and occasionally invited me for a barbecue at his house. Mthuthuzeli Radu organised radio interviews for me in which I highlighted the plight of jailed freedom fighters.

Richard Sizane, one of five PAC Members of Parliament in Cape Town, used to take me for drives on weekends. One day we drove through the famous Stellenbosch vineyards. Silent clouds scudded across the sky: thunderclaps are rare in the Cape. Acres of lush green rolled far and wide. Wine estates, mostly with Dutch names and eighteenth-century architecture, were scattered on this backdrop of green. We stopped to buy grapes from a stall.

As we leaned against the car, enjoying the grapes and the landscape, Sizane said: "Do you see how beautiful this place is?"

"Yes," I said.

"Now, let's face it comrade. Do you think that whites will give up without a fight? Yes, they can accommodate some of us in Parliament. They can even allow an African government to run the country so long as it doesn't interfere with their grip on the land. For your information, Cape Town is for sale and Europeans, especially the Germans, are buying it, thanks to the strength of their currency and the weakness of the rand. The Canadians have imposed a moratorium on the sale of land to foreigners. I'm not inciting you, comrade, but it will take a real revolution to liberate this beauty. Anyway, I'm not going to take part in that revolution because I have sworn to remain loyal to the government of the day."

I became a regular visitor to Cape Town, the headquarters of the

Truth and Reconciliation Commission (TRC). I would go there to submit amnesty application forms from jailed Apla cadres.

The Apla attacks on the St James Church and the Heidelberg Tavern in 1993 had been condemned locally and internationally. The PAC was among the first to condemn the attack in the church, and some members of the Apla High Command distanced the guerrilla army from the attack.

On the other hand, prominent businessmen in Umtata gave their nod to the attacks when they delivered large supplies of groceries to Apla cadres in the town. They always did this after any spectacular Apla operation.

I've never shied away from taking responsibility for Apla activities at the time I was Director of Operations. I'm proud to have been part of such a heroic army. At the time the Heidelberg Tavern was attacked I had issued an order suspending attacks on civilian targets. However, I had waived this order after the murder of five schoolchildren by the SADF in Umtata. Even then I said the security forces had to be our primary targets.

On the night of the attack on the tavern, an army base and a police station were also attacked by Apla, but the media, and later the TRC, chose to focus on the tavern attack. This was part of the attempt to paint Apla as a bunch of cowards who were good only at attacking innocent revellers. The media and the TRC did nothing to unearth the truth about SADF attacking schoolchildren in their sleep.

The Apla operatives who carried out the attacks on the St James Church, the King William's Town Golf Club and the Heidelberg Tavern were taken out of prison cells, paraded before the world as murderers and herded back into their cells to wait for the outcome of their amnesty applications. Not a single member of the SADF is in prison for killing schoolchildren in Umtata, Soweto, Umlazi, Langa and many other townships and villages.

April 1994 was a hollow victory.

A few years after the St James attack, I met Charl van Wyk, one of the survivors and the man who returned fire and wounded Apla cadre Gcinikhaya Makoma slightly. Makoma's blood samples were to be crucial in the subsequent trial. The meeting with Charl was facilitated by journalists who had previously interviewed him and me separately. We met in the PAC offices in Parliament in Cape Town. In front of TV cameras we shook hands and shared our experiences from our different viewpoints.

That was the beginning of the exciting journey I was to travel with

Charl. A few days after our meeting he invited me to a restaurant where we chatted over a snack. As we ate, the excited waitresses hung around, pointing at us and whispering among themselves. We concluded they had seen us on TV.

Charl said that although he didn't agree with my cause and the means of achieving it, he respected my forthrightness. He said he hated spineless politicians. He said former Ciskei military leader Oupa Gqozo was a strong leader who stood his ground to the finish.

"I hate spineless people," Charl said, tensing his small body and clenching his hands. His eyes were alert. I congratulated him on his courage and assured him that love, not hatred, was the fuel on which our ship of liberation sailed. I said that we need more contact and mutual understanding rather than the rehearsed phrase of "I'm sorry". I said it was not enough to talk reconciliation: we must walk it and meet each other half way.

Before we parted, Charl asked me to accompany him to a Sunday church service. I told him that as an atheist I didn't attend church, but for his sake I would attend the service. The great Sunday arrived. I asked my host in Cape Town, Nqaba Gubanca, to go with me, since I had long forgotten church etiquette. And the rituals began right in his house in Khayelitsha: he wore a dark suit and a tie and wanted me to wear the same. He wanted to lend me a suit, but I settled for the jacket without a tie.

We rode the train from the township to Cape Town station, where Charl came to fetch us. He took us to an Anglican Church in Tableview. Gubanca and I looked alien in the church: two Africans in a sea of white. We were the only people wearing jackets, and only Gubanca and the youthful priest wore ties. I looked at Gubanca, tugged at the lapel of my jacket and grinned mischievously. But he was unfazed. An elder of the Methodist Church, he had been wearing his jacket during services long before I was born.

The priest delivered a sermon I had heard many times before: Fear of the Lord . . . Christ was crucified for our sins . . . The Day of Judgment is coming . . .

The songs were moving and the beat was lively. I joined in the singing, as the lyrics were projected on the wall. I enjoyed the hymns immensely, and after the service I asked Charl to get me the cassettes of the songs. He did, and whenever I play them, I relive that service on a hot Cape Peninsula day. My friends keep asking me how I reconcile my atheism with my love for gospel music. My answer is simple: I love human emotions expressed through music.

From the church service, Charl drove us to Victor Verster Prison to see Gcinikhaya.

"For an atheist like you," Charl said with a contented smile, "this was a spiritual ambush."

"A spiritual ambush indeed," I said and congratulated him for a mission accomplished. At the prison entrance, warders asked if we had firearms on us. Speaking for the group I said no, since I didn't expect people to emerge from a church service armed with guns. But Charl said he had one. He said he carried it wherever he went, even to a church service. He left it at the entrance.

"I guess you will be armed even at Heaven's gates," I teased him.

"Yes, of course. You never know. There may be Apla hanging around the gates and one would have to defend Heaven."

"I don't think God would give a poor shot like you the task of defending Heaven's gates. Otherwise Apla would overrun them."

We laughed.

Charl told us he was carrying the same revolver on the night of the attack on the St James Church.

Dressed in green overalls, young and tall, Gcinikhaya was happy to see us. Charl was visibly moved by the sight of the young man he was forced to shoot in defence of Heaven's gates. Charl encouraged Khaya to study and promised to pay the costs. Khaya assured Charl that he did not hate him as a person, but what he had done was the result of years of oppression and racial discrimination. He thanked him for his help and promised to further his studies. Although Khaya had been speaking to the prison authorities about studying, all they did was give him an Afrikaans-speaking tutor and plenty of Afrikaans books. He didn't know Afrikaans and the whole exercise failed.

We shook hands with Khaya and Charl drove us to Khayelitsha.

Later, when I needed books for a community library, Charl contributed a cardboard box full of books, mostly Christian literature. Charl is a great survivor, and not merely a survivor of an Apla attack on the St James Church. He does not harbour hatred.

His attitude helped me to discover my contradictory personalities: that of a man pouring out vengeful rhetoric on public platforms, and that of a man who feels for the people hurt and maimed thanks to orders I gave.

My visits to prisons were punctuated by invitations to address various gatherings. The Student Representative Council of Rhodes University, for example, invited me to speak on Women's Day. Grahamstown, the seat of the university, with its old buildings and only a few cars on its wide streets, looked deserted.

A PASO student at the campus told me to brace myself for hecklers, mostly from the ANC. I felt I could cope with them.

The audience was small, but the joke of jokes was that in spite of being a Women's Day event, there was only one woman present and she left before I concluded my extemporaneous speech.

The audience enlivened the occasion with their questions. One student asked me what I thought of ubuntu. I said ubuntu, humaneness, is not exclusively African but a universal human quality found among the Chinese, Indians and all other peoples. It is learned behaviour. A basic and simple economy, vulnerable to the hostile elements, glued Africans together and made them dependent on one another's support in ploughing, weeding, harvesting, hunting and even in arts like music and dancing. A child was not the child of its parents but the child of the community. Today, in the cut-throat scramble for private property, it would be unfair and exceptionally naïve to expect people living in slums and ghettos to practise ubuntu. Shantytowns are social jungles that produce armed robbers and car hijackers. These beasts are miles from ubuntu, but the deadliest beasts are not in the shantytowns – they are in the boardrooms of multinational companies and on the stolen farmlands. These greedy bloodsuckers, clinging to the property of society as their own, are the real murderers of ubuntu. It will not flourish till we fix the economics of our country. The profits of collective labour must be held as the property of society.

A student from Kenya wanted to know my views on the TRC. I said nobody in his right senses could reject truth and reconciliation. However, reconciliation had to rest on the pillars of economic, political and social justice. There can be no reconciliation between land robber and his victim until the robber returns the land to its rightful owner. The TRC disregarded African history and was blind to the causes of violence and strife. Instead, the commission demanded that all those who were involved in violence apply for amnesty. It didn't differentiate between the violence of a colonised people, committed in self-defence, and that of the coloniser. You cannot equate a disease with its cure, poison with its antidote.

The TRC Act defined gross human rights violations narrowly. The truth is that colonialism by its very nature is a gross violation of the rights of the conquered people. Land dispossession, the migratory labour system, Bantu Education, the Group Areas Act, the pass laws, the disenfranchisement of the Africans, forced removals, job reservation – all these and many more grossly violated the rights of the indigenous African people.

Again, the TRC covered a narrow period: between 1960, when the oppressed Africans took up arms against the settler-colonial oppressor, and 1994, when the oppressed laid down their arms. This creates the false impression that there were no gross human rights violations before the oppressed Africans stirred and challenged the oppressor's guns, beginning with the PAC's marches to police stations on March 21, 1960, demanding the abolition of pass laws.

The TRC fanatics say the process was healing, but that is untrue. It tore off the comforting bandages of time and again exposed the wounds, but did nothing to heal them. You can't heal the landless and the poor by parading them before media cameras, letting them relive their anguish and burst into harrowing tears, and then leaving them in the condition in which you found them before they told their stories.

I answered many other questions but there wasn't a single heckler. I was later driven to Port Elizabeth, where I boarded an evening flight to Johannesburg.

Colonel Odirile Moalafi, his wife and their two daughters fetched me from the airport. As Matshidiso was serving supper, Odirile asked me where I'd had my breakfast.

"In Cape Town. I had lunch in Grahamstown and now supper in Soweto," I said.

There was action in Gauteng. Members of the PAC marched, picketed and held night vigils to put pressure on the government to release jailed freedom fighters. Cape Town, Port Elizabeth, Bisho, Umtata, Durban, Bloemfontein, Pietersburg and other towns followed.

The engines behind this campaign were Nozuko Ramokhele, Marcus Makhari and George Mkhwanazi, who criss-crossed the country delivering banners and placards. Motsoko Pheko was the voice of the campaign.

Ike Mthimunye, the PAC chairman in Gauteng and one of the first six political prisoners to be sentenced to life by the South African regime in the twentieth century, was also among the leaders of the campaign. Many other people contributed, but the man who touched my heart was Ben Khumalo, a security guard at the Johannesburg building where the PAC had offices. Mtungwa (Khumalo's clan name) would always contribute some money before a march and share his food with the hungry militants when they returned.

The residents of the shantytown of Phola Park in Umtata, organised by Sipho Memani and Majola Mfihlo, raised over three thousand rand at a party to contribute to the twelve thousand rand needed for bail for Nkopane Diahomonaheng. Businessman Mashumi Ndzuzo contributed most of the money. A Rastafarian band played till late that night, and I addressed the patrons of the party before they dispersed.

Archbishop Njongonkulu Ndungane, head of the Anglican Church in southern Africa, and Bishop Mvume Dandala, head of the Methodist Church in South Africa, donated money to assist the Apla freedom fighters who had been recently released. The South African Council of Churches didn't even have the courtesy to acknowledge receipt of our hand-delivered letters.

Umtata businessmen and professionals always responded positively when money was needed for legal fees or bail – thanks to Gilbert Sineke and Komsana, who convened meetings to inform them. Cunningham Ngcukana and Mahlomola Skhosana of the National Council of Trade Unions and their staff went out of their way to support the cause of the jailed freedom fighters. When we were desperately in need of ten thousand rand to bail out Luyanda Gqomfa, Cunningham took me to Dikgang Moseneke and Peter Vundla, prominent businessmen, to ask for contributions. Dikgang gave us six thousand rand and Peter one thousand rand. Thoko Obisanya, Marcus Makhari and Cunningham also contributed one thousand rand each. The following day I was on my way to Bloemfontein to pay the bail.

In and outside Parliament, the PAC is spearheading the campaign for the release of Apla, MK and AZANLA cadres. Other sections of the liberation movement are quiet except for the courageous voice of Makhenkesi Stofile, the ANC premier of the Eastern Cape. Stofile argues that some of the imprisoned ANC cadres were arrested after taking orders from him. He says he is ashamed to face them while he is serving in a government that is keeping them in jail.

President Nelson Mandela broke our hearts.

He snubbed us when we marched to Mahlamba Ndlopfu, his official residence in Pretoria. Our memorandum was received by a junior official. While he was snubbing us, Mandela was calling on Zimbabwe President Robert Mugabe to release Kevin Woods, who is serving a long prison term for attacking Azanian freedom fighters in that country. We wondered if Mandela valued the well-being of whites above that of his people.

White soldiers and their generals who had murdered and maimed hundreds of thousands in the Southern African sub-continent were sitting pretty in the comfort of their own homes, while soldiers for justice and liberation were rotting in jails. While freedom fighters were struggling on their own to pay incredibly high legal fees and bail, the State paid for the defence of the servants of apartheid.

General Magnus Malan, one of the most notorious apartheid-era figures, used to fly in a chartered plane between Pretoria and Durban for his trial. During the trial he was accommodated in a posh seaside government house and a chauffeur drove him to court. The State spent three million rand on his legal fees. He was subsequently acquitted. It's therefore not surprising that he praised and thanked Mandela after the acquittal.

While South African taxpayers' money pampered Malan, I had to board a third-class train, a taxi or a bus, or hitch a ride to my court appearances in Bloemfontein. I got to Bloemfontein from different directions, depending on where I had been before my appearance.

One winter morning, Pasika Nontshiza drove me from Umtata to Bloemfontein via Queenstown. We travelled in a van and gave people lifts along the way to get money for petrol. It had snowed around Queenstown and the mountains were wearing beautiful white caps. When we arrived in Sterkspruit, the van sounded like a low-flying helicopter because its exhaust pipe had broken. We stayed the night, and the following day Phambili Mei drove us to Bloemfontein.

We had left our car in Sterkspruit and arranged for it to be fixed. When we returned we found the welder still struggling to fix it. It was dark and he didn't have a torch. His helper struck one match after another until he emptied the box. The welder had broken the exhaust pipe into two pieces and was struggling to return them to their place. He had the gall to charge us fifty rand for damaging the car.

I wanted us to stay another night but Pasika refused, saying he had to be at work the following day. The car made a deafening noise as we drove and we had to shout to hear each other. Guzzling petrol like a dry sponge, we crawled slowly till we passed Barkley East. As we headed down to Elliot, we heard a loud explosion and the car careened. Pasika fought the steering wheel until the car stopped. The worn-out rear tyre had burst. We had a spare wheel, but no jack. It was dark and an owl was hooting to compound the mysteries of the night.

It was cold. We tried to stop passing motorists but they thundered past. Two African men, flashing hazards in the middle of nowhere, waving down cars to stop at midnight – we must have looked like criminals. A police car flashing a blue light approached us and our hearts leaped with expectation. We waved and the car slowed down, and then suddenly accelerated and screamed off into the cold dark night.

"These are stupid police," Pasika cursed as he wrapped himself tightly in his sleeping bag. "If they had been clever, they'd have arrested us. I'm sure it's less cold in the police cells."

He fell asleep in the back of the van – I used to tease him that he could sleep through an earthquake. I got into the driver's seat and watched the police car as it drove up and down that road, as if mocking us. The windscreen misted over and a crust of ice formed over the car. I had just fallen asleep too when I heard a gentle knock on the window. I wound it down and saw a white man standing there. My heart lost a beat.

"Hi! I'm Captain Whitehouse of Charlie Company, Six South African Infantry Battalion. Can I be of help to you?"

"Yes," I said as I opened the door. Pasika and I agreed that he would remain with the car while I went to Barkley East with Captain Whitehouse and his colleague. The two soldiers didn't have a jack either.

"How long have you been stuck here?" Captain Whitehouse asked as the military truck cut through the cold early morning air.

"Since nine last night," I said.

"From nine to one o'clock!" his colleague exclaimed.

"Wait a minute – just before we met you, we saw a police patrol car heading towards Elliot. Why didn't you ask them for help?" the captain asked.

"They've been going up and down this road and ignoring us," I said.

"I see," the captain nodded. "The police are interested in stock theft only. People stuck in cars in this cold mean nothing to them."

Captain Whitehouse described how cold Barkley East could be. He said in winter the army vehicles used jet fuel because ordinary fuel froze at night. He told us the prices of houses in the town were very low because of the cold climate, and there were times when it snowed in December.

As we drove into Barkley East the captain asked his colleague to drive to the police station. We found three policemen warming themselves at a big gas heater, wearing large coats and cooper hats and scarves around their necks. The place was warm.

After the greetings, Captain Whitehouse asked them to help me, a member of the public. He told them my story but they refused to help even with a jack. They said they could only accommodate me in the charge office till sunrise.

The captain got angry and shouted: "You call yourselves South African Police Services but you refuse to serve a member of the public. What a disgrace!"

They would not even contact their patrol car by radio to help Pasika. When tempers rose, the language switched to Afrikaans. Then the captain would change back into English, I guessed for my benefit.

"Okay gentlemen, if you can't help a member of the public, then lend me a jack," the captain said in a mild and conciliatory voice. Still the police refused. The captain flung his hands in the air and shouted: "Write down in the occurrence book that I, Captain Whitehouse of the SANDF, came here for help and you refused."

One of the policemen scribbled something in the book, and the captain demanded to see what it was. He read what the policeman had written, shook his head in anger, and gestured to me to leave.

We went to the army camp, and the captain dispatched two indigenous African soldiers with a jack to go back with me to the car.

We got back on our journey to Umtata at four in the morning. Later I wrote a letter to the commander of Six South African Infantry Battalion, Lieutenant-Colonel E Rabie, thanking Captain Whitehouse and his Charlie Company, and faxed the letter to the headquarters of the battalion in Grahamstown.

— Aluta Continua —

EVERY TIME I've appeared in court, my case has been adjourned to wait for the results of my application to the TRC for amnesty. The TRC finally closed down, while still demanding that I make "full disclosure" of my "crimes". I on the other hand insisted that I had waged a just war that shouldn't be treated as a crime.

I'm still waiting for the next move from the prosecutors.

The constant postponements give me a chance to visit Manaleng. I am lucky to be reunited with my family, friends and neighbours. Many of my comrades died and were buried by the roadside during the tortuous march to freedom. As I lie in the bed, gazing at the rafters of the corrugated iron roof, their faces flash across my mind.

The mournful tolling of a bell forces itself on my attention. I also hear Mother outside, asking Father if he knows who died. Fright chokes me. I can't get used to this tolling; I can't silence it the way I switch off a radio when obituaries are read.

The tolling has become regular; batho re a fela – we are being wiped out. Many say the numbers will climb because we have turned our backs on our ancestors, and others say the prophecies in the Holy Book are being fulfilled. My materialist outlook has set me free. I no longer attribute sickness and death to sin or failure to pacify the ancestors.

The HIV/Aids virus is running rampant in our land. The pandemic has fed on our economic helplessness. In the USA an HIV-positive person can live for up to twenty years after infection, while in African countries like Zimbabwe he or she lives on average for just three years.

The abject poverty afflicting the continent and inflated Aids drug prices condemn Africans to early death. Even if HIV/Aids were to be cured by simply taking a glass of clean water, millions of Africans would still die because clean water is very scarce.

I am back home, back in Manaleng, with its tolling bells and giant mountains that delay the rising of the sun and hasten its setting. My journey has come full circle. Since I left, I have grown. The struggle has taught me that I am neither inferior nor superior to anyone else. I assert my equality to all other human beings. I have learnt that change is constant, but we can steer it or be its passive victims.

I'm proud to have been part of the PAC, an organisation that once strode centre stage of South African politics with confidence. The PAC is now reduced to a shadow, thanks to its unusual birth as well as other self-inflicted ills.

It had a short legal existence – eleven months before it was banned and driven underground into guerrilla war. It didn't live long enough to develop its own culture and a leadership core. Exile and the underground are the worst places to try and mould an organisation. Many took advantage of its shadowy existence to further their personal agendas.

It's sad that, to this day, we haven't had a PAC postmortem of our struggle to liberate Azania. We as an organisation and as a country were too quick to pop the champagne bottles.

The PAC ought to call a big indaba and honestly answer some hard questions. Is the organisation still relevant and necessary? If the organisation thinks it has to continue, what does it need to say to South Africans? What must it do for them, and with them?

The PAC might find it has to hold hands with others on the left of the political spectrum. It makes me angry that the right is seen as the only alternative to the present ruling party.

We need to be refocusing our people and getting them into the new battlefields: the war to control the economy of this country and this continent.

Yes, we have chalked up the April 1994 victory, but aluta continua!

As the sun climbs up the sky here in Manaleng, the corrugated iron sheets crackle as they expand. I can't stand this stifling heat, and I go outside and sit under the morula, facing the ever-brooding Molongoane. Memories of childhood climb to its summit. I stand at the top, happy to be home – but the damned bell doesn't want to be silent.

Molongoane whispers: "Welcome home, child of the soil."

— Acknowledgements —

THIS BOOK would not have been what it is if it weren't for the insightful first editing by Joe Thloloe. Working with Bra Joe has been quite a revelation: I found myself back in the classroom listening attentively to a great teacher.

Nozibele Ndlumbini also encouraged and advised me. Indefatigably she typed the original manuscript, and thanks to her vigilance it survived a police raid.

Jaki Seroke shared his literary experience generously, and Dan Mdluli restored my faith in the manuscript when he commented that it was "un-put-downable". Zipho Mtshali was competent and patient as he, too, typed and scanned the manuscript.

Phangisile Mtshali made available her farm, where we worked long hours and enjoyed delicious meals and the serenity of scenic Kwa-Zulu-Natal.

My thanks go to every cadre of the Azanian People's Liberation Army, Umkhonto we Sizwe and the Azanian National Liberation Army for their courage and sacrifices. Their inadequately told story pushed me to contribute this book, and I hope many more will be written to immortalise their heroic deeds. Countless well-dones to the members of the Transkei Defence Force and the Transkei Police for hiding me and thus ensuring that I lived to write the book.

I owe a great debt to many families who adopted me during my fugitive days. The list is very long and it is impossible to mention all of them. Among them are the families Ncukana, Kantolo, Koko, Tyhilana, Roloti, Mabula, Mbuli, Maqwara, Ndzaba, Moleko, Magengenene, Sefatsa, Ndamase, Ndlovu, Maseko and Mphats'oe in Azania; Simelane in Swaziland; Ncube in Zimbabwe; Mothopeng, Jakalas and Dube in Botswana; and Mothobi, Motlatsi and Matosela in Lesotho.

A million thanks to Antjie Krog, Henrietta Rose-Innes and Annari van der Merwe for their sterling efforts to get the manuscript published. Henrietta is a sensitive final editor and Annari is a diligent publisher and I thank her for constantly informing me about the progress of the book.

So many people have encouraged me to tell this story and my gratitude goes to them all. Among them are Phyllius Ntwanambi, Mpho Phatudi, Bambo Qonqo, Narius Moloto, Zuko Camagu, Blacks Joyi, Lungisa Ntintili, Simphiwe Sesanti and Pat Dooms.

Many names have been omitted to make the book readable. However, the people whose names have been omitted are as important to me as those whose names are included.

LETLAPA MPHAHLELE